W9-BUH-094

# LIVE TO RIDE

## ALSO BY WAYNE JOHNSON

*White Heat*

*The Devil You Know*

*Six Crooked Highways*

*Don't Think Twice*

*Deluge* (as A. Strong)

*The Snake Game*

# LIVE

*to*

# RIDE

### The Rumbling, Roaring World of Speed, Escape, and Adventure on Two Wheels

## WAYNE JOHNSON

**ATRIA** BOOKS

New York    London    Toronto    Sydney

**ATRIA** BOOKS

A Division of Simon & Schuster, Inc.
1230 Avenue of the Americas
New York, NY 10020

Copyright © 2010 by Wayne Johnson

First Atria Books hardcover edition June 2010

**ATRIA** B O O K S and colophon are trademarks of Simon & Schuster, Inc.

For information about special discounts for bulk purchases,
please contact Simon & Schuster Special Sales at
1-866-506-1949 or business@simonandschuster.com.

The Simon & Schuster Speakers Bureau can bring authors to your
live event. For more information or to book an event contact the
Simon & Schuster Speakers Bureau at 1-866-248-3049 or visit our
website at www.simonspeakers.com.

Designed by Elliott Beard

Manufactured in the United States of America

10 9 8 7 6 5 4 3 2 1

Library of Congress Cataloging-in-Publication Data

Johnson, Wayne.
   Live to ride: The rumbling, roaring world of speed, escape, and adventure on
two wheels / Wayne Johnson.
      p. cm.
1.  Motorcycling.  2.  Motorcycle touring.  I. Title.
GV1059.5.J62 2010
796.7'5—dc22

2009043983

ISBN 978-1-4165-5032-7
ISBN 978-1-4391-7715-0 (ebook)

**As always, for Karen**

# CONTENTS

Author's Note     ix

**1**   The Call of the Open Road     1

**2**   The Riders of the Apocalypse Find a New Mount     11

**3**   Road Racing: Sex on Wheels     57

**4**   Why Don't We Do It in the Dirt?     99

**5**   MCers, 1%ers, Outlaw Bikers, and Club Riders: Brando, Barger, Balls, and Bluster     137

**6**   Widowmaker: Hill-Climbing Killer Extraordinaire     177

**7**   At the Last, Fastest Place on Earth: Salt Fever     203

**8**   The Ultimate Freedom Machine: (Just) Getting Out There     245

Acknowledgments     273

# AUTHOR'S NOTE

This book is about bikes, from the first golden-era motor-bicycles to today's high-performance, head-spinningly fast rockets. I have wrenched on, ridden, and loved motorcycles now for more than forty years—motorcycles of *all* kinds, from Honda Cub 50s, such as the one my cousins and I, with all our crashing, and riding three up, and dirt donking, didn't manage to break, to the beautiful Ducatis I've owned and repaired since the middle eighties. More so than being about bikes, though, *Live to Ride* is about the experience of riding, and about riders—some of historical note, some just enthusiasts, and some just plain old crazy or mean as junkyard dogs. Want to know what it's like to canyon race at 150 miles per hour? Open the pages here and pilot a Ducati ST4 up Wolf Creek in Utah's Wasatch mountains. Ride flat-track on cement, motocross on dirt. Take a tour of the Rockies and brave a run with the West Bank Motorcycle Club. And, finally, take a trip to the last and fastest place on earth, the Bonneville Salt Flats, and rub shoulders with the anointed motorcycle speed crazies there (350.88 miles per hour on a motorcycle?!).

Motorcycling opens up an astoundingly big and wonderful world. If after having read *Live to Ride* you feel compelled to get out there on a two-wheeled adventure yourself, all the better.

That big, wide world is waiting, and all you need to enter it is your trusty steed.

Happy riding!

# LIVE TO RIDE

# 1

# The Call of the Open Road

Picture a vast, open landscape with towering snow-capped peaks in the distance. In the foreground is a winding two-lane road. You are on that road, which curves left now, and you lean with the road as if carried on a breeze.

You, in this landscape, are not in a car, but riding feet off the road as if on some magic carpet, the pavement rushing by lazily under your feet.

The wind tosses your hair. The sun shines warmly on your face. On either side of you is sage, blue-green and sweet smelling.

You may or may not be smiling, but there is something glowing within you regardless, some deep, elemental satisfaction here.

Here you are *in* it, this landscape, not just passing through. If you reached out, you could touch that blooming sage which is dotted with bright yellow flowers. In fact, to remind yourself of that, you drop your boots down until they are roughly abraded by the asphalt under you.

Where the road dips the air is cooler, refreshing, a scent of water in it.

Here there are no windows to see through. No windshield between you and what is before you.

You can smell everything, taste it, touch it. This landscape writes itself on your body, mile after mile.

Because you are riding *in* it on a motorcycle—a machine that is both mechanical miracle and oddity. After all, why would anyone choose to travel unprotected like this, out in the open, when the comforts of a car are available?

Earlier, and for some still, in this dream landscape the rider would be on a horse.

But that is what a motorcycle is, after all, an iron horse, and our bikers cowboys of another age.

We dream of riding, in landscapes and through them. Of adventures. Of mountain heights and desert stretches.

Motorcycles enable us to enter landscapes that are both real and imagined.

If you are an American, or anyone thrilling to the myth of the American frontier, you are astride a Harley-Davidson, the motor an enormous V-twin threading you through this landscape with an accompanying rumble—*rolling thunder*, enthusiasts call it.

Traveling at a leisurely sixty miles per hour in fifth gear, you drop down to fourth and crack open the throttle.

Now the engine, once loping, surges, vibrating with a certain intoxicating violence.

Explosive.

Seventy, eighty, ninety. One hundred miles per hour. Now the landscape has taken on another quality entirely. Those once gentle sweeping turns are flying at you, you forcing the bike through them, hard left, now hard right, your right foot peg grinding into the pavement, this turn a long sweeper of decreasing radius, forcing you with each second to angle the bike over further, your body tensed.

You can only glide so far to the outside of the turn before you run out of pavement, a consequence of this kind of turn.

Traveling at one hundred miles per hour, the wind is a veritable gale in your face, which you lean into as if some great weight.

Instead of hitting your brakes, and hard, you push your luck.

The sweeper empties into a long straightaway. Victory!

Orienting yourself over the bike as if using a gun sight, hunched over the gas tank, you twist the throttle full open.

Your horse, your scooter, your bike surges, the speedometer still climbing—110, 115, 120 miles per hour.

For a dresser like you are on, this is about the limit.

And it's plenty. That breeze is a hurricane now, threatening to knock you right off the bike. The bike is vibrating like some demented tuning fork. You can't see anything in the rearview mirrors, the bike shakes so fiercely. A bug hits you in the face with the force of a bullet. Your heart is clunking away in your chest, your hands shaking as if palsied, something in you needing to engage in this boxing match with the bike, which forces you to hold the 120 just over the upcoming rise in the road, and here you are over it, headed down, and down, and down, nearly weightless, backing off the throttle and that big V-twin engine "compression rapping," making a pretty staccato sound, the engine slowing the bike as if you'd thrown out an anchor.

And, in seconds, you are again just lazily approaching the mountains rising out of this plain around you, but now with this sweet, satisfied something in you, the residue of your burst of speed. And here in the heat there is a certain joy in knowing you will soon be there, the air so cool you will have to stop the bike and put on your heavier jacket.

In the mountains the air will smell of snowmelt, and fresh, resinous pine, and wet earth.

Stopped along the shoulder, headed into those mountains, you'll lean against your bike feeling like Brando in *The Wild One*, Winnebagos, buses, cars going by, kids waving to you and their parents scolding them for drawing your attention to them. You'll light up a Camel, unfiltered. You don't smoke, but when you ride the bike you do. It reminds you of being twelve, or fifteen, or twenty, you and your buddies riding dirt bikes, cadging cigarettes from one another, smoking them with a certain bravado.

Here, on the Harley, the world opens to you. New again like that.

You have just what you need and no more. A tent and camping gear. Some cash in your pocket: for gas, and for meals, dinner perhaps, at a ramshackle restaurant that looks pretty much as it did in the thirties. Peeling paint. A cockeyed porch, over it a buzzing neon sign, here, in the Rockies, that sign announcing Ruth's Kitchen (Salt Lake City, Utah), or the Overland Express (Bozeman, Montana), or the Renegade (Rock Springs, Wyoming). You'll order a steak and baked potato, put the sour cream on the potato—and it won't be low-fat, it'll be full-fat, rich, creamy, satisfying. There will be families around the other tables, efficient-looking parents in travel-crumpled clothes, and the kids will give you surreptitious glances, afraid but curious, and the parents will steer them away from looking, you in your leathers, spotted with bits of bugs, oil-stained and wrench-roughened, dangerous.

You'll smile. It's a sweet smile, too. It says, If you dare, come on. There's a life outside the box waiting for you. Think about it, kid.

Most turn away, shy.

Freedom, you know, is dangerous. It may cost you your life. But then, since the motorcycle bug bit you decades earlier, you've accepted that.

It's the price you pay for riding.

But there is this about touring: What you've just experienced, getting out there into that mountain landscape (which, incidentally, is the most common *dream* of motorcycling, is just one kind among tens of kinds of riding)—

No such riding exists.


Real touring is both better *and* worse than the dream of it. It is something that cannot be fully imagined, has to be experienced. Because riders, most anyway, won't give you the whole picture.

The flip side.

Here, you leave some major city, yearning for open spaces and to connect with something elemental—*visceral*, one of my Ivy League colleagues called it, his lip curling with contempt, this colleague someone who wouldn't so much as think to get on a bike.

Let's say you want to head to the Rockies as in the Great American Touring Dream you've just experienced. You're in Chicago, down from the Twin Cities to pick up your old friend Rat, who was to go with you and take some of the edge off. Rat, though, has bowed out. Too much work, matters off-kilter at home. So you're alone, which makes things easier and excites you.

Now, you're really Bronson, from that starry-eyed early-seventies soft metaphysical show *Then Came Bronson*, where Bronson, week after week, rode the lonely highways on his Harley, saving distressed maidens in halter tops, calming mayhem, giving displays of his karate skills, and offering profound Zen motorcycle insights like, "If it's meant to be, it'll be," throwing his leg over the saddle and riding off into the sunset unblemished (but for a bruise or two on his hands from throwing those perfectly timed karate chops), his jeans neatly pressed and his hair looking perfect.

But for you, in typical midwest August fashion, the mercury's been hovering around one hundred, the humidity the same.

It's been a dry summer, so you've reasoned an old rain suit you've borrowed will do the trick in a pinch. No need to go out and buy rainproof booties to cover your engineer boots, either, or a vest to put under your jacket if it gets too cold. You can't even think in terms of rain, much less cold.

You've bolted a rack on your bike, strapped a pack to it, in the pack your ground pad, sleeping bag, tent, canteen, cooking gear, and one-burner Coleman stove. You've got a radio that operates off your bike, speakers in your helmet. You've got all the clothes you need. The lighter clothes and your hiking boots are in your tank bag, and on the top of it, under a clear plastic cover, your map, now Illinois.

All that gear makes your bike handle differently, a bit top heavy.

You kiss the wife, husband, lover, girlfriend, boyfriend good-bye. (Or, here, shake hands with Rat.)

You throw your leg over the saddle and hit the starter button. Boy, is this the bee's knees, you think!

But you have to get moving, and quick—out in the sun in your black leather you'll die of heat prostration if you don't.

So you head out onto the Lincoln Expressway just after seven, and some crazed commuter bored with his job decides he'll spice up his morning by seeing how close he can get the bumper of his Hummer to your rear tire. (Or it's some retro Gen Xer in a lavender Pacer trying to shake off last night's ketamine high, glued off your rear, eyes wide as saucers.)

You grit your teeth and bear it. Chicagoans, for some demented reason, will tailgate anything—get ten inches right off the bumper of a Mack truck and stay there, hurtling along blind at eighty and trusting to providence. Maybe they're drafting—saving a few cents on gas that way?

Most cities have their challenges: In Pittsburgh, for example, you are often lost, as they skimp on road signs. In San Francisco, you have hills so steep you can't see over the crests. In L.A. the speed limit signs are fictions, as everything there seems to be.

But those Chicago tailgaters: If they'll do it with trucks they can't see around, how much closer will they get to a motorcycle?

You blip the throttle and get the kid off your rear, but a girl veers in now, a '57 Dodge, fins. Purple hair.

If that girl's bumper hits your rear tire, you're dead in this traffic, which makes this length of your ride more than a little tense, especially when you see, in your rearview mirror, that she's got a whole wad of Juicy Fruit in her mouth and is painting her toenails and having a fist-shaking chat on her cell phone. She must be steering with her knee, you think.

Thirty minutes go by, navigating traffic in a greasy sweat. You have never been so focused.

When you can take it no longer, these tailgaters, you crack open the throttle, cut between lanes, racing ahead, and where there's a space in the lane to your right, you zoom back in. Now some dead ringer for Richard Nixon wearing an overly dark toupee and driving a car with the license plate 1BG DCK is tailgating you.

You hunch lower over your bike, switch on the radio: some inane talk show couple discussing the freak clouds that just blew in.

You scan the road to the west, and, sure enough, it's socked in by heavy gray clouds all the way to the horizon, Hurricane Katrina dark.

But here is your exit to those two-laners William Least Heat Moon had you yearning for in *Blue Highways*.

You happily exit, and for a full twenty minutes you weave ecstatically left, right, left, reminding yourself why you love motorcycles.

They're just . . . *intoxicating* to ride. And the very moment you're back in the swing of riding—God, but you're having fun!—that's when the skies open up.

On this little road in Illinois farming country you're doing just sixty or so. But the raindrops, if you're sitting upright, strike you in the face like nails from one of those pneumatic guns carpenters use.

And they are cold! Colder than you could possibly have imagined. They strike your face at fifty degrees or so, but immediately, with the wind, and the effect of evaporation, cut the temperature to just over freezing.

You stop alongside the road and tug on your rain suit.

Then, back on the bike, you discover to your dismay that your rain suit is poorly made, that water runs down your neck from your helmet. And up your sleeves, and down your legs. In fact, in thirty minutes, not a square inch of you is dry. And now the center of the road is greased watermelon slick where the oil from most cars and trucks drips down. And there's a car behind you, his lights boring into your back, so you stay in the right or left rut, off the greased crown of your lane, but in the ruts there's water, and now you are getting a bit of a wobbly hydroplaning feel if you ride over sixty.

Which, *feel*, you don't have much of in your hands anymore.

Leather gloves, no matter what color, make great sponges, you've discovered.

And your feet? What feet? Your legs, encased in soggy denim and black leather, are like two logs resting on your foot pegs. When you reach for the rear brake (right side in front of the foot peg), it is as if your entire leg has fallen asleep.

You've been on the bike three hours. Your butt's complaining, your ears picking up engine sounds you never wanted to hear. Clashing, gnashing, grating sounds, and there is this general hum that has numbed you over all.

You hope the *ping!* that you think you really probably didn't hear came from something other than your bike.

Your radio you turned off long ago, about the time you heard the tenth advertisement for Albert Hobbernockin's Super Labor Day Twenty-Four-Hour Monster Truck Sale-a-thon!

Up ahead is a glowing sign: *EAT.* You pull off the road, rev your bike to get up the poorly paved driveway to this diner, the rear tire breaking loose the dirt at the top. When the tire cuts down to pavement, it nearly propels the bike, and you on it, broadside into the front door, a fate you avoid through the most adroit use of your brakes.

You park under the carport, alongside an orange Ford Festiva.

Walking to the door, you study the waitress in the front window. Framed there in her white apron, she's sizing you up. You're moving like some somnambulant or drunk—or like a biker who's been out in the rain, glued to his ride, half frozen. In August.

You don't know if that waitress is going to go for the twelve-gauge Winchester below your line of sight, like Schwarzenegger in *The Terminator,* or open the door.

But it's the door.

Inside you doff your helmet. It's blessed quiet, and some golden oldie is playing in the kitchen.

"Getcha something?" the waitress says. While you stand there, too dazed to think, she'll get you a bowl of soup, which makes way for a hamburger, a piece of pie, à la mode, and about half a gallon of coffee. You've never been so hungry.

You watch it rain outside.

You have just had the best bowl of soup in your whole life, and the burger wasn't far behind. What amazes you is that the soup was Campbell's, and the burger some frozen patty.

Your sense of smell is incredible. New lumber. Pepper, from the shaker in front of you. Pickle, which you removed from your burger, but nibble on now. Cinnamon from the donuts in the counter case.

Wiping his hands on a towel, the fry cook comes out, stands off the end of your table.

"Hey," you say.

"How far you ride?"

"Just from Chicago," you tell him.

"How far you goin'?"

"Montana," you say, savoring the word. "Colorado—Estes Park, Rocky Mountains, then back through Wyoming. Right now, though, up to the Twin Cities."

This fry cook, no doubt the waitress's husband, will look out the windows of the restaurant with terrible longing. Which you feel again now, down to your very boots, as you did before you left Chicago.

"Always wanted to do that. Buy a bike and just . . ."

"Ride off into the sunset," you finish for him. A cliché that is both an embarrassment and reality.

For that's the odd thing—here, early on in your touring career and poorly prepared—even given the tailgaters on the expressway, that patch of greasy road that nearly put you in the ditch, and the rain and mild hypothermia, *something* in you wants to get back on that motorcycle and *just go.*

Even down to . . . *Patagonia.* Don't they ride llamas down there? Or herd them, those South American cowboys? Gauchos? And things have gotten mighty complicated at your home, too, not just your friend's.

You could do it. Just . . . keep . . . going.

Your pants are filthy and covered with wet dirt. You've sweated something awful, guiding the bike along on those treacherously slick spots.

But you experienced it all: touched, smelled, saw, heard. The rain on your face was real rain. Here, in Illinois, the landscape is nothing spectacular, but even here, you already know, there is something . . . *addictive* about this motorcycle touring.

Riding, you're *not* waiting to get somewhere. Not waiting for something to happen. Not waiting for some one or some thing.

You're having an adventure, *right now, right here.*

Every mile is written on you, from your first, shocking hours' long stretch, this motorcycling business dirtier, rougher, less comfortable, and more dangerous than you thought.

And, almost perversely, you love it all the more for it.

The riding itself—roaring up hills, gauging how fast to enter unmarked turns, navigating traffic, staying focused and sharp—is all reward in itself.

Being *on the bike* is a thing unto itself. Which creates this love of the bike—if your bike is a good one, and you can trust it, it comes to be wedded to you and to your adventures.

If you race, a bike comes to be an extension of your very body.

And when you return from that first tour over a month later, countless adventures under your belt, and someone says with a starry look in his or her eyes, "I've always wanted to do that, just . . . take off and ride," you'll want to tell them, "That kind of riding you're thinking of doesn't exist." All that clean, *Then Came Bronson* nonsense. But you'll want to add, too, "No, that's all a load of dreaming. But what riding is really like is so much better, *you can't imagine.*"

Motorcycling is intoxicating.

It should be, as bikes are the stuff of dreams, and their creators meant them to be just that.

# 2

# The Riders of the Apocalypse
# Find a New Mount

**Y**ou are at a stop light in your Toyota Camry, patiently waiting for the light to change, when you hear some commotion, first to your rear, then alongside you. A roaring, clattering . . . *something.* You carefully glance to your right, see some character in black leather astride—

A motorcycle! To the uninitiated, the nonmotorcyclist, they all look the same, sound the same.

You can't look too long. And certainly you can't put anything you're feeling into your look, this complex knot of irritation, disapproval, fear, and—yes—envy. Secretly you wish you could be brave enough (or is it dumb enough?) to ride the wind, to head out into that great world of nowhere and everywhere just for the going. Well, you think, I can do that with my Toyota, but in that same second, you acknowledge that, no, that is not the same thing at all. But why not?

Instinctively you know these two things are worlds apart.

And the fear component at the light now is simple. You're wondering if your glance will incite this . . . nut, daredevil, social miscreant, or deviant to leap onto the hood of your car, where he (or is it a *she*?) will pound on your hood with a gloved fist. You don't know why, but people who ride motorcycles are unpredictable. They have some screws loose, are playing with less than a full deck, are a wee bit more than a few fries short of a Happy Meal. All this is part and parcel of the common, socially agreed upon perception of motorcyclists.

Another glance will tell you this: No tattoos. No "colors" (insignia, such as the best-known and dreaded *Hells Angels*, or *Pagans*, or *Satans Soldiers*) on the jacket, no Maltese cross on some sissy bar. So, at least this rider, this character alongside you, is not some gangbanger biker (see chapter 5), that American cult figure felt to justifiably arouse sweaty, white-knuckled fear, but just your appropriately attired motorcyclist.

And it *is* a guy this time, tinkering with something on the top of that stupid engine he's sitting on, the motor sputtering, then roaring.

The light changes, the biker bends over his handlebars, and, as if shot from a slingshot, he's gone.

And once again, the nonrider wonders, What is it with all that?

## The Unbelievable Yet True Story of the Birth of the Motorcycle

That two-wheeled noisemaker with the miscreant on it, which inspired so many (mostly negative) feelings in you, the nonrider, is the love child of the bicycle and, initially, the steam engine, now celebrating its 142nd birthday.

That's right: The motorcycle is 142 years old.

Though if the true origin of the motorcycle is to be found in the bicycle (which you thought to be, maybe, just as old as your grandparents), then the motorcycle is nearly two hundred years old—and possibly even older, tomb paintings from as early as ancient Egypt suggesting precursors.

Without the development of, and earlier fervor for, the bicycle, the motorcycle would not exist.

And how did this all start? With the eruption of Tambora on the island of Sumbawa in Indonesia.

An auspicious origin for such a machine as the motorcycle.

Purportedly ten times larger than that of Krakatoa, and one hundred times that of Mount St. Helens, Tambora's eruption spewed almost forty cubic miles of ash thirty miles into the atmosphere, causing in 1816 what has since been called by historians "The Year Without a Summer." Famine followed, and people all across Europe were reduced to eating whatever they could find, including roots and rodents. But not before they had resorted to the widespread slaughtering of horses for meat—leaving those accustomed to coach and horseback to travel on foot.

To replace the horse, Karl Drais, of Karlsruhe, Germany, invented a *Laufmaschine* (or "running-machine"), which had two wheels with a diameter roughly equal to the length of the operator's legs, a wooden bar connecting the wheels on which the rider sat, and a steerable front wheel, as found on bicycles to this day. The operator of Drais's machine, though, kept his feet firmly on the ground, propelling the vehicle with his legs Fred Flintstone style. The "dandy horse" (or *draisienne* in France) became so popular that by the autumn of 1817 laws became necessary to prevent over-enthusiastic "gentleman riders of breeding" from knocking good citizens from sidewalks—these vehicles by this time having been given the more dignified name *vélocipèdes*.

Sound familiar? Rebels on velocipedes. Taking over the streets. Raising mayhem and the dander of good citizens!

From the first, riders of velocipedes greatly enjoyed the sensations of zooming, veering, and gliding. So much so that riding "academies" sprang up all over Europe, and designers marketed ever new versions. Attaching pedals to the front wheel (1863) allowed riders to propel themselves without their feet touching the ground, and overnight it was discovered, rudimentary math being sufficient, that if the front wheel was pedaled, the drive wheel could nearly double in size. This improvement in design increased the speeds at which these new velocipedes could be ridden.

Which required taking them to the streets, where they again were to be found everywhere.

*Fad* does not do justice to the public fervor for velocipedes.

These "new velocipedes" had heavy steel frames and steel wheels with solid tires, the pneumatic tire not having been invented yet. Europe at this time had cobbled streets (composed of brick). Hence, these new machines were called "boneshakers."

And boneshake they did.

Far from the machines we think of today as a poor man's means of transportation, though, these "high-wheelers" were popular with people of means (and, importantly, nearly all these early riders were *men*). And in that, they garnered looks of envy as well as admiration, these machines costing what the average worker of the time would make in *six months*.

Still sound familiar? A current Ducati Desmosedici, at around $70,000, is all but unobtainable for the average wage earner.

This high-wheeler was the first machine to be called a "bi-cycle." In the decade that followed, ball bearings were invented, the caliper brake, the first change-speed gear, and the continuous chain, which spawned the bicycle as we know it today (and, really, the motorcycle), with wheels again slightly smaller in diameter than the length of the rider's legs, the rear wheel driven by a chain, and the pedals mounted at the bottom-most point of a diamond-shaped frame.

This new machine was called a "bicyclette" to distinguish it from the "ordinary" (seen commonly) high-wheeler.

Enter here a most crucial element: women.

Not to be left out of the fun, women took up riding adult tricycles (1880). And given a taste of—yes, what motorcyclists most cherish—*freedom*, there was no turning back, even though much bicycle and tricycle riding was still confined to parks.

Bicycle societies sprang up to provide social outlets for enthusiasts, but even more so now to remedy the "boneshaker" problem of these machines, though through a seemingly almost ridiculous means: paving the roads!

*Bicyclists* were the first to lobby for paved roads. After all, they needed them to get out of the parks they were stuck in. (Though some, such as Thomas Stevens of San Francisco, simply got out anyway. Stevens, on a solid-wheeled bicycle, left San Francisco on April 22, 1884. Traveling eastward, he reached Boston 3,700 miles later, on August 4. Not content to have made the first transcontinental bicycle ride, he continued eastward, circumnavigating the globe itself and returning to San Francisco by boat from the "Orient" on December 24, 1886, some twenty-seven years before it was done on a motorcycle.)

Enter an Irish veterinarian and his sickly son. The father, wanting to make the son a more comfortable tricycle, inflated lengths of surgical rubber tubing and fixed it to the wheels of his son's machine, and—*voila!* The pneumatic tire was born. The veterinarian's name? Dunlop.

Now the *comfort and performance* of the high-wheeler could be had with *convenience and style* in one machine. The year? 1888.

The pump had been primed, from dandy horse to high-wheeler to bicyclette, for the next, and latest development, the "safety bicycle," from which the modern motorcycle directly descends (the high-wheelers, when they hit a rut in the road or a pothole, would unceremoniously trap the rider under the handlebars and hurl him into the pavement headfirst—a profoundly unsafe accident known at the time as a "header").

The safety bicycle had a diamond-shaped frame, multiple gears, brakes, and pneumatic tires.

This safety bicycle hit Europe and America like a bomb. It has been estimated that by 1896 Americans alone had spent $300 million on bicycles and $200 million on accessories. Harry Dacre, a songwriter coming to America in 1892, brought with him a bicycle. His friend joked that he was lucky it wasn't a bicycle built for two, or he would have had to pay double duty on it, which led Dacre to write "Daisy Bell," which, more than one hundred years later, any Brit or American can sing the refrain of:

*Daisy, Daisy, give me your answer do*
*I'm half crazy all for the love of you.*

*It won't be a stylish marriage*
*I can't afford a carriage.*
*But you'll look sweet upon the seat*
*of a bicycle built for two.*

This now so-simple-seeming machine spawned nothing short of a revolution, both *practical* (affordable bicycles allowed extraordinary mobility for an unprecedented number of people) and *social* (the people riding these newfangled bicycles went places on them they hadn't before, literally and metaphorically). Said one clergy member: "Man is a locomotive machine of nature's own making, not to be improved by the addition of any cranks or wheels of mortal invention." So great was the initial backlash against these early bicyclists that they were set upon by mobs. Others hoped the bicycle would "take men away from the gambling rooms and rum shops, out into God's light and sunshine." Most simply cherished the freedom of motion they brought.

But it was women, particularly the suffragettes, who most seized upon the bicycle as the instrument of their emancipation. It is hard to imagine now, but urban women had been forced into a style of dress so physically restrictive (with whalebone corsets, bustles, gathered waists so small in diameter that they damaged the wearer's spine and internal organs, and shoes so narrow they made it difficult to walk in them) that a "commonsense dressing" movement was spawned around the bicycle. To ride the new safety bicycles, women for the first time wore a form of pants, really a skirt divided into midsection lengths for legs, called bloomers. Most popular were "Betty's Bloomers." Born with the bicycle was the "new woman," who replaced the staid, Victorian Gibson Girl of the prior two decades. Detractors called the image of the new woman—capable, educated, even daring—poisonous.

Said the feminist figurehead Susan B. Anthony in a *New York World* interview (February 2, 1896), "Let me tell you what I think of bicycling. I think it has done more to emancipate women than anything else in the world. . . . I stand and rejoice every time I see a woman ride by on a wheel

. . . the picture of free, untrammeled womanhood." This same year, a Baltimore minister went on record saying bicycles were a "diabolical device of the demon of darkness . . . imbued with a wild and Satanic nature."

Male undergraduates at Cambridge University, protesting the admission of women to their college, hung an effigy of a woman in the town square: a woman *on a bicycle.*

During the bicycle craze, manufacturing and metalworking techniques were being developed, as well as components (ball bearings, sprockets, drive shafts), that would find their use in motorcycles, essentially overnight.

Early "moto" cycles were really bicycles with some profoundly crude form of mechanical propulsion, and the first was possibly built by the inventor Sylvester Roper of Francestown, New Hampshire, in 1867, employing existing steam engine technology. Roper, a mechanical genius (he also invented a hand-stitch sewing machine, a machine for making screws, and a folding fire escape), built a small steam engine that he bolted into the frame of a boneshaker. Powered by coal, and requiring both a boiler and water tank, the machine was initially impractical, though by the early 1890s Roper had mounted an improved and more compact engine in a safety bicycle he wished to market to the public.

And where was the best place to showcase his invention? A board track for bicycle racing, given that thousands attended the events held at them.

By the mid-1890s, more than five hundred companies manufactured bicycles in the United States alone, more than one hundred in Chicago, and bicycle racing was big money. A racing bike at this time cost, in today's currency, $27,450.

The cost of Roper's invention? Inestimable. Roper, in 1896, attended such a board track event, bringing with him a two-cylinder version of his "steam bike," which he intended to race against the best bicyclists of the time.

Roper, seventy-three, was laughed off the track.

However, when he was finally allowed on, not only did he keep pace with the bicyclists, but he gained a fair lead over three laps, winning his race—at a speed of about thirty miles per hour. Roper, not content to leave things there, tried for higher average speeds that night, his front wheel coming loose and his "steamcycle" throwing him into the sand surrounding the track.

When Roper was reached by spectators it was found he was dead—though it was later determined he had been killed by heart failure, not the accident itself.

Roper's triumph did not go unnoticed, though, his invention inspiring the German Gottlieb Daimler, who had worked with Nicolaus Otto on a four-stroke engine. Daimler, in 1885, attached an "Otto Cycle" engine to a wooden boneshaker with outrider "stabilizer wheels," thus creating the first gasoline-powered cycle, which Daimler's son rode a whopping six miles. (Daimler, realizing the advantages in the Otto Cycle engine for general use, and acknowledging the poor vehicle the powered boneshaker was, chose to focus his efforts on the horseless carriage. In 1900 Daimler had Wilhelm Maybach, another of Otto's former cohorts, design an engine for his company. Emil Jellinek, an entrepreneur on the board of Daimler's company, demanded the new engine be named after his daughter, here the origin of the "Mercedes" in the name Daimler's company adopted, after a merger, in 1926—Mercedes-Benz.)

Still, the notion of powering bicycles with Otto engines had been seized upon, and no end of engineers and inventors began experimenting with specific applications, most significantly in France, where Count Albert de Dion and the toy maker Georges Bouton created a single-cylinder, half-horsepower Otto Cycle engine, air cooled, upright, and using a battery-and-coil ignition system, later dubbed the De Dion–Bouton. Most early "motor-bicycle" configurations placed this fairly heavy engine over the front wheel, which negatively impacted the handling. No matter, bicycle enthusiasts bought either factory-adapted bicycles or kits for adapting De Dion engines to bicycles with a passion bordering on mania. The British magazine *Engineering* at the time described this new "moto-cycling" fad as "a form of entertainment that can appeal only to the most enthusiastic of mechanical eccentrics," expressing doubt that it would have any lasting widespread "favour" with the public.

"Puttering" took hold in Britain and in America.

About this time in America, the inventor E. J. "Airship" Pennington patented the first "Motor Cycle," in 1893, which, like his proposed dirigible that was to travel to the moon at a speed of two hundred miles per minute, was mechanically unsound. Some claim Pennington, a charismatic fraud, was the inspiration for L. Frank Baum's Wizard of Oz. Those working with him commented: "he furnished experience and the other furnished capital, with a reverse of the conditions at the finish."

Hildebrand and Wolfmüller, properly reading the puttering rage, released the world's first *production* motorcycle in 1894. Powered by a 1,428 cc Otto Cycle engine, it put out 2.5 horsepower and had a top speed of twenty-five miles per hour, a problem in Britain, given existing speed laws: such "fast" vehicles were to travel preceded by a man waving a red flag.

"Moto" cycling became the new rage, and to accommodate the new "moto-cyclists," new laws were written nearly overnight.

Manufacturers sprang up everywhere—which, from our contemporary perspective, is nothing significant. Consider this, though: By the late 1950s, Harley-Davidson was the only surviving manufacturer of motorcycles in the United States. By the end of the 1970s, all of Britain's bike manufacturers had gone under due to Japanese pressure, exerted by makes even nonriders can identify—Honda, Yamaha, Kawasaki, and Suzuki. The big four. And by 1980 in Italy, there existed (as major producers) just Ducati and Moto Guzzi.

Imagine this then: "Moto" cycles, until assembly-line construction brought the relative cost of automobiles down in the 1920s, were so popular that, to accommodate the early, "golden years" demand, more than *three thousand* individual manufacturers existed. More than seven hundred in the United Kingdom alone, and well over a hundred in the United States.

And where did these riders take their machines? There were the already existing venues for bicycles—countless miles of *paved* roads, and for racers, velodromes, which became "motordromes." And when "moto" cycle performance improved significantly, these early motordrome designs were expanded until board tracks measured miles, and stars were lapping them at insane speeds. In 1920, the champion board-tracker Gene Walker was clocked at 136 miles per hour at a Daytona, Florida track—on a stripped-down machine with no brakes. Board tracks killed so many riders that motorcycle racing was moved to horse tracks and pavement. Oddly, given its two-decade worldwide popularity, only *one* motion picture of board-track racing is known to exist, and that just minutes long and silent.

But to return to the development of the motorcycle. Notice the cubic displacement of the Hildebrand and Wolfmüller engine: 1,428 cc. That, even today, is an enormous engine for a motorcycle. Also notice its horse-power and top speed, 2.5 and 25 m.p.h. respectively. Has the writer here gotten his decimal points in the wrong place, you might ask.

No.

Let's take this year's off-the-showroom-floor 1,400 cc motorcycle, the Kawasaki ZX-14, for comparison. Horsepower? Around 200. Top speed? Over 180 m.p.h. or, really, as fast as you dare to go on it. (On the Bonne-ville Salt Flats, ZX-14s have done well over 200 m.p.h.)

So, why the difference in performance given that these two engines operate on the same principles, burn the same fuel, and are even made from the same materials? Why?

A necessary anecdote here:

Months ago, I attended a party in Park City, Utah, one thrown by a motorcycle enthusiast to celebrate the arrival of his new industrial lathe and machining tool, which could mill metal to millionths of an inch. That lathe and tool, I saw right away, was the size of a thirties Buick; it had been bought from some manufacturer in Vladivostok or Irkutsk, and looked it.

Tom had gotten this monster to make parts no longer available for his vintage bikes. And he had them, twenty or so. Beautiful bikes: a Norton International, early-model Ducatis, and bikes no one has heard of but bike nuts—Bianchis, Velos, Crockers, and a Brough Superior.

They all ran, or were in restoration.

These were bikes I'd ridden, like the Velo, some I'd seen and badly wanted to ride, like the Brough and the Vincent. Legends. Lacquer shiny, meticulously pinstriped tanks. Megaphone exhaust pipes. Sand-cast casings. Hand machined and assembled. Tom's bikes were just so much motorcycle jewelry.

An older, pot-bellied guy with short, iron gray hair to my left, who'd ridden in on the latest BMW tourer, which, I could see from his thumb-fingered hands, he'd never so much as touched with a wrench, said, surveying all these motorcycle works of art, "They were pieces of shit then, and they're pieces of shit now."

All of us within earshot laughed.

Here was *easily* a half million dollars' worth of bikes (a Vincent Black Shadow alone is worth about $55,000).

What did this guy mean, and why did we all laugh?

This takes us right back to the Hildebrand and Wolfmüller motorcycle. Only someone acquainted with these machines can know how absolutely cantankerous they were, just sometimes nearly impossible, and the earlier, the more so. The H&W machine, for example, had its connecting rods running *directly* to a ratcheted crank on the rear wheel, obviating the need for a transmission and in effect making the bike *direct drive*—each combustion stroke of the engine spun the rear wheel. *Kerpow!* And away you were propelled—which must have made for some wild ride. And to add to this, instead of using a flywheel to conserve energy between the power strokes of the engine, H&W used elastic cords. Lovely!

This first generation of motorcycles didn't stay in tune (most early engines used what was called hot tube ignition, a flame in a tube fitted to the intake valve, attached to it an induction vaporizer, a small bowl of liquid benzene, the benzene's higher vapor pressure alone atomizing and creating an air-fuel mixture). These machines leaked oil (total-loss lubrication was typical early on, operated by the rider, who pumped it through the engine via a stob on the gas tank, the surplus oil exiting the engine onto the road), stank, backfired, seized up altogether (once a Matchless I was riding seized a piston, locking up the rear wheel at sixty or so, but before I went down, I—instinctively—pulled in the clutch and saved myself that otherwise certain road rash). They wobbled, shook, and shimmied; the cables broke, the levers warped, and the tires blew out.

And, jumpin' jeepers, if we weren't having the time of our lives riding those bikes from their inception. You don't believe me? Then ask yourself why three thousand companies would make them? People wanted *moto cycles*.

Yup, they broke all right. But when they ran, rumbled, tore off into space with you hanging to the handlebars for dear life, there was *nothing* like them. Even a pathetic little Briggs and Stratton-powered minibike, to a ten-year-old, is pure intoxication. I should know, I had a few.

So, 2.5 horsepower, at the turn of the century, out in the open, roaring along, was nothing to sneer at.

But the question remains: Why this performance, given the displacement? Why *so much more motor* in the modern motorcycle?


### The Motor in *Motor*cycles, and Other Engineering Marvels of the Breed. (Or, Why Does That Thing Have to Shake Like That and Make So Much Noise?)

Given that the bicycle was undeniably a thing unto itself long before Roper or Daimler got their hands on it (and given that the bicycle remains today in the same form), it is the *motor* that makes the motorcycle—here, motor meaning an *engine*.

The word *motor* is derived from the noun form of the Latin verb *movere*, meaning "to move." The root form of *movere* is *mew* or *meu*, meaning "to push away." From this root we derive the words *momentum, mobile,* and *motive*—if you're in the mood for murder!—and *commotion, emotion, promote,* and *remove.*

*Engine,* now a synonym of *motor,* is of a different lineage. The word entered our language through Middle English, from Old French (where it meant "skill" or "invention"), its earliest source being, of course, Latin: *ingenium,* meaning "inborn talent," "skill," or "power" (also giving us the word *genius*). Thus *engine*, in its earlier forms, meant a force (sometimes of an invisible, even spiritual, nature). An engine, then, was some *driving force*. As in "the *engine* of robust commerce *drove* the Gay Nineties."

(It is interesting to note, here, that it was George Hendee of the Indian Motorcycle Company who first conjoined the words *moto* and *cycle* to create *moto-cycle*. Prior to this, powered bicycles were called "motor-bicycles.")

And did this lump of fire-breathing, stinking, thundering iron, this motor, this engine, simply appear for tinkerers to drop into the frames of so-called safety bicycles? Obviously not.

So let's go back a bit, and follow the development of the engine to the point where Roper and Daimler jammed it into their boneshakers. Again, a device we've come to take for granted (and arguably the single most world-changing invention in modern history) had its origins in the most humble of circumstances.

How about this—the internal combustion engine had its birth in a gadget called the steam digester, which was used to extract the fat from bones, leaving them brittle enough to make bonemeal. Think of a motor-cycle named the Steam Digester. Sexy.

Denis Papin, an associate of the physicist Robert Boyle, and familiar with Boyle's newly formulated gas law, which states, "for a fixed amount of gas kept at a fixed temperature, pressure and volume are inversely proportional" realized that if he could create a "sealed cooker," thus increasing pressure, he could also raise in it the operating temperature, which, in any open system (standard atmospheric pressure), was limited to 212 degrees Fahrenheit, give or take a degree or two for altitude.

Papin's steam digester was really the world's first pressure cooker.

And how do you get from this *digester pressure cooker* to bearded dudes on Harley-Knuckleheads?

Papin found, predictably, that in his contained system the pressure increased with the temperature, but also that sometimes his digesters exploded, and with unhappy results, users sporting scars from shrapnel if they survived. To solve this problem, Papin designed a steam release valve. (Some time ago I had a wonderful roommate, Vikas, from India. Vik's mother, cooking lentils in her pressure cooker one afternoon, blew a hole six feet in diameter in the kitchen ceiling, this after my roommate had laughed at me for ducking under the table the first time the valve let off a plume of steam.)

Papin, watching this new valve on his digester open and close (1679), conceived of a piston-and-cylinder engine. He even drew up plans, though the means to convert the linear motion of the piston for usable power eluded him. That remained for Thomas Savery to invent (1697), though he used what he called a "beam," all steam engines from that time being *beam* engines (primarily used to pump water from mines). Simply imagine a beam—a bar of steel—on a pivot about midway along its length, a piston fixed to one end, forcing the beam down. The unattached end of the beam, then, was available to do "work": pump water, grind grain, and so on. The valves necessary to admit steam into the engine, and to exhaust it, were operated manually. James Watt, from whom we get the term *watt* as a measure of power, realizing the limited application of this early steam engine's beam, patented sun-and-planet gears (1781), which produced from the linear piston movement *rotational motion*—thus birthing the "engine" (cylinder, piston, connecting rod, crankshaft) as we know it.

Historians cite this one invention, the modern steam engine, with Watt's gears, as giving birth to the industrial revolution.

Steam engines. Now a thing of the past, right? Wrong. Even nuclear power plants are just fancy steam engines, using fission, rather than coal, to boil water to spin turbines. And, really, steam pressure as a force to do work has been with us far longer than its use by Papin. In Roman Egypt it was used to open temple doors ("Pay no attention to that man behind the curtain! I am the Great Flim Flam!"). Taqi al-din, an Ottoman Arab in the sixteenth century, utilized a crude steam turbine to rotate spits of roasting meat, these early devices employing steam power called "mills." Oddly, *mill* is now an archaic term of affection for tweaked engines used by hot-rodders, auto and biker alike. ("It's got a bitchin' mill, man, that'll blow your mind!")

Robert Fulton, who is sometimes thought of as the inventor of the steam engine, was no such thing (such credit is often attributed to James Watt). Fulton, in 1807, used a Watt steam engine in his paddleboat, though unlike Richard Trevithik, a predecessor, he made them commercially practical, which in turn led to the development of the steam locomotive, and all things steam-powered—the rest is, again, history.

Still, a crucial design limitation remained regarding the development and use of the reciprocating-piston steam engine. The steam engine is an *external-combustion* heat engine, and requires an external boiler and water tank.

A near parallel development, but one operating on a refined formulation of Boyle's gas law, was the *internal-combustion* engine. By 1834, Benoît Clapeyron, through experiment, had found that the state of an amount of gas is determined by its pressure, volume, and temperature. (Clapeyron's formula is simple enough: $PV=nRT$, where P is the absolute pressure, V is the volume of the vessel, n is the number of moles of gas, R is the universal gas constant, and T is the absolute temperature.) What this simple-seeming equation suggested was that gas could be introduced to a closed system, such as that already existing in Watt's steam engine, and if cataclysmically heated, would expand cataclysmically, this explosion driving the piston as did steam introduced from outside an engine. Simple enough? And how to heat such gas? Burn it. *Add oxygen.* Only, simply adding oxygen isn't sufficient to initiate oxidation, a problem in an altogether closed system.

It is amusing now to note that deriving mechanical power from this sort of contained explosion had been in engineers' minds for centuries. As early as 1206, the Persian Al-Jazari envisioned a pump with a reciprocating piston-and-connecting-rod mechanism—the insoluble problem being how to initiate the explosion inside the cylinder/chamber. Likewise, Leonardo da Vinci, in his papers, toyed with the idea of a compressionless engine, as did the physicist Christian Huygens, neither resolving the problem Al-Jazari encountered. Basically, how do you "light" a fire inside a sealed chamber? No solution existed, until Alessandro Volta (from whom we get the term *volt* as a measure of electrical power) found it, his first application being in the most humble of devices.

So, as with the steam engine, having its first application in Papin's digester, the internal-combustion engine had its first use in a parlor trick, one employing a toy gun. Volta, using newfound technology, electricity, exploded within the sealed barrel of a gun a mixture of air and hydrogen, popping into the hands of his audience—a *cork*. Here was the birth of the spark plug.

Development of the compressionless internal-combustion engine from this point was unceasing, these early engines operating on any number of fuels, most often hydrogen (it didn't leave "pernicious residues" in the cylinder as did gunpowder, milled saltpeter, and so on). And while as early as 1824 the French physicist Sadi Carnot established through thermodynamic theory that *compression* was necessary to create a powerful internal-combustion engine, no application resulted until nearly fifty years later.

If you compare the timelines of the two developments, external-combustion engine (steam) and internal-combustion, it is easy to see why the internal-combustion engine lagged behind in use. Steam engines could run on fuels already at hand, such as coal, wood, industrial scrap—literally anything that would burn. They were easy to build, simple, and suited heavy use (boats, trains, industrial applications). By comparison, compressionless internal-combustion engines didn't develop much power; they overheated; and their by-necessity far more complicated internal parts suffered destructive friction created by the crude fuels burned in them. So comparatively efficient was steam power that engineers focused on it, one company, Stanley, producing steam-powered cars up until about 1920, by which time they had become badly antiquated.

Enter, of course, petroleum, used at first almost exclusively for lighting and lubrication (industrial and domestic). In 1854 the Italians Barsanti and Matteucci patented the first engine of its kind fueled by the new petrol—here, a squirt in a sealed-by-valves firing chamber.

There followed, of course, Otto's engine (four-stroke, and having in-cylinder compression, 1876), and the Atkinson engine (a profoundly crude two-stroke, also having in-cylinder compression, 1882), both heavy, under-powered, and unreliable.

By 1882 steam-engine development was at its zenith. Steam-powered battleships, trains, and electrical power stations were in use worldwide. Steam ruled the world. But steam power, suitable for heavy applications—such as seen in the steam locomotive—proved unwieldy for smaller ones. Say, a horseless carriage or motor-bicycle. Or for a portable power source.

Hence, a whole coterie of engineers was bent on solving the basic problem inherent in the internal-combustion engine as they knew it. Why was the caloric (energy) value of this hydrocarbon they were using for fuel (petroleum) not expressed in the output of their engines?

From the inception of the motorcycle, engines designed to power them have of necessity been models of efficiency. The motorcycle engineer Walter Kaaden's two-stroke, for example (for a real-world application, see chapter 4), was the first to put out 200 horsepower per liter. All of this no small feat really, it became rocket science, and remains so today.

Realize that a 30 percent efficiency figure (meaning power derived from the engine in relation to the energy value of the fuel) for an internal-combustion engine is *high*. Peak efficiency, even at this present date, is about 37 percent. So where does all that energy go? Recall that what is useful in an internal-combustion engine is *not* the combustion, the burning, of the fuel. What *is* useful is the expansion of the gas in that sealed system, which, in turn, is converted to mechanical "work." Heat, then, is a by-product of combustion, and is lost in the engine's exhaust, as well as radiated by the engine itself. Friction and so on takes another good portion of power. So early engines had, possibly, as low as 5 percent efficiency.

Again, necessity proves the mother of invention. Enter the science of fluid dynamics. Technically, even vaporized gas is still a fluid, so the internal-combustion engine is a *fluid* engine.

If you're running Z gazillion kcals of fuel through an engine and the engine is only producing A units of power, even taking into account the loss due to heat, what's the problem? Factoring for the basic inefficiency of the internal-combustion engine due to heat loss, friction, and so on, the answer is, primarily, inefficient "burning" of the fuel.

Not very helpful, right?

Consider that Harley-Davidson's first carburetor was (reputedly) made from a tomato can (1903). And why not? Petroleum was nearly useless. Rockefeller, when he first struck the big time in Pennsylvania, had no idea how to market the stuff, so the more the merrier, right?

No. The challenge simply became one of *fluid flow*, complicated by other factors that made designing gasoline engines not only a science, but an *art*—an unbelievably complex art. And especially so for the moto-cycle. Because, for the moto-cycle, on top of the first challenge of improving efficiency was the question of *fitness for use*, which we'll get to in all its various, sometimes hilarious forms, an example here of poor fitness for use being the ill-fated mid-thirties Indian Exhaust-Over-Inlet Four, which produced more horsepower than its Inlet-Over-Exhaust predecessor, though it also barbequed its cylinder head and valves as well as riders' legs. And there was the aesthetic issue—these engines were going to be out in the open, *looked at*, even admired and lusted after, hopefully.

Already the bicycle at this point was an object of aesthetic interest, and all that was lovely in the bicycle immediately applied to the moto-cycle, but now with all the mechanical appurtenances of this newly invented "engine."

Because horsepower output was so low, pedals were left on these turn-of-the-century motorcycles so that when their engines/drive trains were insufficient for mounting the most gentle of hills, the operator could resort to assisting with the pedals. And even given the effort at making these machines light, they still weighed in the neighborhood of three hundred pounds. Imagine pedaling a three-hundred-pound, balloon-tired bicycle up a hill. Such experiences, no doubt, fueled in riders visions of roaring up hills in blazes of dirt and exhaust, which they later did (see chapter 6).

So how do you effectively move gases through an internal-combustion engine, increasing usable power output? Here we'll address the Otto Cycle engine. Otto, considering this problem, arrived at the presently most widely used solution, a four-stroke (sometimes called "cycle") engine. During (1) the *intake stroke* the piston moves down from the top of the cylinder, creating an increase in volume, and so a decrease in pressure, a mixture of air and fuel entering the engine through a valve, which closes once the piston reaches the bottom of the phase. In (2) the *compression stroke* the piston begins moving up, until it again reaches the top of the cylinder, the cylinder again at its smallest volume and the air-fuel mixture under significant pressure. In (3) the *power stroke*, a version of Volt's gadget, the spark plug, at the precise moment the piston is at the top of the stroke, fires, igniting the air-fuel mixture, causing a catastrophic contained explosion, the oxidizing (burning) air-fuel mixture expanding exponentially over a fraction of a second, creating enormous pressure, which, again, drives the piston down to the bottom-most point (the cylinder at its largest volume). At which time, in (4) the *exhaust stroke*, a valve opens, the piston coming up again, decreasing the volume of the cylinder, thereby forcing out the burned gases from combustion. (Harley riders call these strokes "suck, squeeze, bang, and blow.")

In theory this seems simple enough. Still, real-world application is worse than problematic. First, consider here that only one phase (stroke) of all this moving metal adds energy to the system, the "power" stroke. And, granted two principles of the laws of thermodynamics—energy is neither created nor destroyed and all systems tend to rest unless acted upon—what's acting upon the system to move all that engine mass in the first and second (intake and compression) and fourth (exhaust) strokes? Of course, that energy must come from an *outside source*—initially, with a motorcycle, either human energy ("kick starting") or an electrical "starter" turns the engine. So what happens when it's "running"? You still need something that *conserves energy* from the power stroke to provide the energy in the three strokes of the engine not creating it. So? A big, heavy flywheel.

However, another problem is created by using the flywheel—you've just added an enormous amount of inertial mass to the engine. If you want to speed the rate at which the engine goes through the cycles, and thus create more power (explosions per minute) you have to work against the limitations of getting that heavy flywheel spinning *faster* but also *in less time.*

Think of a bicycle with really heavy balloon tires versus one of those street-racing wonders. Compare the amount of energy it takes to get either up to speed, say, twenty-five miles per hour. And how about stopping either? In both cases, it takes more energy with more inertial mass (here, the heavier tires).

So these early Otto engines ran, but that was about all. The earliest examples operated at one rate of revolutions per minute—rpm—which was around 1,500. This was not much over the number of revolutions required to generate enough momentum in the flywheel to carry these early engines through the three "dead" strokes of the four. For some time it was thought that the theoretical absolute revolution limit of an Otto Cycle engine was 3,000 rpm. Sport bike engines now commonly turn at over 15,000 rpm. And, if you couldn't rev the engine to "burn" more fuel to generate more power, how could you get more power?

Simple solution: Make the damn thing bigger! But how, and what part of the engine? At this point in the development of the internal-combustion engine, industrial and agricultural applications became common everywhere through what was called the "one lung" engine. These engines had pistons the size of Folger's coffee cans, flywheels on them—larger for larger displacement—weighing anything from a few hundred pounds to a ton, and operated at sufficient rpm to keep their flywheels spinning, essentially making these engines "flywheel momentum engines." In remote areas, they were everywhere you couldn't get power lines in, and were in use well into the first few years of the sixties, when I saw them run generators in northern Minnesota, Michigan, and Wisconsin.

So, as Americans like to think—bigger is better, right? Again, no. This engine must, after all, fit into a vehicle—and in the case of a motorcycle, a very small one. And what, after all, does this engine size come from? One liter, four liters, 455 cubic inches, and so on? What does it *mean*? For purposes of simplicity, let's consider the most common early engine having only one cylinder, such as the massive one-lunger just mentioned. The "displacement" of such an engine is the cubic dimension of the closed cylinder with the piston at the bottom of the intake stroke. Or, more accurately, the volume the enlarging motion (stroke) of the piston has created given the diameter of the cylinder (known as the engine's bore). So, Bore x Stroke = cubic displacement. Math is not even necessary here: The bigger the container, the more it can contain. So, if it is an explosive, the bigger the charge, the more power when it explodes, right? Think Quaker Oats: with the small size you get five cups of oats; with the big, budget daddy, you get twenty.

So, thinking of those oats, you dump the twenty cups in that cylinder, instead of the five, and all other things being equal (the same density of air-fuel mixture, and so on), you'll get four times the bang from that larger engine, right?

Yet again, *wrong.*

And here's another thing that drove early engineers crazy. Okay, you make a big whopper of an engine, here a single cylinder. Realize that when you use a gorilla-sized piston, that piston, once it's moving, is going to hit like a gorilla, too. Up, down, up, down.

How do you deal with unidirectional, unequal force? Some of these early engines had such terrible balance that they would lift the wheels of the machines they were mounted to off the ground.

Remember those sun-and-planet gears from James Watt? The ones that converted the piston's up-and-down motion into rotational motion, leading to the development of the steam engine as we know it? The piston is connected to a "connecting rod" or "con rod." The con rod is connected to a "throw" (what looks like a shallow U) on a crankshaft, so that as the piston moves up and down, the connecting rod rotates the crankshaft.

Imagine, then, as the piston moves up, a mass equal to that of the piston, but fixed to the crankshaft, rotating down in exact synchronized opposite motion—thus "counterbalancing" the inertial mass (moving mass) of the piston. Great idea, right? Problem solved. Only, no, this *didn't* solve the problem—it only made the problem something operators could live with. Counterbalancing reduced the problem of the inertial momentum of the piston, but engineers discovered that there remained phases in the cycle wherein there was little or no "counterbalancing" taking place, given the "vector" (direction) of the counterbalancing force. With a single-cylinder engine, this imbalance is always worst midway in the piston's movement from Top Dead Center to Bottom Dead Center, given that the vector of the counterbalancer is then in part lateral to the motion of the piston. Make the piston bigger, and the inertial imbalance is magnified.

Bigger motor, bigger shaker. The more and faster the revolutions per minute, the greater the off-direction inertial imbalance. A problem that, to this day, still hasn't really been solved in certain engines. A 1960s Norton Commando engine, a simultaneous twin, at 4,000–6,000 rpm, shakes the frame it is mounted in so badly that the rearview mirrors are all but useless, the images in them blurred beyond recognition. Is riding that Commando fun? Absolutely! But you'd have to "safety-wire" it, drill holes through critical nuts and bolts and run wire through them, to prevent vibration from shaking nuts loose from critical controlling "bits," or these monsters would come apart as you rode them.

Also, if your engine has greater inertial mass, added to by the use of counterbalancing, don't forget, you then need a flywheel with greater mass to carry that new, larger mass through those three "dead" strokes.

And all this is just *balancing* the engine—the problem of efficient fluid flow has been in no way solved. How do you most *effectively* get the air-fuel mixture into the engine, burn it, and get it out? To do this, the Otto Cycle engine needs mechanical valves (unburned air-fuel in, burned exhaust out), and a modified form of Volta's spark gadget to set off the explosion. From a theoretical standpoint, again, all simple enough, though, early on, to produce *ideal* results in real-world application was all but impossible. To fire the spark plug, for example, about 40,000 volts are required. Since in these early years the alternator as we know it did not exist, all ignition systems (induction coils) ran off batteries—this system was called "total loss ignition," since the batteries were depleted in the process—and early batteries were *awful*.

Since the primary problem to solve with an internal-combustion engine is effective fluid flow, though, let's go back to the valves. Engineers initially struck on an "atmospheric" valve to get the air-fuel mixture into the cylinder, that valve opening during the first phase of the Otto Cycle—*intake*. With an atmospheric intake valve, the rapidly increasing volume of the sealed cylinder creates a partial vacuum, thus *pulling* the valve open against the weak spring that otherwise holds it closed. The problem here being that when engine balance was improved, and along with it air-fuel vaporization, the engine could turn at 3,000 or more rpm, but this atmospheric valve couldn't close quickly enough, so hot exhaust gases and unburned air-fuel mixed, creating "precombustion," which all but stopped the engine. And there was this, too: Given that there is no spring strong enough to hold outward-opening valves (both intake and exhaust) closed against the violence of the "power" stroke explosion, the valves had to open *inward*. But if you wanted better engine performance, greater compression was necessary, which meant the piston forced the air-fuel mixture into a smaller space at the top of the compression stroke, which made it possible, if the timing of the valves was off even in the slightest, for the piston to strike the valves—causing engine failure. Or the spark plug, too low in the firing chamber, could melt the piston, since one way to deal with the problem of inertial mass was to make the pistons lighter, out of aluminum—but then they *melted* under less-than-ideal conditions.

As a result, during this stage of early motorcycle engine development even metallurgy posed severe design limitations—parts melted in high heat, fractured under stress, or simply wore thin due to lack of hardness. The tough but light alloys that we take for granted now, such as titanium alloys, did not exist. Hydraulics were not in common use until after World War II. And marvels such as EFI (electronically metered fuel injection), much less microchip-monitored engine functions, were far, far beyond the most advanced mechanical engineer's wildest dreams.

So early engineers focused on balancing and aspirating engines, while keeping them small, of tractable character, and somewhat reliable.

All this is just scratching the surface of the difficulties this "motor" presented designers. Driven by market demands, early manufacturers cranked out versions for the public that were little more than experiments. As a result, these early engines, as well as the motorcycles they were in overall, were engineering marvels but mechanical nightmares, as some remain to this day. They had more congenital defects than a factory-defect Yugo. And what about the other half of that first question? Why does that damn thing have to make so much noise?

From the first, noise and power were associated. How does a muffler work? By passing that explosive exhaust gas through a series of baffles, the percussive sound waves are turned against themselves, though in the process the baffles create "back pressure," which in turn impedes the effective flow of gases through the engine. So the most effective engine runs without a muffler.

Loud came to mean *powerful*—whether the public liked it or not. Noise abatement was an issue from the birth of the motorcycle, and was paramount in the formation of one of the first, and now the largest, motorcycling organizations in the world, the American Motorcycling Association.

All this had occurred by shortly after the turn of the century. The bicycle had paved the way (literally), and continued to have popularity, but the motorcycle quickly became a worldwide, near-hysterical craze. In this early, now dubbed Golden Age, period, people went crazy for motorcycles, cantankerous or not.

The public response was unprecedented. Otherwise taciturn Brits, phlegmatic Frenchmen, and practical Americans turned into moto-maniacs overnight. And moto-cycles, at this time, were not a fashion statement, but a vehicle of both utility (doctors rode them, as did delivery people, suffragettes, and tradesmen) *and* pure sport.

Everywhere, heck was a-poppin'. In 1893, at the World's Columbian Exposition held in Chicago to celebrate the four hundredth anniversary of Columbus's "discovery" of the New World, the public was introduced to the White City (which Walt Disney's father had helped build, and which would influence Walt's creation of Disneyland fifty-some years later), lit not by Edison's direct current, but Westinghouse's alternating current. Also introduced at the Columbian Exposition were the zoopraxiscope (which would inspire Edison's first moving film machine, the Kineto-scope); Nikola Tesla's first fluorescent lighting; George Ferris's "Wheel," or the Ferris wheel; and household items still with us today, the hamburger (or hamburg steak), Juicy Fruit gum, Quaker Oats, Cream of Wheat, and Cracker Jacks.

And the automobile and moto-cycle.

Engineers and inventors had nearly gone mad trying to solve the early problems of four- and two-wheeled propulsion and displayed all kinds. But lost to history is the victory of the motorcycle. (Even a decade later, there were only five thousand native-built cars in the United States, all toys of the wealthy.) Early moto-cycles, even beset by engineering difficulties as they were, could be had at a fraction of the cost of a car, though, even more important, they gave tens of thousands of owners previously undreamed-of mobility, and with it the thrilling sensation of riding in the wind.

The "iron horse" had been born, and *people loved it.*

Moto-cycle companies sprang up overnight to meet the public demand, each touting some new "advancement" in design, some new form, a great many of which are still with us today, such as the opposed, or "boxer," twin. Recall that single-piston engine and the balancing problems it had? Engineers thought, Why not run an identical piston opposite it, thus canceling the directional momentum of both pistons? But then how to time the firing of the two? This proved simple enough—though there remained the "dead" strokes, for each side of the engine, as well as the off-vector energy, which again necessitated counterbalancing and a significant flywheel.

One company, drawing from then current aviation technology, thought to use a rotary engine. Here "rotary" does *not* refer to a decades-later invention, the Wankel engine, as used in experimental Nortons and the production Suzuki RE-5. In aviation, an early design was the "radial" engine, with the pistons running off a crankshaft like spokes on a wheel. With the radial engine, the *block* was mounted to the firewall of the airplane, and the crankshaft turned the propeller. Some engineers (particularly at Le Rhône, in France), though, soon realized they could solve a host of problems the radial engine suffered (overheating, vibration, and lubrication) by mounting the *crankshaft* to the firewall and having the *engine in its massive entirety*—pistons, cylinders, and valve gear; carburetor ducting, spark plugs, and oil lines—*spinning at aviation speed*, around 1,200 to 1,400 rpm. In this rotary engine, centrifugal force gave excellent oil pressure to all moving parts distant from the crankshaft/axis and negated the off-balance beats of the engine; and the spinning of the engine drew an infinitely larger volume of air over the engine's fins, allowing them to cool the engine more effectively. And, given all that spinning mass, the Le Rhône engine *didn't need a flywheel*—so it could be *hundreds* of pounds lighter.

This was the engine that, later, powered a significant portion of World War I fighter planes. The machine guns on these planes, mounted at the pilot's eye level, had to be synchronized to fire not into but *through* the blades of their propellers—earlier aces engaged in combat having found themselves suddenly without a propeller. And also suffering diarrhea, from having inhaled and swallowed their engine's total-loss lubrication—castor oil.

Sounds like a great engine for a motorcycle, right? (No.) And how would you mount it in a bicycle of the time?

Such an engine was put in the Millet, a five-cylinder rotary, with the fixed crankshaft as the hub of the rear wheel, *the rotating cylinders being spokes*. Not ones to be outdone by the French, the German company Megola produced its own version, which had no clutch and no gearbox. But instead of making the rotary (spinning) engine a component of the rear wheel, as had Millet, Megola put the engine in the front wheel *and* geared the engine to counterrotate the direction of the front wheel, six times for every turn of the wheel. The engine weighed in the neighborhood of 150 pounds. Having no gearbox or clutch, you started the Megola by running alongside it, then jumping on and "bump" starting it. Megola produced this little monster into the 1930s, when a rider set a speed record with it—ninety-six miles per hour. Multiply that times six, and you get an idea how fast that little rotary engine was spinning in the Megola's front wheel. Scary? Proponents boasted that the Megola, once running, could be piloted by anyone, and was so stable it could be operated on loose sand—just think of all that centrifugal force generated by that spinning engine. (For those interested, Alan Cathcart, a motor journalist, has chronicled his contemporary impressions of riding a Megola in an article titled "Megola Maniac." Cathcart, Alan. "Megola Maniac," *Motorcycle Classics*, Dec. 1997.)

Needless to say, the rotary-engine motorcycle is not still with us, though Killinger and Freund, Germans again, built a two-stroke version in 1938 that would have gone into production but for the advent of WWII. Nor is its cousin, the radial-engine motorcycle built by Redrup and others into the teens, still with us.

And while "brands" have come to be associated with one given engine layout or approach—Harley-Davidson, the 45-degree V-twin; BMW, the opposed twin, transverse in the frame; Honda, Yamaha, Suzuki, Kawasaki, in line fours, mounted transversely; Ducati, the L-twin; and Triumph, BSA, Norton, and so on, the vertical/simultaneous twin—no such distinctions existed early on.

All of these companies made engines of all sorts, nearly all motorcycle trends having originated prior to WWI. Harley-Davidson, for example, was the first company to build a production-model horizontal opposed twin, more than a decade before BMW, and most of the British companies built V-twins at one time or another.

## Morphological Considerations: Or, the *Racer* in Road Racer and the *Chop* in Chopper, and the Development of the "Ideal" Motorcycle

Right about here, you might be thinking, but *why*? Why all these different engines? Why all these different ways to stuff them into bicycles? What *difference* can any of it make? Gas goes in, the engine makes power that drives the vehicle, just like it does for a car. The less you know the engine is there at all, the better.

Wrong.

Given the physical operating difference between four wheels (which define a "plane" on which the vehicle rests) and two wheels (which are kept upright through the gyroscopic force of those wheels), and given the motorcycle's smaller mass, where and how—exactly—the engine sits in the machine, and *how* the engine makes power, profoundly affects how it will ride.

Here is another critical thing to consider: the motorcycle's frame. Think of a child's bicycle. The child can confidently pedal it to a little over walking speed. Ever seen what happens when the child decides to coast that little bicycle down a slope and turn it? At fifteen miles per hour, that little bike's front wheel "crabs," throwing bicycle and child onto their sides. No, that fall is *not* the fault of the juvenile rider. That fall is the result of steering head geometry not appropriate for speed.

The steering head, to which the front wheel is mounted (via a fork), is angled, or "raked," so the child's bicycle turns best at *walking speeds*. At nearly zero degrees of rake, the momentum at a higher speed (and therefore mass, but more so force, given the child and bicycle are moving) when the bike turns is directed at an angle counter to the centrifugal force of the wheels—the forward energy cutting through the plane of the centrifugal. So the bike falls.

Now imagine this. You take a bicycle made to operate at, perhaps, twenty-five to thirty miles per hour. Put an engine in it, as did Clement of France in 1902, a 1,000 cc V4. The motorcycle can now "go" at seventy-one miles per hour. But if you turn it, what happens? The motorcycle goes wildly out of control and falls.

So manufacturers raked their motorcycles appropriately for speed, only to discover, through further poor functioning and disaster, that yet another factor was critical to handling: "trail." And what is trail? To measure trail you drop a perpendicular line through the hub of the motorcycle's front wheel, and mark that spot P. Now you run a line down through the front fork, extending that line until it hits the ground at point Q. The distance between P and Q is the "trail." If your forks are particularly long, as on some choppers, the trail is large. Choppers got their name from bikers cutting, or "chopping," the steering heads from the frames of standard motorcycles and reattaching them at that now characteristic chopper/cruiser long, low, lean, "raked" angle. If short, as on a motorcycle for slow speeds (as for observed trials, addressed in chapter 4), there's very little trail.

Choppers, with their raked and extended forks and armchair, laid-back style, are *made for going in straight lines.* So a chopper can't compete with a sport motorcycle a third its size on a curvy mountain road.

Early designers tried to find some golden mean, which came to be roughly 30 degrees of steering head rake and 80 mm of trail. (Now, too, as then, all motorcycles, with the exception of minicycles for children, have a wheelbase somewhere between fifty and sixty inches, with wheels sixteen to eighteen inches in diameter.)

Roughly, it works like this: for rake, the higher the steering angle (the closer to vertical), the quicker the steering; the lower, the slower; for trail, the longer, the more stable the handling (and heavier), the shorter, the quicker (but more unstable, or "squirrelly").

When you combine the two, you have an infinite range of possibilities, and this is complicated by yet another factor. If you take that old bike with pneumatic tires, run it at fifty, sixty, and even seventy miles per hour, and it hits, say, a shallow divot in the pavement, the force generated is transmitted directly into, first, the wheels; second, the motorcycle; and third, the rider, these forces becoming proportionally larger with increased speed—wheel- and bone-breaking larger.

"Suspension," a way for the motorcycle to absorb or transform this road energy, became critical then, especially for the front, steering wheel (many bikes remained "hardtails" until the fifties), as a shallow pothole could cause a blowout or hard fall if struck with sufficient force head on.

The first sort of suspension for motorcycles consisted of "springer" forks, which simply added a second fork with springs, parallel to the already existing fork, the wheel either mounted to that sprung fork or to the end of arms connecting the two. Simple enough, but, of course, this device changed the steering "trail" and wheelbase, and made bikes thus suspended handle . . . let's say, sometimes unpredictably. And these forks had no hydraulic or other dampening, so when compressed, they worked a bit like stiff Slinkys or pogo sticks. Long after you hit something, these bikes were still bouncing. And there were other front-wheel suspensions: the Castle fork, as fitted to the Rolls-Royce of motorcycles, the Brough (pronounced "Bruff") Superior; the "girder" fork, attached to just about everything else; and the late girder fork in the Vincent, dampened hydraulically. Finally, by the late thirties, the telescopic fork, which is on most motorcycles now, came to be the best solution to this problem of front suspension. And there have been yet more types since, the Earle, or leading link fork, which BMW used for years, now called Telelever suspension, as on BMW GS models—even a hub-steered setup, which was used at one time in Yamaha's premier touring bike.

Add to these frame-design considerations the center-of-gravity issue. Given that the engine constitutes as much as (and on these very early motorcycles more than) half the weight of the machine, the location of it in the motorcycle's frame becomes critical. As mentioned before, the De Dion–Bouton, or variations of it, was widely used, first placed over the front wheel, which, at least initially, made the most sense, given that the steering head appeared to be structurally the strongest place to mount it.

Did you ever sit on the handlebars of a bicycle while your good friend pedaled it behind you? Both of you laughing hysterically because . . . ? The bike became nearly uncontrollable and you were, unless you exercised extreme caution, destined to crash. Very funny at ten miles per hour, but not very funny at sixty.

So the positioning of the engine in the frame also made enormous differences in the way the motorcycle handled.

The racing-bicycle builder Oscar Hedstrom, in Middletown, Connecticut, fabricating a moto-cycle for pacing his racers in 1901, cut the rear tube of a safety bicycle's diamond frame, installing there a De Dion–Bouton engine. Now the mass of the engine was midway between, and slightly above, the hubs of the motorcycle's wheels. Hedstrom's design was so superior—tractable, with good handling; a joy—that the Springfield, Massachusetts, entrepreneur and bicycle racer George Hendee persuaded a reluctant Hedstrom to manufacture versions of his bicycle pacer for the public at large, the two naming their company Indian Motorcycle. Here was the first major production American motorcycle. Indian played on the "iron horse" theme, marketing its racy red motorcycles as "Crimson Steeds of Steel." Until World War I, Indian was the world's largest manufacturer of motorcycles, at its peak producing more than 20,000 bikes per annum, and in one year 41,000. Many classic motorcycle aficionados today rate the Indian Chief, with its streamlined fenders, the most beautiful motorcycle ever built. Indian was also the first to introduce the "loop" frame, swing-arm suspension, electric starting, and lights. By 1923, Indian alone had sold more than a quarter of a million motorcycles.

William Harley and Arthur Davidson, in 1901, were, like Hedstrom, experimenting with motorized bicycles using an upright, single-cylinder version of the De Dion–Bouton engine, producing by 1905 (a figure adjusted by historians) their first signature model, the "Silent Gray Fellow," so named for its quiet exhaust note and subdued (gray) paint scheme, sold under the name Harley-Davidson.

Both companies, Indian and Harley-Davidson, following their early success, brought in mechanical engineers. Both began producing (roughly) 45-degree V-twins, with the plane of the engine in line with the frame, the crankcase bolted now into the bottom of the classic frame's diamond, giving both companies' motorcycles excellent balance.

What was *not* in balance was the engine itself. Recall that business about engine balancing and vectors of force. With a 45-degree V, no amount of counterbalancing at the crankshaft can balance the lateral vector forces. Consequently, the 45-degree V engine has congenital imbalance that increases proportionally as engine speeds increase. Hot-rod the engine, and it produces even more vibration.

Far from alienating riders from Indian or Harley-Davidson motorcycles, their characteristic "powerful," "wild" character created cults of die-hard riders (see MCers, 1%ers). Recently, when Japanese manufacturers attempted to replicate the rough-idling Harley-Davidson exhaust note, the company filed a lawsuit against them, attempting all the while to patent their signature sound (unsuccessfully). What is that sound? *Potato-potato-potato-potato!*

A third company in the early American triumvirate was Excelsior-Henderson. Excelsior, founded in the late 1800s to build bicycles, got into the moto-cycle business about the time Indian and Harley did, producing a single-cylinder motorcycle popular with the public. Ignaz Schwinn of the Schwinn Bicycle Company in Chicago, wanting to profit from the moto-cycle craze, bought Excelsior in 1911. At that time Henderson was an independent manufacturer, and both companies knocked down significant world-class records: Excelsior was the first to produce a motorcycle to officially exceed 100 mph (1912); and a Henderson in-line four, piloted by the enthusiast Tom Clancy, was the first motorcycle to circumnavigate the globe (1913), a journey of eighteen thousand miles. (While the four-cylinder engine, invented over a decade earlier by the British engineer Frederick Lanchester, had the advantage of creating near continuous power pulses, it also produced secondary vibration, a problem that couldn't be corrected with counterbalancing at the crankshaft and caused them to run "rough as a cobb" until the vibration was negated through the use of independent, eccentric, counterrotating balance shafts.) Henderson, despite competitive performance, suffered supply difficulties during WWI, which led Schwinn, wanting to expand his motorcycle empire, to buy Henderson in 1917, forming Excelsior-Henderson, after which Henderson came to manufacture the first motorcycle with "full-pressure" lubrication.

As a publicity stunt to advertise the Henderson motorcycle's virtues, August E. "Blick" Wolter in 1918 rode Schwinn's latest Henderson for two laps around the highest roller coaster then in Los Angeles, including those sections that required him to ride upside down. Excelsior-Henderson likewise shattered Cannon Ball Baker's earlier transcontinental record set on a Harley-Davidson. And, particularly significant, Excelsior-Henderson boasted of being the first company to produce motorcycles with all the controls (clutch, front brake, and throttle) on the handlebars.

Excelsior-Henderson, through the twenties, was thought to produce some of the finest motorcycles in the world, particularly the Excelsior Super X, on which my grandfather, Robert Emil, was photographed. Nothing sells motorcycles like testimonials. My grandfather's? "That Super X went like the wind. I *loved* it."

Still, in 1931, returning to Chicago from a trip to Washington, where he saw the recession that had hit America was only going to worsen, Schwinn told his engineers, simply, "Gentlemen, today we quit."

Which Indian and Harley did not do.

And overseas? Overseas, moto-cycle development and fervor was even *greater* than in the United States. Realize that steam-power development there preceded parallel development in the States by nearly two decades— no surprise, since what passed for high-technology research at the time was done in Europe. For that reason, and due to the dire need for affordable public transportation, the United Kingdom, Germany, France, and Italy were poised for nothing short of a society-wide love affair with the motorcycle. The bicycle had been in production in Europe since the 1870s, hundreds of manufacturers producing them. Significantly, though, the European orientation to the motorcycle evolved out of somewhat different origins than its American counterpart.

Motor fanatics in Europe have long been everything from the fishmonger to the titled gentleman, who just had more money for more exclusive wheels, such as the Brough Superior. And while Europeans to this day find fascination in the American notion of the motorcyclist as outsider. (I can't recall how many Europeans, when they find that I am a motorcyclist, have shared with me their dreams of riding a Harley, wild and free across the American "West"), theirs is a tradition having near identical development history, but very dissimilar social assumptions.

Motorcyclists in Europe (and that includes Britain) are generally not thought of as miscreants or outsiders, with the exception of those intending to be outsiders, such as the Rockers in Britain. Europeans didn't adopt the "iron horse" notion Americans took from the just "closed" frontier, replete with its Noble Savages and "lawless" open spaces, something Indian, of course, encouraged, even naming their factory the "Wigwam." Europeans, as always, emphasized lineage and class.

An advertisement from the builder of the Brough Superior (at the time the most "exclusive" and expensive motorcycle in the world), George Brough, serves to illustrate this European orientation, even where motorcycles are concerned:

> If [my] lack of modesty offends you, let me say that at one time we tried—really quite hard—to be modest. It couldn't be done. The lads who bought and rode my bikes systematically went about giving us swollen heads. Whenever we lay our trumpets down for a spell, Brough Superior enthusiasts take them up and blow themselves hoarse. Modesty is all very well up to a point, but one mustn't lose a sense of realities. If I, after 27 years as Designer-Manufacturer-Rider, couldn't offer you something pretty exceptional in the way of fast, luxurious motorcycles, the time would obviously have come for me to study the "Situations Vacant" column. You see, nobody on earth has been designing and manufacturing riding bikes as long as yours truly, G.B.

—an advertisement decidedly unfit for this side of the Atlantic. And Europeans were from the first obsessed with the *sport* of motorcycling, with racing, as were American fans also, but in a different landscape. In Britain, in particular, they did not take to motordromes or dirt tracks as in America, but to local roads, narrow, winding roads, fraught with hairpin turns, blind turns, off-camber turns. Beginning with the same De Dion–Bouton engines and safety bicycles, Europeans adapted their motorcycles for this challenging environment. European bikes had to be maneuverable, easy to stop, and light, as well as durable and powerful. And while manufacturers such as Triumph (now the last surviving of hundreds of British marques) built V-twins, the character of that engine did not especially suit the European rider. What came to be typical of Britain was first the lightweight single, and later the vertical twin, particularly as designed for Triumph by Edward Turner, an engine that in smaller displacements, up to 500 cc, was balanced well enough, but when made larger and more powerful became ferocious, as in the aforementioned Norton Commando. Vertical twins powered hundreds of thousands of British bikes from their first popularity in the early 1930s to the very demise of the British motorcycle in the late 1970s.

And, again, elsewhere other solutions proved more appropriate.

BMW in Germany, which produced airplane engines (hence the "propeller" tank badge), began production with a V-twin, though here a two-stroke. The machine was so inferior that BMW didn't sell it under its own name. So BMW took from the British company Douglas the opposed twin boxer layout, though turning the engine 90 degrees, so the cylinders jutted out from either side of the frame, which made it possible for the BMW to have a shorter, more functional wheelbase, and better engine cooling. This motorcycle, the classic BMW "boxer" they still make today, was first released in 1921.

And the Italians? Of course, the Italians were all Verdi, and Puccini, and Scarlatti—their "motors" employing the same basic functional layouts, but taken to extremes, as the Moto Guzzi supercharged V8, so powerful it was banned from international events. Or MV's (Meccànica Verghera) transversely mounted fours, Italians priding themselves on superior power output, though employing sometimes highly fragile and stressed engine components to get it.

And what do all these manufacturers have in common? They were each, in their own way, trying to create the ideal motorcycle—which now, as back then, *does not exist*. This takes us back to the very beginning, because, as most motorcycle historians have stated, *all* motorcycle trends were established before WWI, but most critically this:

Morphology. Overall, taken from the bicycle, but with the motorcycle, *motor morphology*.

In total, the variables in design are nearly infinite. For example, a most basic, though often not understood, aspect of engine character is torque. Recall old Archimedes? "Give me a long enough lever and I'll move the world"? Going back to the most basic parts of the internal-combustion engine, we have the piston in its cylinder, and the rod connecting it to the throw on the crankshaft. If you design an engine with an especially long stroke, the throw on the crankshaft is proportionally longer also—meaning you have a longer lever when the power stroke takes place. Hence, more torque. So engines with a longer stroke-to-bore ratio are "torquey." You can, at very low rpms, pull confidently away from a dead stop. This kind of engine is called "undersquare." If you reverse this proportion, you have an "oversquare" engine, and also one that revs more readily, because there isn't as much linear piston motion for each revolution of the crankshaft. In a "square" engine, the bore-stroke dimensions are equal.

So, enough engineering. What does all this *mean*?

It means, a now fifty-year-old bike such as the Matchless G-80, with its overlong stroke, will yield a motorcycle that will feel like it can pull stumps. That engine won't rev well, by comparison to contemporary machines, but it will pull the G-80 up hills effortlessly and without much fuss. Shifting is not critical, as the engine, lump that it is, will lug along throughout the rpm range, one that, in part due to its long stroke, tops out at roughly 5,000. New Yamaha bullet bikes, with oversquare bores, can redline at nearly 17,000 rpm, and will feel hyperresponsive. A bike with an oversquare engine in it will require constant shifting to keep the engine operating in its optimal power-producing rpm range, so, consequently, it will also have a close-ratio transmission, but also one with more gears—Honda having used as many as nine on their high-revving racers.

A contemporary four-cylinder engine, such as that found in Kawasaki's Z-1 R, will put out *four* times the horsepower (per cubic centimeter of displacement) of 1950s-era engines, but will have little torque at near idle rpm.

And given that observation, it's time to address the Japanese.

Coming late into the game, really after WWII, the Japanese refined existing designs. The square four engine, two pistons front/two rear configuration, as in Suzuki's world-beating RG 500 road racer? Introduced by Ariel in 1930 (designed by Edward Turner, who went on to design the archetypal vertical twin for Triumph). The horizontal single-cylinder (facing front) as on Honda's Passport series (used particularly in Asia), of which more have been built than any other motorcycle? Moto-Guzzi refined the concept in the early 1950s, the idea having been around since the 1910s. The boxer four-cylinder, as on Honda's Aspencade? Brough Superior and others had built them by the 1930s. Blisteringly fast rotary valve and piston ported two strokes? Pioneered by Walter Kaaden in the 1950s.

Each design was *not* just a way to make power, but to make power in a *use-specific* way.

T. E. Lawrence, or Lawrence of Arabia, an avid motorcyclist, wrote in "The Road" (a chapter of *The Mint*) of riding Boanerges, one of his Brough Superiors:

> Boa is a top-gear machine, as sweet in that as most single-cylinders in middle. I chug lordily past the guard-room and through the speed limit at no more than sixteen. Round the bend, past the farm, and the way straightens. Now for it. The engine's final development is fifty-two horsepower. A miracle that all this docile strength waits behind one tiny lever for the pleasure of my hand.
>
> Another bend: and I have the good honour of one of England's straightest and fastest roads. The burble of my exhaust unwound like a long cord behind me. Soon my speed snapped it, and I heard only the cry of the wind which my battering head split and fended aside. The cry rose with my speed to a shriek: while the air's coldness streaked like two jets of water into my dissolving eyes. I screwed them to slits, and focused my sight two hundred yards ahead of me on the empty mosaic of the tar's graveled undulations.
>
> . . . Over the first pot-hole Boanerges screamed in surprise, its mudguard bottoming with a yawp upon the tyre. Through the plunges of the next ten seconds I clung on, wedging my gloved hand into the throttle lever so that no bump should close it and spoil our speed. . .

A skittish motor-bike with a touch of blood in it is better than all
the riding animals on earth, because of its logical extension of our
faculties, and the hint, the provocations, to excess conferred by its
honeyed untiring smoothness.

And in this is the crux of motorcycle history and design—the machine
itself being, as Lawrence put it, a "logical extension of our faculties."

But *whose*? And with *what technology*? And why choose one form of
power over another?

Charles Redrup, for example, coming from aviation, built motorcycles
in the late teens and twenties having in them three-cylinder radial engines,
smaller versions of those he had designed for aircraft. Marine Turbine
Technology, likewise using aviation technology for a power source, has
fit a Rolls-Royce/Allison turbine into their Y2K motorcycle, for sale to the
public at $150,000. Is MTT's motorcycle heavy, having a turbine engine
it it? No. The engine weighs only 136 pounds, turns at 60,000 rpm, and
puts out 320 horsepower, making the Y2K the world's most powerful production motorcycle. Design problems with this motorcycle? At lower rpms
the engine produces very little power and the throttle response is worse
than sluggish (and this turbine guzzles gas by the gallon). Jay Leno, host
of the *Tonight* show and a motorcycle collector, owns one. And what is it
like to ride? Said John Cantlie of *Motor Cycle News*: "It's bloody mad and
extremely scary . . . it feels like bungie-jumping, except with the bungie
pulling you forwards and not upwards."

Would the average motorcyclist want to ride such a motorcycle as the
Y2K? Some would. I would. But, even granted the resources, would they
want to *own* it?

Motorcyclists over time develop relationships with their machines.
If you race, or tour, or ride regularly, they become *an extension of your
body.*

*Character* is the secret, is the draw. Motorcycles have *character*. Some
you instinctively hate, some you love, this being specific to the rider, of
course. (Lawrence went so far as to *name* each of his Brough Superiors—

George I through George VII, after their manufacturer, George Brough, each of them Boanerges, or God of thunder.)

Each and every bike built is built out of some rider-designer-engineer collaboration, for some specific use; for the pavement, sport bikes, cruisers, and choppers; for off road, motocross bikes, supermotos, and trials; for both dirt and pavement, enduros, dual sports, and adventure touring; and for cheap, in-town transportation there are scooters of all kinds.

All of this means nothing until you *ride* these machines, which a friend and I did religiously over a period of years, the two of us, through dealers, riders selling bikes through newspapers, and friends' bikes, test-riding before we were even twenty well over a hundred motorcycles, and that at a time when the "old generation" bikes were still around. I loved every minute of it, as each new machine provided a specific and novel thrill.

This is the reason why some riders, as my Salt Lake City friend Rick put it, are motorcycle polygamists. You want different experiences in motorcycling. (The actor Steve McQueen at one time owned more than two hundred motorcycles. Leno's collection is easily as large, or larger.)

And always, at the heart of each motorcycle is the *motor.*

Every Sunday, weather permitting, my friend Jerry and I would ride at least three bikes. One afternoon we rode a forties Knucklehead Harley (terrified of dropping it, as the owner was a bona fide tattooed Hells Angel), a Royal Enfield Interceptor, and a Yamaha RD 350. The Harley roared, spit, coughed, lunged, and loped. The Enfield pulled like a freight train, at which time I encountered railroad tracks, the slope up to them sending me airborne at seventy or eighty. And the tiny, boxy Yamaha two-stroke made the first two, even though being one third the displacement of the Harley and half of the Enfield, seem like 1950s school buses. That little Yamaha would do zero to sixty in the twist of your wrist, its engine piston-slapping and ring-dinging like two mad chain saws under your private parts, thrilling for two seventeen-year-olds.

The Kawasaki H1 "Widowmaker," a 500 cc two-stroke triple, we discovered, had a bone-chilling exhaust note, a whirring, throaty howl, and a tendency to wheelie on on-ramps and wobble at high speeds. There was the Suzuki Cyclone 400, which had almost no flywheel, a dirt bike that when it "got on the pipe" at 4,500 rpm went insane on you, the engine suddenly producing not ten horsepower but forty—in a machine weighing two hundred pounds—the engine so peaky you rode it as if *not* with a variable throttle but with an *on/off switch.*

Each bike was a joy, such as the Ariel Square Four, which had a character like no other. Rumbling, burbling, patrician. There were all the BSAs (such as the Rocket A75 I so took to that I had to have one, and did). Velocettes, Nortons, Triumphs. Velocettes, being singles, thumped (hence the name for them: "thumpers"), then rapped when you rode them hard. The Nortons, Triumphs, and BSAs, all simultaneous twins, had a muscular, throbbing feel that became more pronounced, even intoxicating, at speed.

Enthusiasts (see MCers) riding in groups around one particular manufacturer aren't crazy—they just like what they like. Honda Aspencade owners, for example, like machines that are two-wheeled cars—no exhaust noise, no vibration, no leaking oil, no rattling chains (or clutches), a good stereo between the handlebars. Here no character *is* character, these bikes weighing in with stereo, navigation systems, and hydraulic load-leveling over eight hundred pounds. Silent, gliding, quiet—and again, immensely heavy.

This lack of character became a complaint—not really valid today—in the seventies and eighties about Japanese machines overall. So determined were Honda, Yamaha, Kawasaki, and Suzuki to make their machines for the broadest range of riders that they created instead what critics called the UJM—short for Universal Japanese Motorcycle—all transverse fours (after Honda's CB 750 released in 1969, really a copy of MV's Augusta 750), weighing around five hundred pounds.

They ran, produced very respectable power (and more each year), had middle-of-the-road heavy but predictable handling, and were stone-axe reliable, which was a relief after dealing with British bikes, which, among other things, suffered Lucas electrical systems so unreliable that owners joked: Lucas, Lord of Darkness! But Brit bikes were nimble, powerful (by standards of the day), and, to the initiated, easy to repair when they, inevitably, broke. Those built on Fridays or Mondays were more prone to congenital defects, given union working blokes' pub habits, a nip or five or six for the way on Friday, a hair of the dog that bit you on Monday.

British bike owners liked to say their bikes oozed class—really oil, due to their crankcases being split vertically, and gaskets being inadequate to make up for milling irregularities. Their vertical twins with dual carbs "hunted" (intermittently lunged) if those carbs weren't synchronized, which was easy enough to do, until the too-soft "pot metal" al-yoo-min-ee-um they had been cast from was no longer airtight (jets and needles no longer positively seated), making tuning them impossible. Some thumb-fisted owners then threw up their hands. Trash! Out with it! You could buy these bikes from such owners for what a lawnmower would cost, get a new set of carbs on them in an hour, and roar off into the sunset with cash in your pocket for travel. I never paid more than six hundred dollars for a British bike in the 1970s—though I spent countless times that modifying bikes for myself and customers to get the performance we wanted out of them.

Bikes are *not* appliances to their riders, who have fierce preferences.

Otto-engined bikes (four-strokes) roar, pull hard, have torque; two-strokes "ring-ding" and have "peaky," narrow power bands, but are astonishingly light and quick, racing models having head-snapping acceleration.

Now, as always, motorcycle design is driven by cutting-edge technology. The most sophisticated motorcycles have computer-monitored electronic fuel injection (you can simply change the engine control unit chip to alter your engine's characteristics); antilocking brakes; and the new, inverted slider forks, adjustable for rebound and damping properties, as are their cousins on the rear. Some bikes, to reduce weight, use single-side rear swing arms (BMW) or have a faux gas tank, so gas can be placed nearer the bike's crankshaft, thus lowering the "wet" weight center of gravity. Disk brake calipers, instead of having one piston, can have four to six, giving these new brakes extraordinary power. And, of particular significance, and new, is Ducati's "black box" traction control, or DTC, which will monitor (see chapter 3) road contact forces, to prevent catastrophic loss of traction, this system programmable for the street rider and racer alike—the latter now able to "keep the throttle pinned until traction [is] found," a stunt that would have guaranteed the non-DTC rider a high side crash. Ducati is the only company in the world to use this radical system (the Japanese Big Four are too conscious of litigation, given their experience with three-wheeled ATVs, to cross this line), now in its $25,000 1098 S. The 1098 S is an L-twin descendant of the early seventies 750 SS, or, a good ol' V-twin, as have been around from motorcycling's day one. Magic wrested (by the Italians again) from a dinosaur design.

Yamaha now builds a dirt bike that has power at both front and rear wheels (yes, Rokon had this in the seventies, but in a tank of a motorcycle); and Piaggio a scooter with two front wheels in a four-joint parallelogram that allows freedom of movement like that of a skier's legs. While leaning—which it can do extraordinarily well, since it has double the front-end traction of the standard motorcycle—the inside wheel goes up, while the outer wheel is pushed down. Riders express nothing short of astonishment at this scooter's handling, and nonbikers take one look at it and say, "I could ride that."

Some engineers believe this two-front-wheel configuration represents the future. Quiet, smooth, having incredible traction. But some riders don't want quiet. Some riders will buy a Ducati, for example, simply for the music it makes, a harmonized thundering.

Singles putter and thump. Twins create harmonized explosion (with the exception of alternating twins, which whir). Triples resonate like half of a big inline six, and roar at speed. Transverse fours howl at low rpms, shriek at high, and so on. Each "motor," each heart, creates a significantly different experience for the rider, in some cases a day and night difference.

Which is best? There is no best. The choice is always the rider's, now, one in ten of them being women. And the motorcycle's fitness to his or her purpose dictates form (city streets, open road, road racing, dirt, dirt racing). Style, inevitably, evolves from this—for example, the sixties counterculture chopper, with its easy-chair (European sport riders call it the "sit and beg") riding posture, suggests indifference, rather than vigilance, a devil-may-care attitude as opposed to alertness, a "to hell with handling and whoever doesn't approve of me" ethic. By contrast, a Sears Allstate "twingle" (an Austrian-made Puch) of the same period, with its curved lines closing in on themselves, and upright rider position over the handle-bars, suggests tidiness and control, economy and a natty élan.

European bikes and American bikes from the first have embodied a certain design aesthetic, usually the work of one individual. For that reason, everything on these classic motorcycles is in proportion, making early European and American motorcycles things of great beauty. When the Japanese began designing motorcycles after WWII, committees of en-gineers, such as at Honda, built them from disparate aesthetics as well as engineering (and industrial) sources, giving early Hondas a certain "parts bin" appearance that didn't sell well overseas. Their fenders, for example, were said to look like "pelican bills" or "Roman helmets." To this day, the Japanese motorcycle design aesthetic can be questionable, as demon-strated in the Yamaha Virago, or Honda Magna, parts-bin bikes if there ever were such.

Some bikes are so beautiful that they are not ridden but are simply on display in owners' homes, such as old Vincents, Velos, or the Indian Streamliner Chief or Harley-Davidson Knucklehead (1936). The Guggen-heim Museum recently had an "Art of the Motorcycle" exhibit, in which bikes from an 1868 Michaux-Perreaux (contender with Roper's steam ve-locipede for first motorcycle) to a 1998 MV Augusta F4 were showcased.

Motorcycles are time machines, each generation of bike embodying the zeitgeist peculiar to its builders. Motor-bicycles (to 1915) became board-track racers (to 1920) became streamlined road tourers and speed-sters (to WWII) became counterculture choppers (1960s) became Italian dream machines (1970s) became appliances (1980s) became state-of-the-art road racers (1990), and now, drawing from all these sources, they are all things—counterculture machine (Ducati Monster), dirt bike extreme (KTM 999 Duke), posh tourer (Honda Aspencade), or killer all-out race bike (Ducati 1098 with DTC).

The best, as the Guggenheim's curators affirmed in their show, are technical and aesthetic works of art: Pinstriped, brilliant in glossy paint, and with that aluminum alloy, iron, brass, stainless steel, and chrome monster at its center. The *motor* in *motorcycle*.

You can call it style, as did Christopher Caldwell, incorrectly, in a *New York Times Magazine* article titled "Geezery Rider." But where the motorcycle is concerned, pure style is for the *poseur*, the nonrider.

What it really comes down to, again, is *character*, born out of this century-and-a-half public affair with the motorcycle, with *riding them*, to this day, the motorcycle thrilling us, amusing us, and, to an extraordinary degree (as in Asia), just getting us cheaply somewhere with our family, friends, and, possibly, ten chickens in cages on the back. And even those forced to use them come to revel in them.

Since the collapse of the "practical" excuse for the motorcycle, which took place when cheap automobiles became available in large numbers, motorcycles have existed for *sport*. For the love of them. *That's* part of what that complex feeling is when one pulls up alongside you in your Camry. "Camry," jokes Rick, my "motorcycle-polygamist" friend who owns fourteen motorcycles, two of them race-ready Ducatis, is Japanese for dependable, boring, and . . . well, *no balls. No music.*

You resent someone doing something unnecessary—and, in the United States, perhaps even more so, generally socially frowned upon. Something exhilarating but dangerous. Why should that creepy-looking thug in his dirty black leather have all the fun?

Which takes us back to the beginning.

There's this whole history of social irritation with motorcycles, with those Wild Ones out there, those Hollister characters and bikers in black leather passing you as if you were standing still (and, in California, sharing lanes). You'd have to buy a million-dollar Bugatti W16 to simply keep up with that stinker on his Jap Bullet bike he bought for three thousand dollars—or, as I did, got for free, when the owner couldn't get it to run.

The bike might look like molten sex, like a Ducati Desmosedici; or like some netherworld black-and-chrome apparition, a Harley Chopper, a bearded biker draped over it.

All are descendants of the bicycle and the "motor," of this century-and-a-half love of two-wheeled motion.

Roaring along, free and outside!

But maybe what most creates those complex feelings is this:

The biker's got some . . . grin on his or her face. If you happen to talk to him at a gas station, he'll say, "Wow! What a great day for riding! You oughta try it!"

Riding.

And right there you wonder, maybe, just maybe, I should. That's the part that really irritates. That *maybe*. Because you just know it would be something that would shake you, once again, intoxicatingly, and perhaps frighteningly, *alive*.

And wouldn't that be something? What *then*?

# 3

# Road Racing

## SEX ON WHEELS

### Hot Tar, Cool Cash

*How'd you like to make 30 million cool ones—a season?*

That's what the top-ranked motorcycle road racer Valentino Rossi socked away in 2009, and the Italian tax authorities are after him, claiming that between 2000 and 2004 he underrepresented his income to the tune of $160 million (112 million euros). Many in the business are convinced Rossi had even greater income derived from endorsements and spin-offs. Currently Rossi is ranked number 11 in world athlete income (number 2 outside the United States), just a stretch behind Tiger Woods.

Chances are, though, you've never heard of Valentino Rossi. Nor, most likely, are you aware that in the United States alone, according to U.S. Motorcycle Market research, more than $4.6 billion is spent every year on motorcycles, roughly 1 million of them new road bikes. And this figure does not take into account after-market accessories. A tiny company such as Atomic Motorcycle, with five employees, is selling $1 million of swag per annum.

In Britain, as has already been noted, during the sixties only export sales of cars and whisky exceeded that of motorcycles. So where are all those Brit bikes now? And what about the Japanese Big Four, how did they earn such clout? Or Ducati, for example? And who is this Valentino Rossi?

The answer is in road racing.

## Taking It to the Street

While "road racing" is now a catch-all expression for any competition done on pavement, including amateur "stop-light" sprints, drag racing, Super Sport events, and even Grand Prix, it once meant exactly *road* racing—racing on circuits of closed public roads. This was a direct result of the threat motorcyclists were posing to pedestrians and other users of roadways. So much so that the parliament of the Isle of Man, the Tynwald, passed legislation to close public roads on Tuesday, May 28, 1907, to hold the first International Auto-Cycle Club Tourist Trophy, the world's first sanctioned road race.

The course comprised ten laps of a fifteen-mile "short route," entrants riding road-legal moto-cycles, the emphasis being on touring and fuel efficiency. There were two classes: a single-cylinder class, which, this first year, was won by Charlie Collier riding a Matchless (his time was four hours, eight minutes, and eight seconds, for an average speed of 38.21 mph); and a twin class, which was won by Rem Fowler riding a Peugeot-engined Norton (his time was four hours, twenty-one minutes, and fifty-two seconds, for an average speed of 36.1 mph). Collier was declared the overall winner and was presented with a trophy of winged Hermes by the Marquis de Mouzilly St. Mars.

Sounds like a great deal of hoo-ha for nothing, right? By today's standards, possibly even pathetic. But think about it for a moment. First of all, Collier's average speed was 38 mph, which meant for portions of those four hours he was doing well above that speed on roads that had been cut into the Isle of Man for horses. Roads that were off-camber, sand-covered, sometimes wet, sometimes even rocky (the IOM route wouldn't be all "tarmac" until 1925).

Americans have difficulty visualizing the British landscape until they have been there. For one, the population density is much greater, and roads exist everywhere in Britain (as in Europe), dating back to the time of those greatest of road builders, the Romans. Even in what those sunny-climate Romans must have considered the outpost from hell, rainy, chilly, cloudy Great Britain, they built roads almost everywhere. Winding. Up hills and down. Through landscape that was not flattened or bulldozed. Through forests.

Imagine, now, the most challenging, curvy stretch of public road you've been on, some of it cobbled, and your bike has no suspension. Set some charming cottages along its length, tea shops, an apothecary or three, trees, potholes filled with rain, and hundreds upon hundreds of cheering spectators.

Mount a Schwinn balloon-tired bicycle with a gas tank strapped to the crossbar, a hopped-up lawn-mower engine bolted between your ankles, and kick off with fifty-odd riders trying to run over you. It's raining, off and on. Sometimes a terrible headwind is blowing, or a side wind. At times you are going nearly 60 mph on that Schwinn, the engine between your ankles vibrating with such ferocity it shakes bolts loose. That at-first-intoxicating exhaust note after a very short time becomes deafening. Imagine cornering such a bike at 45 or 50 mph. Wow. What fun! Now stay in front of those fifty other crazed zealots behind you for a mere four hours, eight minutes, and eight seconds.

And you win the trophy of winged Hermes.

Granted you do so on your Matchless, what motorcycle will a good half of the following year's contestants be riding? The winged M. Matchless. And, Matchless, with more money in its pockets from those increased sales, will make improvements to its bikes, while Norton will nearly go into foreclosure spending money it did not earn that year on engineering and development.

In 1908 the use of pedals was banned; in 1909 fuel-consumption considerations were abandoned, along with exhaust silencers; and the IOM game was on. From the first it was international. In 1911, for example, the American company Indian won with the rider Oliver Godfrey, his average speed being 47.63 mph.

A hundred years later, the machines have changed radically, the riders somewhat, but the equation remains the same: Racing success = domestic and international sales. Racing breeds technology for the streets. And racing is *sexy*. Slap a decal on your bike claiming it has won the IOM, and you're guaranteed to sell volume. (Recall that there have been as many as three thousand motorcycle manufacturers.) And in the balance are riders' lives. From its inception, riders have died yearly at the IOM, currently more than a hundred in total. Giacomo Agostini, after a friend was killed at the IOM, refused to race there. Currently, the fastest IOM lap *average* speed (set by John McGuinness of Honda) is 128.6 mph, while *top* speeds have become nearly astronomical. So, for competitors, racing, such as at the IOM, is dangerous, and then some.

But for that other 99.99 percent of riders, racing is boon and benefit: all that rocket-scientist technology brought to bear on the endeavor to dominate road-racing events ends up in bikes built for us, we amateurs and wannabes—who, when riding, dream we are riders such as Valentino.

Road racing, more than any other form of competition, drives motorcycle technology. After all, three quarters of all bikes sold worldwide are road bikes.

And in the process, human history is made.

## A Bit of the Old Stiff Upper Lip, TT Style

If any racing venue brings up images of motorcycle racers in black-leather one-piece riding suits, "pudding-pie" helmets, and double-lensed racing goggles, hunched over ferocious motorcycles, it is the post-board-track Isle of Man of the thirties, late forties, and early fifties.

Yearly, the route changed, with new sections added, such as the Snae-fell Mountain Course, the routes themselves now having a quaint sound to them: "competitors guided hard left at Cronk-ny-Mona then went straight-away on A18 to Governor's Bridge and on to the finish line at Glencrutch-ery Road."

What say? Out of a field of manufacturers, including Cotton, Levis, Humber, and others now extinct, a breed of British bikes emerged, duking it out for survival: Triumph, BSA, Norton, and the not so well known Ve-locette, AJS, Sunbeam, and Douglas.

Would you believe me if I told you that a 1960s Triumph Bonneville was, for all practical purposes, designed in the mid-1930s? (Edward Turner, former Ariel engineer, unveiled Triumph's Speed Twin in 1937, which was changed very little to the end of its run in 1978.) As were all the bikes Britain was manufacturing up until the demise of the British motorcycle industry in the mid- to late-1970s (but which had really started around 1959).

Ten years from its inauguration, the IOM had become road racing's most prestigious and extreme testing ground, and it is still thought to be so today. Year after year, manufacturers made changes to existing technology, so refining their bikes' handling characteristics that it would not be until nearly four decades later that these companies battling for IOM supremacy would be forever surpassed by the upstart Japanese. Early on, even Indian successfully raced on the isle, its rider, Jacob De Rosier, exclaiming before the press, "This ain't going to be no tea party," giving Brits an expression that is still in use today.

All European manufacturers made yearly appearances there, the pres-tige of the IOM races such that by the mid-twenties the Italian manufac-turers Moto Guzzi, Bianchi, and Garelli entered riders—ones who lapped the isle at average speeds over 70 mph. Simple side-valve and overhead-valve engines were replaced with overhead-cam engines, springer forks with telescopic forks, rigid rear ends with plunger suspension. The Ger-mans, too, entered the fray, in the form of BMW, DKW, and NSU. Here was an international coterie of riders, engineers, and marketers, bent on dominating the IOM. Defections were common, as riders, unsatisfied with their mounts, switched teams, as did Stanley Woods (who had won four TT races for Norton), switching to Moto Guzzi in 1935. The word *revenge* was commonly used when teams "shown up" one year returned to take the IOM, as Norton did in 1936. As a result, fierce international rivalry sprang up, tens of thousands of spectators lining the course on hillsides, picnicking, drinking wine, and singing, usually cheerfully enough, patriotic songs directed at rival teams' fans.

*This* was sport European-style: sophisticated, colorful, exciting (personages such as Prince George, the Duke of Kent, attended), so much so that the American filmmaker George Formby used the 1935 IOM as the backdrop for his feature *No Limit*. Even Germany's National Socialist party, the Nazis, took an interest in IOM events, Hitler himself espousing a mandate to dominate world sports and motorsports events. In this climate, Germany's BMW won the 1939 Senior Event. The British company Velocette at the time was experimenting with a supercharged 500 cc twin, the "Roarer," a sure bet for the 1940 TT, but German hostilities curtailed further development. Even given all this, the Isle of Man's golden period did not come until racing resumed there following WWII in 1946.

Here, really, was where road racing as we know it today began, and where the British domination of motorcycle racing was lost in the face of competition from the Continent, particularly Italy.

Streamlining was used, in the form of what were called "dustbin" fairings, such as on Moto Guzzi's bikes, which also covered the wheels, sometimes with disastrous results. A bike called the NSU "Flying Hammock" crashed due to faulty aerodynamics, killing the designer. Side winds, with those fairings not tested in a wind tunnel, could be fatal. Still, so successful were these "streamlined" machines that *all* IOM races in 1957 were won by them. Detractors feared spectators would not be able to see riders, but then, as now, these fairings so improved performance that they became indispensable, tighter, more compact versions being developed in wind tunnels, resulting in the fairings we have now. In 1958, race officials outlawed the wheel-covered dustbin fairings, and that year Moto Guzzi, the progenitor of the design, withdrew from racing.

Of particular interest here is this: Guzzi had developed the dustbin fairing for its V8 engined racer, which was so powerful, it was virtually beyond the capacity of the tires of the time.

While the British were running single-cylinder Norton Manxes, or twins, such as the AJS Porcupine, the Italians had built a water-cooled, double-overhead-cam V8 (that's right, eight-cylinder) motorcycle engine that put out 68 brake horsepower (horsepower is measured at the crankshaft; brake horsepower, usually being about 15 percent lower, at the rear wheel), when other bikes were producing 50. The real miracle was quartering the size of all the components of a comparable full-sized V8, and coming up with an engine that would work in a motorcycle frame, leaving room for eight carburetors, a massive distributor, and all the hoses to cool and lubricate it. The engine weighed just under one hundred pounds, and gave the dustbin racer a top speed of 190 mph, something that GP bikes wouldn't be capable of for another thirty years. Too much technology for the time, the Guzzi V8 was only in production from 1955 to 1958, then disappeared, along with Guzzi, from international racing.

This end-of-the-fifties period was a turning point for Great Britain, which had, since the thirties, enjoyed phenomenal success in world road racing. Walter Kaaden was testing his two-strokes at the IOM, and others, including the Japanese, their multicylinder engines. And now, after WWII, road races laid out on public roads and running through local villages were held elsewhere, such as the East German Motorcycle Grand Prix at Sachsenring, Hohenstein-Ernstthal (beginning in 1962), but also in Italy, West Germany, and France. All of this culminated in the formation of a round of competitions held globally, from Suzuka, Japan, to Opatija, Yugoslavia, to Laguna Seca, U.S.A. The current grand prix takes place on no less than eighteen disparate tracks worldwide.

While this World GP racing circuit was taking shape, nothing short of a revolution, cultural as well as engineering, was forever changing the landscape of motorcycling: as Kaaden's two-strokes changed the face of dirt racing, so would they change grand prix road racing. Two-strokes would conquer all.

But not before Honda had its first golden period in world road-racing circles. Honda, just two years prior to Suzuki getting Kaaden's two-stroke (1959), released its step-through Cub 50 cc. The Cub, a clever amalgam of scooter (it had a unibody, painted a cheerful blue, and valenced fenders) and motorcycle (the engine was still down by the rider's feet, visible, with a stylish exhaust pipe and chrome muffler), created Honda as we know it today, a megalithic, powerhouse manufacturer. To say it was popular would be a gross understatement. Fifty years on, they are still making them. At this writing, more than 60 million Cubs (this one model alone) have been sold worldwide, more than any other single model of bike. This was from a company the West had never heard of, and whose president, Sochiro Honda, had said his efforts to that point had been a terrible failure. (Honda had run a number of other ill-fated enterprises before turning to the manufacture of motorcycles.)

What Honda did, wisely, was dump enormous amounts of his Cub-earned revenue into research and development. And while the Japanese at this time were not great innovators, they were spectacular refiners. Valve trains that improved performance but were unreliable, levels of complexity that generated great power but had failed outright for British, American, and European manufacturers, were set upon by Honda and perfected. And while Britain and BMW, for example, were refining singles and twins, respectively, designs over two decades old, Honda was building the equivalent of motorcycle Ferraris—and in the most unlikely of machines, the 50 cc. It was a very wise move. After all, quite bluntly, who cared about a "high-performance" 50 cc racing bike? (Gee, and given the sales of the Cub, why did Honda think this fussy little thing might be important?) No one really paid Honda any attention. MZ and Kreidler, with Kaaden's two-stroke, were dominating the class, and here came Honda with his little four-stroke nightmare.

It was called the RC 113 (RC for racing). Recall that four-stroke bikes such as the Brits and Germans were building produced peak power at, maybe, as much as 9,000 rpm, which, given the inherent balancing problems they had, was extreme. And British bikes for the motorcycle market made their peak power under 6,000 rpm. Honda's 50 cc RC 113 produced its 13 horsepower at 18,500 to 20,000 rpm. Where Britain's bikes had four-speed gearboxes, this little Honda had a nine-speed gearbox, and chain-driven dual overhead cams. And it didn't break. The RC 114, the bike that followed, produced 14 horsepower at 23,000 rpm, giving the bike, with its nine-speed gearbox, a top speed of 103 mph.

But what was the point? A late-1920s Brough Superior would do 125 mph. And Kaaden's two-strokes were still outperforming the RC 114—though just barely. So most of the biking world thought, Well, what a load of shit that Honda nonsense is. Sure, their little machines are kind of clever (and in this there was a fair amount of post-WWII bitterness), but what's the use? My BSA Goldstar (500 cc single) would make mincemeat out of that piker.

Brilliant. Honda's strategy was right on. Any engineer, or mechanic, can tell you this: Clever ideas are all fine and good, but it is real-world application that proves the pudding. How hard do the facing surfaces on cams have to be, if they're turning in an engine that produces peak horse-power at 23,000 rpm? How do you lubricate it? Keep it from overheating? What kind of clutch is most effective for it, dry plate or wet? Should a twin, such as the RC 114, use a 360-degree crankshaft (both pistons rising at the same time), as all the Brit twins did (thus necessitating heavy coun-terbalancing), or should they use a new, 180-degree crankshaft (one piston moving up while the other was moving down) that would obviate in part the counterbalancing problem, but create another one in its place, that of slightly off-phase ignition? Honda put all its money on the 180-degree crankshaft (the so-called "alternating" twin).

So Honda's little twins even *sounded* strange—they made a high-pitched spitting noise, which at first, to bike fans, was experienced as just plain awful. It didn't thump, or howl, or even whine in a scary, gnashing fashion as did Kaaden's two-strokes (some blokes in the U.K. had dubbed these two-strokes "meat grinders"). Surely this sound became an acquired taste, such as one acquires a taste for certain poisons, say, a good whisky or single malt scotch. (Honda's alternating-twin sound, even given my nostalgia for these bikes—God knows, I worked on enough of them—I have never taken to.)

Of course, Honda was using his small-displacement bikes to work out real-world performance problems. And then he simply made his engines two and three times larger, and went out and beat the world. In small-displacement motorcycles, no one could beat Honda in the middle years of the sixties. Honda came to dominate *all* classes, with the exception of one. What had been regarded with interest, but scorn, the 50 cc, in its final incarnation put out 320 bhp per liter. And the machine Honda had been told was outdated by the British motorcycle press at the 1959 IOM TT, the 250 cc transverse four-cylinder RC 160, in refined form, and ridden by the world-class racers Jim Redman, Tom Phillis, Bob Brown, and, most important, Giacomo Agostini and Mike Hailwood, proved unbeatable.

By 1965 the Honda R&D department alone had more than four hundred engineers, technicians, and mechanics. By 1966 Honda had unveiled two more wonders, a compact, transverse six-cylinder 250 and a GP five-cylinder racer. Next would have been a three-cylinder 50 cc, and a larger-displacement V8.

And right there, Honda quit—racing, that is—much to the shock of all in the world GP game.

In the years 1959—1966, Honda won sixteen world championships and had 138 grand prix victories—unprecedented and still unmatched. But they had not won a single 500 cc world event.

No matter. The descendants of those race bikes were already everywhere, bought by the "nicest people you meet." Elvis, in one of his beach pictures, rode one, a guitar strapped over his back, singing sappy songs. Out of Soichiro Honda's racing development came a whole generation of nonthreatening, technologically and mechanically superior (to their British, American, and European counterparts) flashy motorcycles—"Dream" Hondas—and in the weirdest displacements: 160 cc, 180 cc, 305 cc.

But unlike their racing bikes, Honda's production "Dream" bikes had goofy faux leading-link front suspension, pressed sheet-metal frames, bulbous fenders, and goofy-looking instrumentation. Most had either a variant of the Cub's little horizontal engine or the race-derived twin—dubbed "coffin heads" due to their rhomboidal shape. These engines turned a gazillion rpm, didn't leak, could be banged around endlessly without breaking, and the sexier, larger-cc twins all made that alternating-twin spitting sound, now associated with world-class racing success.

Riding these bikes, such as the Dream 305, was like riding a pogo stick on two wheels. The Dream 305 wobbled when pressed hard into corners, had speed shakes, and the whole frame flexed. None of this mattered, because Honda's target population, the U.S. rider market, didn't ride like Europeans did and still do. Americans weren't competitive in international motorcycle road racing at the time (with the exception of winning Honda a team prize at the IOM in 1959), and wouldn't be until the seventies, when Kenny Roberts would switch from flat track to World GP. Honda engines just ran, and ran, and ran—making that inoffensive, high-pitched "egg beater" sound.

I suppose that because I was one of the last of the boomers born in my family, and had first cousins a full decade further along, I hung with an older crowd by the time I was in my early teens. Motorcycle people. But not Harley people. (I don't intend anything negative here. Members of my family had been Harley riders. But Harley riders, if they are into modifying their bikes, usually go in the direction of drag racing.) The characters I met had Nortons, Velos, and Triumphs. All were God-honest gearheads. I remember getting my first ride on a modified Triumph Bonneville when I was twelve. Martin, the son of my father's friend Bernie, had hot-rodded it, removing the mufflers. Hurtling up residential streets at three times the legal speed limit, that machine made a masculine, thundering roar that was intoxicating. It throbbed, became ferocious at higher rpms.

It just felt right.

And so I began to haunt motorcycle shops, and to pester mechanics. Where the Elvis-singin', "you meet the nicest people on a Honda" bit didn't appeal to me at all, the mythos of what my friends called *real motorcycles* did. I pored over photos of golden-age road racers in British bike magazines (and didn't mind the plump "birds" slung over those machines either). I didn't want "a motorcycle that wasn't a motorcycle," such as Honda built. I wanted the real thing: fire-breathing, oil-spurting, rip-roaring. Britain made them. (And the Italians made them, these bikes like some species of griffin, or dragon, known of but never seen—bikes like the MV Augusta 4, on which Giacomo "Ago" Agostini and "Mike the Bike" Hailwood had won nearly every open-class World GP in those years of the sixties. My friend Jerry and I, not versed in Italian, called Giacomo "Gee-ah-coe-mo," which amused us no end when we wised up.)

Prior to 1969, there wasn't a road-going Honda, Yamaha, Suzuki, or Kawasaki that could hold a candle to a race-prepared Norton Commando, could navigate a curvy road as could a Velocette Thruxton, could go as flat-out fast as a Vincent (150 mph out at the Bonneville Salt Flats). Domi-nator, Interceptor, Manx; Tiger, Black Lightning, A-65 Rocket, these bikes were legends. My older "friends" had them.

But you had to be a wrench, a gearhead, to keep them running. And when you met one of these men who could, it was like meeting some sor-cerer, some magician. I recall the first time I had such a mechanic repair my minibike. No spark? Let's just pull the flywheel here and see what we've got. There was a grain of sand that had gotten between the ignition points. A cam opened and closed them. See? Ray said, removing it. One wrench, a bit of know-how, and voila! Same principle works everywhere, Ray told me. And he was right, though of course each bike was different in some way.

I was not old enough, nor did I have the money for these mythic mo-torcycles, then, or for a half decade following. I did, though, have money for teenaged kids' shitpiles that had been ruined by hard, ignorant use, like the Kaaden-derived two-strokes that had hit our shores in mass numbers, though not to truly rival those of Honda.

And then, prolonging our lives, the whole dirt-bike revolution hit, and we raced, burned up, blew up, and abused every motocross bike we could get our hands on, starting with Hodakas. This was a reprieve for our par-ents, given that out on a dirt track we couldn't become a hood ornament on some Buick Deuce and a Quarter or Pontiac Safari. But, as addressed

in chapter 4, those bikes were insanely difficult and, with time, only whet-
ted our appetites for the big metal.

And then Honda, according to the popular press, did it again, introducing, in 1969, a revolutionary motorcycle that spelled the death of all that
Great Britain was building then, and had built, and nearly taking down
the Italians as well. Honda's bike was the CB 750, now commonly called
the first "Superbike." It was a 750 cc, single-overhead-camshaft in-line four
(mounted transversely), with four carburetors, putting out around 60 horsepower. Unlike its British and Italian rivals, it didn't leak oil, revved freely
with only high-frequency (an odd, tingling sort of) vibration, and required
almost no maintenance whatsoever. Again, a motorcycle that seemed *not
to be a motorcycle*. You didn't have to know squat about the bike to own or
ride it. All of Honda's research, development, and racing success hit like a
tidal wave in this bulletproof bike.

Britain's last-gasp effort, released the year before, *really* the world's first
superbike, was the Triumph Trident/BSA Rocket 750 cc Triple. While mechanically competitive, the triple was a styling disaster. Wanting something new, and space age, Triumph/BSA had gone to a company that did
design work for automobile manufacturers, Ogle, who gave them the slab-
tanked, ray-gun-mufflered Rocket (and sank the venture by taking eighteen
months to do it). Using components from Triumph's Tiger, but having one
more cylinder, it was sometimes called the "Tiger 100 and a half."

Brits and Americans alike hated the Rocket's styling, called modern
"square." I loved it, and at first sight. It looked like something out of Britain's puppet drama *Fireball XL5*, with that odd British something I found
likewise intriguing in their cars (Jags, Healeys, MGs, TVRs, Lotuses).

My father had, I believe, threatened to kick me out of the house if I
brought a big road bike home, and he and my mother had set limits on the
dirt bikes. (I'd been a Nordic Jumping competitor for some five years by
this time and had made it into the USSA Central Division Tournament in
1975. So leaping off something the size of a twenty-story building at over
seventy miles per hour didn't scare me, or jumping on dirt bikes, either, so
what would I do with a street bike?) My apologies to both.

I saw it, I bought it, I put it in the garage. My father never acknowledged its existence until I had to trailer it to a transmission wizard, one who had the press I was sorely lacking.

The Rocket (even granted it was really derived from mid-1930s engineering) would run circles around the Honda CB 750. Modified by Doug Hele and Rob North, Rockets won races everywhere in Europe, even at the Isle of Man TT—famously so in its "Slippery Sam" guise. In the United States, Dick Mann won the Daytona 200 on a Rocket, against race-prepared CB 750s, BSA using this victory in an advertisement that read: "World's Fastest Production Motorcycle."

I bought mine in 1974, shortly after Kawasaki—longtime producer of insanely fast two-stroke street bikes like the H 1 500 and H 2 750—released its version of Honda's CB, the Z 1 900.

It took the Z 1, a 900 cc four, to beat the Rocket. And that was game over for, by then, so-called Norton Villiers Triumph. But not for gearheads like myself. I sent off to the Nicholson Brothers, in Saskatoon, Saskatchewan, for high-compression pistons; electronic ignition; and bigger carbs, which I installed. I had Ed's Plant, a motorcycle shop in St. Paul, lighten and reinforce the frame.

Really, I thought of myself then as some modern equivalent of Ecossi, Manuel Fangio's mechanic. Nightly, until I drove my neighbors nuts, I polished, tuned, and tinkered with that bike until it scared me.

Back then dynamometers were uncommon, but, given the mods I'd made to that engine, it put out around 80 to 82 horsepower. The bike weighed 400 pounds, which made it a good 140 pounds lighter than the Z 1.

I'd left the "ray gun" silencers on it, having read that even Doug Hele's bike had produced more power with them. I liked them because they looked ridiculous—like some 1930s designer's idea of what mufflers would look like in some future that had never happened. I'd adjusted the valves to the correct few thousandths of an inch; gone over every last bit. I'd safety-wired the criticals.

So, on that May evening when I wheeled it out of the garage and kicked it over, I hoped—hoped I'd gotten the wrist-pin C clips in right; that the compression wouldn't be too much for the main bearings; that the carburetors I'd put on it would be in the neighborhood of functional; as well as twenty other things—just hoped, really, it would so much as start. Which it did, with a roar. (Threes, as I've said before, sound something like half of an in-line six. They resonate at lowish rpms, howl at higher.)

I rode, almost timidly, out beyond the Mississippi River on Highway 62, night coming on. Holding back, I wove the bike down a roller coaster of a road off the highway, hyperaware of the engine. I'd have to lean the air fuel mixture a bit, because I could tell the engine would "bog" now with the larger carburetors if I cracked it open. And, with a rebuild like I'd done on a bike such as the Rocket, you generally want at least three hundred miles for the piston rings to seat.

Just a kid, I managed to hold it under sixty for a little less than an hour (by which time the bike had stopped blowing blue exhaust, a sign the rings had seated). I rode back to the garage and turned all three carburetor air-fuel screws in a third of a turn (one and a half turns out was stock). I gave the throttle a blip, and the engine ran right up to redline and beyond—another thing you shouldn't do with a fresh engine (you want, when you run higher rpms initially, the engine to be under load).

I turned onto Sixty-sixth Street, the ascending aorta of Richfield, headed west toward Portland Avenue, looking to test the bike. One thing that I'd liked about the Rocket, its tall first gear—you could do fifty in first—was now a potential liability (but even more so than I could have imagined) for what I was about to do. I was feeling like John Milner in *American Graffiti,* out in my deuce coupe and looking for action. I was wearing my Bell helmet, my Schott Brothers black leather, and a suicide's leather jackboots. The temperature had dropped, which was a good thing, making the air more dense. In retrospect, of course, all of this seems insanely ill-directed, even dangerous to the point of being stupid—a Darwin Award waiting to happen.

I turned south on Portland, and at a red light stopped alongside a simi-larly race-ready character on a two-stroke "rice burner," a Yamaha RD 350. I glanced at him; he glanced at me.

Your heart, at such a moment, is pounding as if pumping molasses. A strange thing happens to your vision, too—you are so hyperaware that you have a bit of an out-of-body sensation. In stop-light racing, you watch the cross-street light to your right. When it goes yellow, you turn to the road in front of you, still aware of the light in your peripheral vision.

Green light, and we both tore away from the intersection, the Yamaha pulling ahead by three bike lengths, making the next light and leaving me there. That he waved, getting onto the highway, added further insult. I'd never gotten out of first gear, never gotten near the engine's power band.

There were either of two things I needed to do: Get a smaller counter-shaft sprocket if I was going to fool around with stop-light racing, to get that first gear down; or pull brake starts like I'd done hill climbing. When you use a "brake start," you hold the front brake on with your index and second fingers, and roll the throttle with your palm until you're pulling power-band rpms. Your engine is screaming. A split second before the light goes green, you drop the clutch, the front brake still on, and the rear wheel rips loose under you, spinning. You get the green, release the brake, and crack the throttle wide open.

It was one thing to do this on a two-stroke dirt bike, and with a hill coming at you to slow you down. I'd never done it on the street. Not like this.

It also occurred to me I could use some distance, a proper quarter mile at least, to let the Rocket run, and so I found myself back on Sixty-sixth at Portland (the Richfield police station was just a few blocks to my left). By now it was, maybe, a little after ten. The air was cool, even chill. I was thinking maybe I should just head home and call it a night.

A single headlight came at me from the rear, though not a Padiddle, a car with one headlight (as my sisters and I had called them on car trips, seeing who could spot the most). A motorcycle. You could always tell by the height of the light, and by the way it shook slightly. I got the green but didn't go. A guy on a Kawasaki Z 1 pulled up alongside me. Handlebar mustache, frayed cutoffs halfway up his hairy thighs, a purple-and-yellow Vikings sweatshirt, Adidas tennis shoes. The bike was box stock, right off the showroom floor.

Here was one of those "You meet the nicest people on a Honda" riders, a guy who'd never touched a wrench in his life. I didn't have to get closer for the scent of his Brut to waft over. That this Z 1 was undoubtedly his first bike gave me pause (nearly 60 percent of all motorcycle fatalities occur on new bikes, ones the rider has had for less than three months; I knew that, even back then. After I'd almost killed myself on railroad tracks test-riding a Royal Enfield Interceptor, I'd taken that statistic seriously, especially when riding unfamiliar machines).

Yet, when that Marlboro Man *Saturday Night Fever* Disco Dude laughed at me, all that went right out the window.

"What's with the Preston Petty outfit?" he said, blipping his throttle.

I cut my eyes at him and he laughed a second time. Yup, I was kind of ridiculous, flat bars, ray gun mufflers, black leather neck to toe.

The light went yellow crosswise, and we bent over our bikes. I got on the front brake, brought the engine up to four grand, making that three-cylinder yowl. Heart in my throat. Got the green, dumped the clutch, hit the throttle, and pulled away from the light, the rear wheel spinning like mad, jetting out with a warp factor 5 feeling, but the Kaw pulling away until the Rocket hit 6,000 rpm and that engine went mad and I blew by Disco Dude like he was standing still, taking in the speedo (120 something miles per hour) and Nicollet Avenue coming at me.

All in eleven seconds.

I got the bike stopped, shaking from head to toe. I was so adrenaline-juiced I was of two minds. Even then, at eighteen, I knew I was dangerously judgment-impaired. It was as if I were on drugs, just as my friend Bobby had said that day dirt racing (I'd been at it so long that dirt racing felt . . . familiar). Here came Disco Dude, looking serious. One of my two minds said, This is insane, I'm gonna die. Just turn to the right and cut this short. Go home, buddy. And the other said, Give him hell.

The Nicollet-to-Lyndale stretch of Sixty-sixth is nearly a quarter mile, as was Portland to Nicollet, but here there were shops, fast food, a pizza place, and cars, lazily turning here and there. I had one in my lane about halfway to Lyndale.

Disco Dude asked if I wanted a knuckle sandwich. Cute. I told him to put his Kaw where the sun didn't shine. We were both insane. When the light changed, I didn't bother with first gear, I used second, lost time on the start, but blew by him again, and on Lyndale thought, Okay, before this kills you, quit.

I headed for Highway 62, took the ramp, and here came Disco Dude, giving me the finger and pulling up alongside, then going by me, and I thought, Okay. You want to get nasty? I lay on the gas tank, dropped a gear, and brought the bike up to redline, blew by Disco Dude, hit third at 90, hit fourth around 110, the cool air now bitter cold, and that engine howling, and me shaking so badly, whether from the cold, or the speed, I didn't know, that my knees thumped against the tank. The needle swung around the clock.

Smith speedometers run to 150 mph. That had always seemed more than wishful thinking to me, sexy, but almost silly, too, because most of the bikes these speedos were on (Triumph Bonnevilles and Tigers, A 65 BSAs, Velos) would, on a good day, only turn 115. Just. The Rocket was about to peg that speedometer when I got off the highway. Disco Dude was far behind me.

I felt like an utter idiot, yet was beyond thrilled with myself and the machine I'd built. Frightened out of my mind, yet exhilarated.

Wow, I'm still alive, I thought.

I parked the bike in the garage and went inside.

"Did you shut the garage door?" my father called from upstairs.

I told him I had, and lay on my bed. My mind went first to countershaft sprockets—I'd lose top-end speed but would be better off the line—then turned to how, if one of the wrist-pin circlips had come loose, the engine would have seized; or, if that star nut I'd thought I'd dropped into the crankcase had actually done so, and gotten in the big end of the engine, there, too, would have been another catastrophic engine failure. I'd fallen tens of time in the dirt, but doing just under 150? On pavement?

I promised myself I'd take the bike to a drag strip; by the weekend, I was out again, looking for bikes to smoke on Sixty-sixth. I took down a slew of Sportsters, two more Z 1s, was smoked myself by an H2 750 Kaw built for drag racing, ran even with a big-bore Shovel. Outran all manner of bikes on Highways 494, 35W (where the bridge collapsed), 62, and 61, of Bob Dylan "Highway 61 Revisited" fame.

And then there were the accidents.

Drag racing with friends in a '57 Dodge D-500, we belted off that same Portland intersection, were giving the Roadrunner 383 to our left a run for its money, when a guy in a dirty blue Skylark, his wife and baby in the car, pulled in front of us.

We hit the rear of that car with a colossal *bang!* Both cars, ours and the Skylark, skidding down a fair slope of pavement. It was that slope, and the fact we'd just got off the line, that saved us.

We were out of the car in seconds, terrified we had done the family in the Skylark some irremediable harm. The baby was crying. The Super Bee was long gone. The couple had been in some argument, this guy hugging his weeping wife and saying, over and over, he was sorry he hadn't been paying attention, it was all stupid, what had they been fighting for?

The cops came, and we let the guy in the Buick explain the accident. There weren't even any skid marks the police could measure, but the officers gave us suspicious looks, this being one time I definitely wished I wasn't wearing black leather.

A short while later, my friend Chip, out on a double date, was broadsided by a drunk, killing everyone in the car but him; Chip made some Barbara Walters special, the poster-boy vegetable, who, it was argued, should or should not be euthanized. Another boy named Wayne Johnson, who'd gone to Jefferson High and had just graduated, was killed riding some bike, and my friends, hearing it on the news, called my parents to tell them they were sorry I was dead.

I didn't stop-light race again. Not as I had. So I took up with dangerous types, in the form of the West Bank Motorcycle Club, but that is another story.

## Brainerd for a Nerd

I was living a patched-together, sometimes-seeming-schizophrenic life—I didn't know anyone in my ill-directed march through premed who was the least bit interested in motorcycles, or MC clubs, or racing—when I met Peter.

Peter, I was told one afternoon, was tinkering with some old motorcycle in his tiny flat on the third floor of our Lake Street house, had parts strewn all over, which was driving his roommate nuts.

I thought: Piece-of-shit old Honda, Yamaha, or Suzuki, say a Hustler 250 with Posi-lube. Who cared. Still, I bothered to knock on his door. We shook hands. Peter had flaming red hair and those otherworldly agate blue eyes redheads sometimes have.

"Heard you got a bike in here," I said.

He cocked his head to one side. "You ride?"

"Rocket," I replied.

"A Sixty-five or A Seventy-five?"

Right there, I knew this was someone different. I was suddenly interested. I told him an A 75. Plus parts.

"Still running the ray guns?" I nodded, and he motioned with his head for me to step inside.

The place was a mess, but for the living room, where, on a blue milk crate, sat a chrome moly frame. To the right of it was the bike's engine, fresh gaskets drying on the crankcase, the pistons there like two fists.

He didn't ask me if I knew what a Ducati was. I'd nearly driven Leo, at Leo's Cycle Sales, mad sitting on his 750 SS, Leo barking at me, "Don't shift that bike!" and "Is the zipper on that jacket of yours scratching the gas tank?!" Here was one of those griffin motorcycles, a modern-day Black Lightning or Brough Superior 100. Ducatis, I knew, were hand-built in Bologna, had lovely sand-cast crankcases, desmodromic, towershaft bevel-driven cams, were the only 90-degree V-twins in the world able to turn 10,000 rpm. Already, this bike was a legend, the only remaining European ride still taking it to the Japanese fours. The base price on this model, the square-case 900, was, in today's currency, about $15,000. Peter ticked off the parts he'd installed, new big-end bearings, Carillo rods, Venolia pistons. Altogether, the bike, minus labor, was easily worth $25,000.

Peter was studying me.

"I race up at Brainerd. I need pit crew who can wrench," he said. "You interested?"

What I learned from Peter was this: What I didn't know about road racing could fill a book, and then some. What I'd done was dirt and stop-light racing, with a round or two of flat track thrown in.

I knew nothing, really, about GP riding, and almost killed myself the first time I tried to navigate Brainerd International Raceway at speed. Riders on machines half the size of my Rocket were passing me, which made me charge at the challenging 180-degree west-end sweeper to catch up, so I had to hit the brakes so hard I locked up the rear wheel, and then tried, motocross or flat-track style, to power out the far side.

Slow as I was, and sideways too much, I was a danger to myself and to other riders.

Five laps had me exhausted. I headed back to the pits, shaking.

"Ready for a few pointers?" Peter said. He'd been in the grandstand watching me.

What I learned from Peter has lasted a lifetime.

To ride quickly, you have to first of all change your very way of seeing. You have to be looking at the horizon, or, if you are in a turn, at the exit, even while you are approaching that very turn's apex. Imagine you are passing a picket fence. If you turn your head to the side, the individual pickets rush by in a blur. If, however, you focus at a distance, all the pickets stay in focus. (And this carries into road riding, too, as, in a right-hander, if you enter the turn too soon at speed, you can be carried into the oncoming lane just past the apex.)

World GP racers win because their turning lines can be six inches closer to the apex at speed—six inches—which allows for a quicker turn-exit roll on. A half second here can buy you as much as eighty feet, more than enough to win a tight race.

Racing, you can't fix your eyes on anything, especially the rider you want to pass: this is called object fixation. You'll hit him, or whatever you fix your eyes on. And if you don't hit that rider, your speed will match his, which is also a no-win situation. In the end, racing requires a sense of flying with the bike under you, a scary sensation until you're accustomed to it. Being shortsighted will cause you to be late on the throttle coming out of the corners, where races are won.

Given the gyroscopic effect of a motorcycle's wheels, the faster you are going, the more force you need to apply to turn it. Motorcycles, really, are affected by six forces: gravity; kinetic energy; the bike's propensity to continue in a straight line unless acted upon (really, Newton's second law); thermodynamics (braking transforms kinetic energy, making heat that must be taken into consideration); "centrifugal" forces in turning (actually tangential linear forces); and friction (between the tires' "contact" patches and the pavement).

Push left, turn left. Push right, turn right. All bikes "countersteer" at speed. The front wheel "deflects" and the bike leans into the corner. But you can't punch at the handlebars. If you do, and a wobble results, you don't want to stiff-arm the bars to get control, which will just make the wobble worse, and you'll truly be out of control.

Smooth. You want everything smooth.

I had to unlearn a host of motocross riding techniques: sitting bolt upright when sliding the rear tire around corners, scooting back on the seat when riding at speed, skidding the rear wheel to make sharp turns, and leading with my inside foot off the peg as I'd done forever off loamy berms.

A road-racing turn has three parts. You enter it on the brakes and off the throttle, but as soon as you've got the bike over and turning, you want maintenance throttle, so the bike doesn't fall too far to the inside. You can greatly improve your turn by both hanging from the tank to the inside of the turn—your whole body, so far that your inside knee will nearly touch the pavement—while applying pressure with that inside foot to the foot peg, this, maybe at fifty, or sixty, or even eighty miles per hour, the pavement rushing at you. Most people, incorrectly, think that this hanging off the motorcycle brings the bike further over, making it turn more sharply. The opposite is true: the bike will turn more sharply, with less lean angle, when the rider's *mass* is moved to the inside of the turn and off the bike. And the timing of moving your body is critical—if you move too early, the bike will "fade," drop too far, into the turn; too late and you'll have difficulty overcoming the gyroscopic force of the wheels.

You want to point your chin, going like hell, up the track, with your head down and in, while keeping your eyes on the horizon—on the turn's exit.

The apex of the turn is *not* where most people think it is, in the middle. The apex is *three quarters of the way around,* and just reaching it, you want to roll the throttle on. Rolling the throttle on will make the bike stand up, at which point you will have the greatest contact patch, the area where the tire and road meet, on the rear wheel. You can, safely, then give it all you've got.

Dropping off the throttle in the middle of a turn makes the bike fall to the inside of the turn; rolling on the throttle will cause the bike to stand up and take a straight line again. Holding it steady will give you an unvarying lean angle and line. All simple enough, until you enter a turn—which you inevitably do—too early or too late, too slow or too fast, and you have to adjust your line *in* the turn.

Say you're doing one hundred on a straight and you've scared yourself stiff—your eyes will be too low, which will cause you, entering a turn, to enter *too slowly.* Too slowly? That's right—too slowly. Your initial impulse, and a commonsense one, too, is to dive for the turn, leaving yourself the most pavement to the outside to maneuver in, which is altogether wrong on a motorcycle. This makes the radius of the turn smaller, so requires that you either hit the brakes hard and scrub off speed, or use a frightening lean angle, maybe 50 degrees, to negotiate the turn. Some riders encountering the latter will simply ride off the track—of course, this is something that can't be done on the street. Basically the formula is this: Radius = Speed / Speed = Radius. The larger the turn radius, the faster it can be negotiated; the smaller, the slower. So, always, your strategy as a racer is to open up turns as much as possible—that's your entire aim in choosing the best line on a track, or in canyon racing.

But, just now, let's say you stomp on the brakes in a turn you've come into early. You wrestle the bike over, and, suddenly, you're aimed not around the apex but at it, a problem you can correct, somewhat, with throttle steering, standing the bike to take a wider line, though you'll be taken wide out the opposite side.

How to correct that problem? With trail braking—riding the rear brake to lengthen the front forks, which in turn will again give the bike a wider line.

The trick to trail-braking, or any braking in a turn, is this: You have a limit to the traction afforded you. If you are hanging from the tank by your knee at speed, bent over at 50 degrees, you have used nearly all the traction in your tires. If you brake suddenly, the tires will tear free of the pavement. And if you screw on the power suddenly, the rear end will slide away, with you and the bike tumbling down the pavement. Turning, there's that outside-directed force (really not outside at all, but tangential to the turn so seeming outside—what is incorrectly referred to as centrifugal force). As with Newton's law, all bodies tend to move in a uniform direction unless acted upon—motorcycles "want" to go *straight*. And you can't *ride* the brakes, because the heat generated will make your brake fluid boil, rendering your brakes useless.

So you want to hit the brakes approaching a turn, enter the turn wide (opening the radius), aim for the apex with maintenance throttle, and when you've reached it, roll on the throttle as the bike stands up, drifting to the outside.

All seamless, smooth, calculated. To this you can add trail-braking and throttle steering, but only after you've got this right, which some riders never do.

Now add to this rough pavement. Terrifying as it can be, rough pavement is not an excuse to grip the bars to save your life—it won't work, will only further distort the bike's already stressed frame, steering, and suspension components.

And which brake to go heavy on, front or rear?

Seventy percent or more of your braking power in a motorcycle is in your front brake. But if you grab at it, especially in a turn, your front tire will break free, and you'll have what's called a "low side fall." Break loose the rear, and you can have a dangerous, rider-throwing "high side fall."

All of this makes sense when off the track, but on it? When you start racing, everything is off kilter. You make a beautiful, wide, late entry to a turn, doing eighty, head up, looking at the horizon, the apex coming at you to your right, and wanting to pass the little shit on the Yamaha within kicking distance, and think, now, well before the apex is the time to roll on the throttle and pass him, when he's still falling to the inside. What will happen if you do this is you *will* fly by that little shit, but come out of the corner wide, and have to both back off the throttle and lean the bike radically over in order not to fly off the course into the hay bales that might just keep you from killing yourself, that little shit on the RD 350 *zinnnnging!* by you, heading to the next turn, where you will just manage to catch him, since you have 80 horsepower to his 45, but he will be in the perfect groove, and you'll have to fall in behind him. Again.

You can't get around another rider by starting a turn early, or by powering out of one early either. Still, as any racer will tell you, all other things being nearly equal, you win races in the turns.

What to do? You *can't* muscle a bike around a course. It doesn't work.

What you *can* do is ride a cleaner line to the apex of turns, and exactly where you won't run out of pavement accelerating wide, roll on the power, time and time and time again. Kenny Roberts, three times world 500 cc GP champion, said, "It's rolling on the throttle early out of the turn that wins races."

It's also where most riders fall.

When Peter pulled into the pits, I ran to his bike with gasoline, spastically checked and filled his tires, gave him a shove back onto the track, that Ducati bellowing, picking up speed, Peter hanging by his knee for that first turn.

Our third time out, during practice laps, he rolled into the pits and got off the bike, holding it by its clip-on handlebars.

"Yours," he said.

I got on the bike, he gave me a racelike shove, and I headed out onto the track, feeling like Mike Hailwood himself. Or Ago. Into the first turn, the bike fell to the inside so easily, I had the momentary, and terrified, sensation I was dropping Peter's impossibly expensive bike.

I got around the inside of the rider in front of me, and coming at the apex of that turn, rolled on the throttle, and was astounded to pass not just the bike directly to my outside, but three bikes, one of them a Kawasaki Z 1. I was astounded. Where my triple, and every four I had ever ridden, seemed to gather itself in this nanosecond, and then hurl the motorcycle at the limit of traction out of the corner, the Ducati, as if magically, seemed to *walk* out of the corner, the engine pulsation giving perfect traction, especially when the bike was on its side, and the power building in such a way that by the time the bike was up again, it was running near redline and pulling ferociously.

For this reason, Ducati remains one of the few non-Japanese bikes competitive in world superbike racing circles, and really the *only* commercially viable Italian company, Ducati's cutting-edge-technology sport bikes sought after by riders with deep pockets, a present 1098 S (Tricolore) running $25,000. And beautiful? Year after year, Ducati wins international design awards, as it did recently at the World's Most Beautiful Motorcycle

Awards, held at Cortile della Seta, Milan—which, of course, is the heart of clothing fashion as well. Ducati is about *tractable power*. And sex appeal; they are simply beautiful, some collectors not even riding them.

I knew then that I had to have one—for me, this impossibly expensive, handmade Italian motorcycle. It would be ten years before I got mine. By which time, the company had nearly gone under.

### How the Americans Rode Kaaden's Ring-Dings to Fame, and Ducati Made Salami of Honda

If you want to see what's coming to us other 99.99 percent, we road riders, canyon racers, and Fast Freddy wannabes, look to racing—but don't expect what you see on GP tracks to make it to the street for years. For example, that six-cylinder 250 Mike Hailwood was riding for Honda in 1966? Honda released a version of that bike to the public in 1978, the 1,000 cc CBX (Benelli, which had also designed a six, beat Honda by one year, but produced a machine that had congenital flaws).

And all those world-beating Kaaden two-stroke rotary-valve racers? They came to us first from Suzuki as Hustler 250s, and then Yamaha TDs, YMs, and RDs (the Big Bear 305 kick starter had teeth that would break, and an oil pump that stopped when you pulled in the clutch), and Kawasaki H triples. The "blue cloud" racing big three, so named for the clouds of blue exhaust they made. They were seriously scary bikes, and just when we were getting used to them, and performance frames were available (riders didn't call the Kawasaki H 1 500 the "Widowmaker" for nothing), California emissions standards shut them down.

Almost overnight, the Blue Cloud Three began building four-stroke bikes, and by 1980, your average rider thought that was the end of it.

In the class John Q. Public watched most closely, World Superbike, there were few if any competitive two-strokes, which sounded the definitive note on the death of the breed, now thought to be antiquated. The Superbike, unlike the out-on-Mars square four GP two-stroke or "in-line" R series Vs (an in-line V? Is that possible? Yes, but later . . . ) would be found on showroom floors after those models had done battle, successfully or unsuccessfully, on the world Superbike stage. A note here on these "superbikes": For a factory to race a motorcycle in the Superbike class, it must follow what are called "homologation" rules, which stipulate that the manufacturer make a large number of these bikes available to the public, say, five hundred—which, in theory anyway, precludes manufacturers building flat-out racing bikes, which would never be available to the public to win Superbike events. It would just be too expensive to sell five hundred or more bikes costing the factory $100,000 each to the public for a third of that per model. True GP race bikes now cost millions of dollars (including R&D), and are put in the hands of only the most talented and visible riders.

Visibility, possibly, being a problem for Americans. From the first, in Europe, events were held on circuits, like the Isle of Man, of public roads. Americans, on the other hand, went from board track to flat track, where the spectators could watch the riders at all times. In true road racing, spectators choose some spot along a miles-long circuit, say, some particularly difficult hairpin turn followed by a stretch of straight tarmac, get out a bottle of wine, bread and cheese, and make an afternoon of it. At a road-racing track, even one such as Brainerd, they will see only a tenth of the track. Americans, as I did (until I met Peter), drag race. That's really what oval racing is, though over distance. One direction, flat out.

Europeans think this is nonsense. It has little relation to real-world driving conditions, and they don't relate much to it, other than in the form of speedway racing and ice racing. (In Norway, Sweden, and Finland, ice racing—really speedway racing—is done on frozen lakes, ice racers having three-inch spikes in their tires—you'd think the possibility of being turned into Swiss cheese, were you to fall and be run over, would limit the number of competitors to impale yourself against, but such is not the case. Go Team Aquavit!)

Until 1983, when I first drove in Milan, I wondered why Europeans were so indifferent to our national sport of oval track racing, our most visible form now being the ever-so-popular NASCAR races.

I was driving a BMW 520i, rented by my friend Roger, a millionaire and owner of an American fitness company, who was having an affair with Linda, who'd set her lovely chin between the front seats. Roger had just bought himself a Porsche 928 in Stuttgart the day before, and a Volkswagen convertible Rabbit—what the Germans, with great derision, called a "strawberry basket," a girly car—for Linda.

"Get off here," Roger said, but we were doing ninety, and there was no space to maneuver. No one was observing the lanes. In my rearview mirror some idiot was thrusting his fist at me. I broke out in a sudden and intense sweat. I was terrified, never having ridden someone's bumper at ninety while trying to get off a swerving highway.

And then I thought: Not my car. And—*motocross*. I stomped on the brake, to get the asshole off my rear, dropped a gear, and ran the Beemer over redline, swerving between lanes, stomping on the brake, lurching forward again, and not one person beeped at me, was pissed, or even surprised.

On the Autostrada we were doing 130 mph and Maseratis and big Mercedes were passing us as if we were standing still. Linda insisted we stop so she could drive, and when she did, she brought it right up to 130 as I had, chewing her gum, fiddling with the radio, and at one point even putting her left foot up on the dashboard—which terrified me (the car was a manual, and had someone braked in front of us or hit something, long before Linda so much as got her left foot to the clutch we would have expired in a fireball of crushed 520i) and proved something I'd always known.

*Anyone* can put the pedal down in a straight line, or crack open the throttle, making drag racing very much about the machine. This is the very line of thinking Valentino Rossi challenged, leaving Honda after its engineers implied it was the machine, not Rossi, who was winning races. Rossi, jumping to then underdog Yamaha, said: Like hell it is, and went on to prove it.

Europeans pride themselves on aggressive motoring—motoring as *sport*. Skiing in Austria one winter, I met a mother of three who boasted the high-speed road handling of her VW Golf, which seemed to me preposterous, given the ugly box of a car that is a Golf. German design from an aesthetic standpoint? Questionable. The new BMW transverse-four sport bike, the 1200, while putting out 160 horsepower, and having a top speed around 170 mph, looks, as one tester said correctly, "like a magnet dragged through a parts bin."

Having lunch al fresco in Lugano with Roger and Linda, overlooking that beautiful lake, just off a loop of highway that bent back on itself and rose into the mountains, we heard a rumbling, and then a thrumming, and I stood to watch two riders on arrest-me red Ducatis heel over a good 60 degrees, an angle that leaves absolutely no margin for error, navigating that loop at possibly 90 mph (two, three times the speed limit), the riders vying for the best line, then rolling on the throttle at the apex, engines roaring and heading up the mountainside at a good 150 mph.

I was stunned. And in awe. It's one thing to do that on a track, but you are living on a very fine edge doing it on a public highway, but the Italians on the terrace, almost without exception, hadn't so much as lifted their heads. Here this sort of riding was an everyday occurrence.

The woman who did, said to me, *"Che bello, sì?"*

*"Sì."* I said.

## The Modern Era's Greatest Riders in Three Easy Pieces

### Mike the Bike

Were you to give Mike Hailwood's rise to international fame a cursory glance, it would seem that he came fully formed out of Britain, the culmination of five decades of motor-racing obsession, particularly in that most British of creations, the Isle of Man TT. And that wouldn't be far from wrong. Such was his character that before he was tall enough to see over the steering wheel of his mother's Jaguar, he had managed to get the car out of the garage and was caught by neighbors driving it. Hailwood's father owned a large motorcycle distributorship, and Hailwood, long before he had his learner's permit, had ridden a track through the grass in the eight acres behind the Hailwood home in Oxford. No stranger to racing, given his father's work, Hailwood began competing at seventeen, performing so brilliantly that the coming winter, to continue racing, he moved to South Africa, and there became South Africa's national champion, at eighteen. Initially resented for being privileged, Hailwood was found to be a straight-on bloke, a charming person with a big heart for all of Britain. He was modest, friendly, and smart without trying to seem so. And he won races— from the time he was issued a professional license, something he managed to do in months, when other riders took years. He had a disarming smile, looked the part of some happy gladiator in his black leather. The world motorcycle press so loved him they dubbed him, after his first years on the GP circuit, "Mike the Bike." By his second year, he had taken second place in the 250 cc world GP competition, won three British championships and more than seventy-four races.

This was the man Soichiro Honda went to in 1961, finding in Hailwood a rider with the potential to beat all the competition with his then newly built transverse-four 250. We even knew Hailwood in America, given he'd come over to race at Willow Springs, California, and so astonished his competition, that his face was everywhere—the enduring picture for the world of the British rider. He was lanky, soft-spoken, and given to ironic, self-effacing statements that amused the press. In 1962, despite Honda's wooing him, Hailwood signed on with MV Augusta, going on to win four consecutive 500 cc world championships, including the U.S. Grand Prix at Daytona. Wooed back to Honda, Hailwood won another four world titles in all, between 1961 and 1967, nine World Championships, seventy-five grand prix, and twelve Isle of Man TT—at which point, Honda dropped out of competition, leaving Hailwood, still on contract, unable to ride.

Hailwood turned to four wheels, where he enjoyed a degree of success in Formula Two events. In 1973, he was awarded Britain's highest honor for civilian bravery after he rescued Clay Regazzoni in his burning car at the South African Grand Prix, standing in Regazzoni's burning fuel tanks to do it, catching fire himself. The following year, Hailwood, who had never sustained a serious injury, crashed his McLaren at the Nürburgring and had to be cut out of the car, sustaining leg injuries that were thought to have ended his racing career.

While he was living in New Zealand, an Australian company begged him in 1978 to have a go at the Isle of Man TT, and Hailwood reluctantly agreed, granted he could bring in his old mechanic. Like that, the two "old men," as their competitors were calling them (Hailwood was thirty-eight, and with that ruined leg), headed off for that oldest of races, the IOM. There, riding a Ducati 900, Hailwood took his tenth TT in a fairy-tale comeback; he'd last ridden the TT almost twenty years earlier.

Other riders said it was not the machines he rode (aside from Ducati, Honda, and MV, also Norton, Paton, AJS, Benelli, Yamaha, and Suzuki), but Mike himself who won, through "sheer skill and ability."

And Hailwood's end?

This most skilled of motorcycle racers, exiting a takeaway (fast food) shop in Warwickshire with his daughter, Michelle, and son, David, was struck by a delivery truck in a freak accident that killed Hailwood and his daughter instantly.

He was only forty years old. His daughter was nine. David survived and follows in his father's footsteps—marketing Mike Hailwood motorcycle gear.


## AGO

Giacomo Agostini is a fiery Italian if there ever was one, and a road racer whose fans claim as the greatest of all time. Ago has the medals to prove it: fifteen world Grand Prix titles (eight in 500 cc and seven in 350 cc); twelve Isle of Man crowns; and an extraordinary 122 Grand Prix wins, all over a seventeen-year period.

Magnetic and passionate, Ago said of this still unmatched achievement, "Winning is like a drug: The more you win, the more you enjoy it."

Ago, born just two years after Hailwood (1942), became motorcycling's first world superstar. Unlike Hailwood, he did not have the support of his family early on, even given they, like Hailwood's family, had the resources. Infatuated with motorcycles "from the time [he] could think," Ago got an early start riding his Moto Guzzi Lodola (175 cc) on the narrow, winding roads bordering Lago d'Iseo, near the family home in Lovere. So taken was Ago by the notion of racing that he enlisted the help of one of his father's friends in getting his father, Amelio, to sign a race entry document. Amelio signed, thinking his son was *bicycle* racing, and found out what Ago was up to only when he read the race results in the paper. So proud was he, though, that he became from that time a staunch supporter of his son's motorcycle career, which really began with Moto Morino. There Ago showed such promise that MV signed him to understudy Hailwood, Ago himself saying that when Hailwood would ride slower practice laps, he would "tuck in behind [Hailwood] and watch exactly what he did and when he did it . . . and as [time] went on [I] was able to hang on longer and longer."

By 1966, Hailwood was riding for Honda again, Ago staying put with the MV camp. There sprung up a rivalry only to be matched now by Rossi and Biaggi, more than thirty years later. Off the track, though, Hailwood and Ago were good friends. Said Hailwood's father, "Ago was a brilliant, daring rider and one of the nicest guys to know. Mike and [he] were the biggest pals."

After Honda ceased racing in 1967, and Hailwood left the field, Ago on his MVs dominated world GP racing. Ago, until Jarno Saarinen, the "Flying Finn," took up with Yamaha, really had very little competition. Saarinen won the first two rounds of the 1973 season, over Ago, demonstrating the power of Yamaha's new two-stroke 500. And then Saarinen was killed, along with Renzo Pasolini (a smoker, drinker, and wild man loved and reviled by fans), in a twelve-rider crash at Monza brought on by Pasolini's bike's seizing—or by an oil spill left on the course. John Dodds, a fellow rider, had brought the spill to the attention of the authorities, who in turn had only threatened Dodd with disqualification. It was an ugly moment in racing history, and one still debated.

Ago, though, seeing the direction world GP racing was headed, after nearly ten years with MV, signed on with Yamaha. In his first race for the team, at the Daytona 200 (reduced to 180 that year due to the oil embargo), Ago defended his world title against Barry Sheene, Gary Nixon, and Kenny Roberts.

Ago won that Daytona, the "old man" in a field of young riders, then rode one last time at the Nürburgring, winning the last GP for himself, MV, and the two-stroke. Ago retired from racing, and Team Yamaha snapped him up to mentor Yamaha's top talent, as Hailwood had mentored him. This time the talent was Kenny Roberts.

## KING KENNY—KICKIN' IT AMERICAN-STYLE

Kenny Roberts, as you might know, was one of the winningest flat-track racers of all time. Roberts was the first to use "throttle steering" in road racing, which came from his flat-track experience, and "knee balancing" in corners.

From Modesto, California, Roberts really represents the first of the generation of GP riders as we know them now. In his late teens, Roberts began competing in flat-track races on a Suzuki 90. So fast was Kenny that officials handicapped him, having him start a quarter mile behind other racers. Roberts won first place that year, deciding that to really be competitive he would need a larger motorcycle. So he got a Suzuki 250, which he again raced with success.

Determined to go professional, he needed an even larger bike, so went to a local Triumph dealer, seeking sponsorship, and was told he was "too small." At Yamaha, he found a dealer eager to help him, even with a mechanic, and there began King Kenny's association with the Big Yellow and Black (Yamaha). On modified XS 650 twins, Roberts won the AMA Grand National Flat Track Championship in 1973 and 1974, though, by that time, engineers had made improvements to Kenny's competition, Harley-Davidson, specifically the XR 75. Kel Carruthers, a former world 250 GP champion in charge of Yamaha's road racing, in order to give

Roberts a competitive bike, shoe-horned a road-racing engine into a flat-tracker for him to ride at the nationals. In that race he was running last, the machine so ferocious that he was bouncing off the track's perimeter hay bales, squaring the oval, until at the last second he screwed on the power (the engine was so uncontrollable Carruthers had put a switch on the handlebars so Roberts could cut one cylinder on the turns), shooting ahead of Jay Springsteen and winning by two feet.

Some cite this as the moment Roberts quit flat-tracking and began his road-racing career, though he'd really been road racing since a Pan Am pilot, Jim Doyle, had traded him driving time to Daytona for the privilege of racing Doyle's spare 250 cc Suzuki once there. Said Roberts of that race later, it was a mess, and terrified him, riders blowing by him at 130 mph, just inches from him.

"I never want to ride a road racer again," he told Doyle.

However, he did just that, half mile, short track, and TT, taking forty-seven AMA nationals, three of those at Daytona. In road racing alone, Roberts went on to win six Formula One competitions, being one of four riders to win the AMA Grand Slam.

Most significant, though, was his success in Europe, where he became the first American to win the FIM (Fédération Internationale de Motocyclisme) world 500 cc GP, after having broken his back in a preseason high-speed crash. By 1980, he had won three consecutive world 500 Grand Prix championships, all on Yamaha two-strokes, descendants of that TZ 750 that nearly killed him flat-tracking.

His last season, 1983, is remembered by road-racing fans as one of the most memorable in history. Again, "old" King Kenny went up against the upstart "Fast Freddy" Spencer (a rider who had made a meteoric rise to fame), the two duking it out in a yearlong battle for the 500cc world championship, commentators comparing the battle to that in 1967 between Giacomo Agostini and Mike Hailwood. Roberts prevailed, winning his last race at the Italian grand prix as Agostini had when Hailwood was *his* mentor.

And so it goes. King Kenny's sons, Kenny Jr. and Kurtis, have now won world motorcycle road-racing championships, both in 2000, Kenny Jr.'s the 500 cc GP, Kurtis's the 600 cc Supersport.

Roberts, aside from racing, though, did something very American— he got in the faces of the officials of the FIM, as had Jim Dobbs at the time Saarinen and Pasolini died, but Kenny, being the confrontational, and even belligerent, person he can be when certain he is right, forced the moribund FIM to put in place effective safety measures. Before that, "safety measures" had meant hay bales around telephone poles. As the motorsports commentator Dave Despain wrote, Roberts put it to the FIM in classic Roberts fashion: "I'm an American," he told them. "I don't care what you think. We need safety, and we need to *get paid*."

Roberts also bucked the system in creating Team Roberts, his top rider, Wayne Rainey, winning three world 500cc GPs. Rainey, held back by an injured finger before one race, had the finger amputated; preparing for races, he did six hundred sit-ups a day so he could effectively position himself off his motorcycle for the duration of races. Roberts worked with a manufacturer in Malaysia to build road-racing-specific engines for him, also something that had never been done—a privateer going up against the Big Four and Ducati.

## Griffins and Dragons,
## What We'll See Down the Pipe

Ace Cafe riders in Great Britain (the Ace Cafe was for decades the pre- mier watering hole for fast riders), too eager to wait for the *next big thing*, "kitted" out their Trumpets (Triumphs), Nortons, and Beezers (BSAs), or hand-built sport bikes such as Norvins and Tritons (Vincent- and Tri- umph-powered "featherbed"-frame Nortons), and went out riding—all doing "over the ton" (one hundred) in amateur road races.

As a result, riding hot bikes like this came to be called "cafe racing," and so inspired riders worldwide that parts suppliers sprang up everywhere, and magazines printed articles on how to squeeze a few more horsepower out of your ES 2 66 Norton or (pathetically underpowered) Enfield 250. Dreaming of being Hailwood while riding your bike was the whole point, if you were fast—or Ernst Degner, if you went the two-stroke route. It was a sexy, revved-up group, Ace Cafe riders sometimes also being Rockers, who got in bloody—sometimes fatal—confrontations with scooter riders calling themselves Mods.

Around the mid-1970s, manufacturers got wise to this cafe racer market and began to produce "superbikes" with European-style bars, rear set foot pegs, and more challenging power. Honda's 750 Interceptor was such a bike, which required (again, in Honda fashion) no tinkering. The Interceptor's V4 engine put out what my Rocket's had, but with tractor-like durability.

And here was born the "crotch rocket." Every frat boy had to have one, and they were dangerous first bikes. An Indian friend of mine, Rahul, got one, what he thought would be a "small" bike to start on, a 600. And it was small for Rahul, who easily weighed 215 pounds and dwarfed it. When I asked him how he liked it, a week after he'd—with great trepidation—ridden it home from the dealer, his eyes went wide.

"This thing almost killed me!" he said, thrilled but now respectful of his little bike. "It just . . . *goes!*"

I had warned him—but he *was* a guy in his early twenties. ("Learn to stop it first, Rahul," I'd told him. "Heavy on the front brake.")

Crotch rockets, somewhere around 1990, morphed into "bullet bikes." The concept, though, is the same: more technology derived from world GP racers in roadgoing bikes for the rest of us. And for some, bigger and faster is also deadlier. According to U.S. Department of Transportation statistics, only 10 percent of motorcycles on the road now are bullet bikes, but they account for more than 25 percent of rider fatalities. And the total number of rider deaths has doubled since 1997.

These new bikes are deceptively easy to ride—they have superior frames with upside-down forks to reduce unsprung weight (moving mass connected to the frame), far superior braking, and their engines have better primary balance, so vibrate less, and now make horsepower that only GP bikes did years ago. And "endurance" road races, covering vast distances, prove they are durable. The once fearsome Kawasaki Z 1, putting out 80 plus horsepower, seems puny when compared to the new ZX-14, which puts out nearly 200 horsepower, though the ZX is still fairly heavy (weighing nearly 600 pounds).

New materials, particularly carbon fiber, have made it possible to reduce weight, and Ducati, for example, has used them in its spectacularly successful 916, a bike so loved by the motorcycle press and sport riders that Honda went out and built its own L-twin and—shockingly—called it the Honda 916. The first time I saw one, I thought it was some goofball's bike. Slapping that number on a Honda is like slapping a chrome prancing horse—Ferrari—on the hood of a Nissan 300.

Now Ducati's 1098 has made yet another world-class splash, and "race replica" or "homologation special" versions of the Desmosedici (short for "desmodromic distribution with sixteen valves") can be purchased by anyone with the necessary scratch ($70,000). Both bikes weigh in at around 400 pounds, and make 160 and 200 horsepower respectively. *And* there's Ducati's revolutionary traction control (DTC) to help those with a lack of finesse get the bike around corners. These machines are spectacular, but too much for all but a very small percentage of riders, those very riders who rise in the ranks of road racing, really.

And this is just the beginning. All that now "old" racing technology of ten years ago is coming our way, such as that from Honda's uber-successful RC211V, having Honda's flagship VR engine, the before-mentioned "straight V." Volkswagen actually came up with the design, and the *V* stands for "V" engine configuration, *R* for *reihenmotor* (straight motor). So what is this thing? Truly, it is both things. Where in most V engines pistons are offset by 45, 60, or 90 degrees, in the VR they are offset by 10–15 degrees, really creating what is called a "staggered" engine, using an inline firing pattern. Why bother with it? If the engine uses two crankshafts, rotating opposite each other, no balancing shaft is necessary. And, most important, the engine is narrow. In 500 cc engines, this configuration can put out over 200 horsepower (so 400 per liter) in bikes weighing 375 pounds. Honda, around 1977, built, with some success, an engine with ovaloid pistons, one that had thirty-two valves and functioned like a V8. Plagued by problems, it was raced with high hopes until Honda, unwilling to spend more R&D dollars on it, dropped the design.

If, and more likely when, engineers discover a way to remove unwanted emissions from two-stroke GP engines, we'll see versions of them in bullet bikes, or ones such as in Honda's NSR 500, which has won GP races from 1984 to the present, particularly when ridden by Eddie Lawson.

So powerful are these new two-strokes that four-stroke bikes up to 800 cc compete on Moto GP tracks with them. The limit had been 990 cc, but it was found that top speeds of well over 210 mph were too dangerous even for world-class riders. Suzuki's GSV-R puts out 240 horsepower at 16,000 rpm. And Aprilia, with its RS3 "Cube," is experimenting with a "fly-by-wire" throttle system, electronically controlled from the handlebar, as opposed to using some form of cable, this system, in another form, to be found on Yamaha's R1 and R6 sport bikes. Said Aprilia's rider Colin Edwards of the Cube, it was "born bad." In one season Edwards crashed the Cube twenty-eight times. Still, a roadgoing version of the Cube put out 260 horsepower.

Someday we'll see a version of the Cube on showroom floors. Already, in production motorcycles we have Black Box (computer chip) Engine Control Units (ECU) metering electronic fuel injection. "Tuning" fuel delivery now sounds like this as a result: "Yosh Box fuel injection remapping done to improve throttle response," "remapping" here being computer programming, done by engineers selling performance chips. Also to be found on production bikes now are antilock brakes and (Black Box) traction control, and new-generation "sticky" compound tires with infinitely more traction than the old, harder rubber kickers, these sticky tires, though, lasting a fraction of the mileage of the earlier units. A current Kawasaki Ninja ad reads, "Comes with Spare Pair of Shorts." Is this bike fast? How about a wide ten-second quarter mile? Zero to 150 mph in ten seconds, right off the showroom floor.

All this in a tuned frame derived from over a hundred years of development. Sweet stuff, if you can take it. Griffins and winged dragons for those who want to fly.

## Today's Moto GP God, "The Doctor"

Anyone in Europe—or, that is, anyone who reads a paper or watches television—will know of Valentino Rossi. In Europe, Rossi is idolized as much as rock stars. Curly-haired, slight of build (he's five foot nine and 130 pounds), and elfin, Rossi has become the face of twenty-first-century motorcycle road racing, dominating first the ultracompetitive 125 cc class, then 250 cc, and finally 500 cc, which, in 2002, became the Moto GP, then allowing four strokes of up to 990 cc (now reduced to 800 cc).

Rossi, the son of Graziano Rossi, a former motorcycle racer, rode his first mini-moto when he was two. (Warning: parents, that *monkey* bike is *not* safe.) Indifferent to school, by his teens Rossi was spending all his time racing both dirt bikes and go carts, his mother pushing the carts for safety reasons. To no avail. Since the family could not afford both (cart racing, which would have taken Rossi in the direction of Formula One racing, being the more expensive of the two), Rossi concentrated on motorcycles, and before the end of 1991 had won sixteen regional dirt races.

Rossi's road-racing debut was not some angel's glide onto the tarmac and to the winners' podium. A hundred yards out from the pit in his first race, he crashed his Cagiva Mito 125 in the track's first turn; the bike was repaired, and off Rossi went again, crashing this time in turn two. Not an auspicious start. But by the end of that week, Rossi finished ninth, and by the end of the season he was on the podium. In his second year he was provided a factory Mito by Team Cagiva, and "cruised" to the Italian title.

Rossi's game was on. Aprilia, sensing his potential, hired him away from Cagiva to ride world GP while barely in his middle teens. Rossi would run with it, taking the world 125 cc in 1997 and the world 250 cc in 1999, the youngest to ever do so. For his success, Honda hired him in 2000, the team's in-paddock guru, the retired 500 cc world champion Mick Doohan, serving as Rossi's personal mentor. And it was here that Rossi rose to fame, in the kind of battle that had made the earlier Hailwood-Ago and Roberts-Spencer competitions of public interest.

In Max Biaggi, Rossi found a worthy opponent, Rossi the upstart, Biaggi the old man on the way out. While before, Rossi's competition with Biaggi had been a friendly one (even though they'd never raced against each other), now, given that the "arrogant yet loveable" Rossi was pitted against the "proud, king-of-the-hill" Biaggi in the same class, the two became bitter enemies, the press serving to fan the flames of animosity, with real and manufactured gossip, so that the Rossi-Biaggi feud nearly resulted in fistfights, and both were threatened with fines by the FIM for "unbecoming behavior." Biaggi fought back that season, but in nine fierce competitions Rossi won on his Honda. And 2001 was a sweep for Rossi, winning eleven races.

In 2002, the FIM created Moto GP competition, wherein 990 cc four-strokes could compete with 500 cc two-strokes. Honda, going with the larger-displacement four-stroke, put Rossi on their liquid-cooled V5 RC211. Again, Rossi ran away with competitions, racking up eleven victories. In 2003, Rossi shocked the crowd when, after being given a ten-second penalty at the Australian GP for not stopping for a yellow flag (thrown when the Ducati rider Troy Bayliss fell), he pulled ahead of the pack and won by a fifteen-second margin, this with GP bikes reaching speeds of 200 mph.

Rossi promptly quit Honda, by then the equivalent of the road-racing mafia. He dabbled with Ducati, which sent the Italian media into a frenzy, but chose not to ride for that team, given that it seemed to have a similar mind-set to Honda. So he went to Yamaha, which offered him a two-year contract worth in excess of $12 million. Yamaha's best, the M-1, was thought inferior to Honda's RC, and Rossi wanted it that way.

The following year, 2004, on the underdog Yamaha, Rossi battled a field of top talent, including Sete Gibernau, taking nine World GP races, and the World Championship title—and again in 2005. By this time, *Forbes* magazine reported, Rossi was the world's ninth-highest-paid sportsman (equal with Lance Armstrong), making in excess of $28 million. After a less than impressive 2007–2008 season, Rossi, still in his twenties, is considering where he will land next. What he is certain of is that he will ride into his early thirties.

Rossi, for his cool, calculating style has been nicknamed "The Doctor." He races with his father's number: 46. Before every race he goes through a ritual in which he puts on his riding gear in exactly the same order, and reaching his bike, bends over and reaches his boots, then grasps the right foot peg. On his helmet are sun and moon emblems, representative, he says, of his personality. (There is also text, which in Italian reads: *Viva la Figa*, meaning, "Hurray for the Pussy!")

So hounded was Rossi by paparazzi that he moved to London, where he is now based.

Currently the newcomers "The Kentucky Kid" (Nicky Hayden, on Honda) and Casey Stoner of Kurri Kurri, New South Wales, Australia (on Ducati), have Rossi in their sights; it remains to be seen who will prevail.

It is altogether possible that Rossi will surpass Ago's record to become the winningest road racer in history, as he now holds seven world championships, with 87 race wins and 131 podium finishes.

No matter, though, for he's already seared into the minds of those of us who even so much as dream of pulling knee sliders. Canyon racing, or on a track, we dream of being as talented as Hailwood, Ago, Roberts, and Rossi. Bending your bike over, rolling on the throttle, the landscape whirring by, your engine roaring, you imagine the crowds on hillsides, cheering you on. And just then, you're a hero, too.

The real thing.

# 4

# Why Don't We
# Do It in the Dirt?

**Y**ou are perched on a motorcycle with a seat so high that your toes, stretched in your knee-high gladiator motocross boots, barely touch the ground. Your hands, gripping handlebars a good yard across, take in the buttery and brutal heartbeat of your engine, a two-stroke 2008 Yamaha YZ 250, which puts out nearly 50 horsepower at 11,000 rpm. Given the 208-pound weight of your bike, that's a power-to-weight ratio of one horsepower for every 4.16 pounds. Your off-the-showroom-floor Toyota Camry will have a power-to-weight ratio around one horsepower for every 18–20 pounds.

And your YZ engine revs almost instantaneously. You blip the throttle, hoping you won't foul a plug before you can get off the line. To your right, and to your left, are twenty other riders just like yourself, bent over their handlebars, likewise in gladiator gear, their engines ponging at idle, then revving like King Kong–size chain saws.

*Pong, pong, pong—brrrrrrOWWWWWWW!*

Behind you are yet another forty riders. If you fail to charge from the line with every iota of horsepower and skill you have, you will be run over from behind, by big, knobby-tired wheels, or worse, spun over, by rear drive wheels, all powered by bikes like yours: 200 pounds, 350–400 pounds with rider, all sent dashing by rabid 250 cc two-strokes putting out about 50 horsepower and turning at 11,000 rpm, the "pack" accelerating 0–50 mph in loamy dirt in 2.5 to 3 seconds.

Your job here, in this situation of organized mayhem and murder, is to jet ahead of the riders on your left (the "pack"), and where the course drops out of sight, hundreds of spectators watching from a hill overlooking it, hit the berm there on the inside, slide your motorcycle sideways, and crack your throttle full on again—to straighten the bike, before, in the blink of an eye, you back off, then crack the throttle open yet again before the course's first technical jump, so your bike is on the pipe and pulling hard from the rear when you hit it.

You want your bike to launch into the air, front wheel high and leading, bucking-bronco style. Ten feet up, you'll instinctively back off the throttle again, but not too much.

On the starting line, that's as far as you (consciously) think. There is another quarter mile of track after that, and umpteen laps, but you won't let any of that cloud the moment. All of that will take care of itself later. You are in a bubble of eternal *now*.

You *will not* think about what will happen if those top-ranked riders on your left get out ahead of you. But you do have a fall-back strategy that will come into play in the space of a thought if that happens. But only then.

Easing out your clutch, with your front tire you nudge the bright red surgical tubing stretched across the dirt course. The moment expands, behind you and to your side riders' engines fouling plugs and dying, the riders like crazed clowns trying to get them going again. Jumping on kick starters, or running to the rear to give them a bump start. You crack your throttle open, clean it up.

*Brrrrr-OWWWW!*

If you were to use a drop start, as do hill climbers, you'd be run over.

You need a clean pull off the line on this, the only solid ground here.

And there are the trees on either side of the track, oaks. If you really went out of control, at forty, you could hit them. But first the hay bales banked in front would surely reduce your momentum, turning your forward motion into an "endo," a fall in which you are, unceremoniously, sent tumbling end over end, at thirty or forty miles per hour.

Your head is in that cave of your full-face helmet and the bikes behind you are started again. Everything in your vision is set on that point a city block ahead of you where the ground drops off. To your far left, an official in a white shirt holds a green flag at his waist.

You get your left foot up on your foot peg and under the shift lever, ready to go for second. You crack your throttle open, enough to get traction when you let out the clutch, but not so much that you'd get bad wheel spin. Now you are a very high, wobbly tripod. When the official raises the flag over his head, you bend over your handlebars, your weight to the rear of the seat for traction.

Even as the flag is coming down you are simultaneously releasing the clutch, cracking the throttle open, lifting your foot onto the right peg, the rubber tubing snapping out of sight, and you lunge forward insanely, as if shot out of a cannon, to your left your state champion and his pals. You try to cut off the third rider, which you do, but you're behind the first two, and instantaneously, you are seeing everything through an irregular pattern of mud thrown on your face shield, and dirt pelts your chest and arms and legs, but the bike is pulling cleanly, and hard, and this oil-rich exhaust creates a cloud you ride through, now over the hill, two riders in front of you, one going for the high line on the berm, which will give him speed coming out of it, the state champ going for the inside, fast line, which leaves you the middle, which is really only a yard wide, and you crack the throttle open, cranking the handlebars *right* to slide left, and arc around the wet, heavy berm, the two riders inches from you, all engines pulling, and the whole pack behind you roaring. You straighten the bars out of the berm, veer right and cut off the number-two rider, but as a consequence come into the jump too hot, lack the nanosecond to get the bike fully back on the pipe, and so, as number one, *quicker but slower* on the inside, screws it on, goes by you like a shot, both of you are thrown into the air. There is a long, long moment when all that forward motion is turned into breathtaking vertical, both of you landing side by side, but you neutral, so the whoops, undulations, that should be navigated with the engine pulling so hard that the front wheel is off the ground all together, or skimming over the tops of the whoops, instead batters you so harshly you can barely hang on, the bike pounding up under you, so that when you are out of them, and face a right-hander, there another berm with, you can see, a second jump following it. You take the inside, to get your balance back (you *can't* have your head tossed around like this and not need a quarter of a second to reorient), crank the bars left, and slide around the berm, but your better-balanced number one, having the advantage, taking the high line this time, widens his lead, so all you can do is stay on his rear wheel and hope not to hit him. Or, if the pack gets ahead of you, have the guts to pull a "hole shot," accelerate through a slot two feet wide while trusting that no rider crosses in front of you.

You are, at this point, eight seconds into your race. You must negotiate whatever a track throws at you—whoops, jumps, mud, berms, ditches, washboards, and straight sections—at lightning speed. Nonstop. With up to seventy riders around you. Hammered, mud-covered, and loving every second of it. You will, standing on your bike, not let up for the duration of the race.

A single race lasts thirty-five to forty minutes, which is why motocross racers are some of the most physically fit athletes in the world. They have to be. A recent National Health Institute study found that motocross racers' heart rates in competition are up around 180 to 190 beats per minute. And motocross racers do this *twice* in each day of competition, for a combined total of seventy minutes of cardiopulmonary stress. Hence, world-class motocross racers are world-class athletes. And world champions are gods in Europe, multimillionaires and public personalities with the cachet of, say, A-Rod, Joe Montana, or Michael Jordan. Household names.

This is not the case in the United States. But then, motocross is relatively new here, though dirt riding is not. In fact, from the very inception of the motorcycle, riders worldwide have taken to the dirt. Getting it on in the dirt is, arguably, the best fun you can have on two wheels.

## Red, White, and Blue Dirt

Dirt track motorcycle racing is thought of as the bona fide form of American motorcycling competition. This is no surprise, given the motorcycles manufactured here lent themselves to this sort of venue. V-twin, heavy, torquey, and, with some modification, extremely powerful—and without exception four-strokes. Indian, Harley-Davidson, Excelsior-Henderson, Flying Merkel, Crocker, Pope, and Yale all built machines employing cast-iron cylinders and heads, and likewise the heavy valve gear required of four-strokes at that time.

Recall that the earliest motorcycles were taken directly to the board-track "velodromes" already existing for bicycle racing, those velodromes for a good ten years being enlarged until they spanned one-third to half-mile distances (in Brooklyn, New York, one track measured two miles). Early motorcyclists raced on these banked tracks at speeds over one hundred miles per hour, often fatally. Board tracks were famous for putting foot-long splinters through falling riders. Tracks were built from two-by-fours—or sixes—laid lengthwise, the turning ends of these tracks banked at up to 60 degrees.

Board-track racing had started in Europe, though Americans, having been likewise stricken by the bicycle craze, took it up with a passion. American riders of the period were colorful characters, such as Leslie "Red" Parkhurst. Parkhurst quit school at the age of twelve to take odd jobs, one of them delivering stock for a paint company. Allowed to drive the company truck, Parkhurst was arrested so many times for speeding that he was fired. By this time the motorcycle bug had bitten him, though, Parkhurst cadging rides on Harleys from a local dealer who recognized his talent for speed. Lying about his age, as had his hero Jack London, he began his board-racing career at thirteen, as Harley-Davidson's first factory rider. Board-racing motorcycles had no brakes, and usually only two gears. Parkhurst, six foot four and carrot topped, hence "Red," stood out among the other diminutive riders, winning race after race, one in front of eighteen thousand fans at the Two Mile Motordrome in New York. Parkhurst, as a result of his success, became Harley-Davidson's advertising face, one fans saw often. He also made the news for brawling with his pal, then heavyweight champion of the world, Jack Dempsey.

No less colorful was Joe Petrali, who became the bridge rider between board-track and American dirt-track racing. As did Parkhurst, Petrali began riding at a very early age, buying his first Indian single when he was thirteen—a motorcycle he modified for racing with the help of a local dealer, who recognized Petrali's unusual mechanical skills and offered him a job in his shop. Petrali accepted, quitting school and beginning what would be a spectacular career in racing. As Petrali's racing hero, Charles "Fearless" Balke, wore leather pants and puttees, so did Petrali—and a surplus WWI "balloon-jumpers" helmet. In 1925 Petrali was the first to average faster than one hundred miles per hour for an hour on a motorcycle, which he did on a board track in Altoona, Pennsylvania. He won the National Board Track title that year, against the Harley-Davidson "Wrecking Crew," but also began racing on the controversial new "flat" tracks, winning national titles five times from 1931 to 1936. Petrali won nearly seventy national motorcycling titles, also setting a world motorcycle speed record at Daytona Beach in 1936, where, on a Harley Knucklehead streamliner, he went 136.183 mph, a record that stood for eleven years. When he retired from racing, Petrali went to work for Howard Hughes, serving as "flight engineer" on the first and only test of Hughes's *Spruce Goose*.

Still, Petrali's move to the new "flat" tracks signaled the end of something, as he was at that time motorcycling's most visible rider.

About this time, Ignaz Schwinn, then owner of the famed Excelsior-Henderson, catching the board-track fever, had his engineers build an eight-valve racer for competition. Schwinn's machine, with his handpicked rider, proved to be a world beater, all right—though, at the end of the evening, Schwinn's rider took a bad slide that hurled him into the board wall, killing him instantly. And this rider was a family man. His head, spectators said, "burst like a pumpkin." Schwinn shut down his board-racing program on the spot. Board-track racing, really, along with Schwinn's rider, died that night in the United States.

So, given that board tracks were too lethal, with their steep, banked turns, where were these riders to go? Where Petrali had gone: horse tracks. Or, since they didn't have inclined turns on each end, *flat* tracks (sometimes called oval tracks). Where the horse had gone before, so went the iron horse.

Flat, or dirt, track has been since that time the original American racing venue. Americans took to it with a vengeance, owned it from its inception, dirt track racing being as American as NASCAR. Hairy-knuckled, balls out, going like hell.

Now "oval" tracks are everywhere in the United States, also accommodating sprint car racing, stock car, and demolition derby. From Petrali's time, just about any town of size built a track near it where motorcyclists and hot-rodders could race, family-style—take any old beater, two wheels or four, and away they went. Flat tracks for motorcycles sprang up indoors, too—in roller rinks, hockey arenas, any space large enough to set out a track.

At fifteen, I got my first taste of flat-tracking through a friend who owned a Harley "quarter liter," really an Italian-made Aermacchi 250 TT. Then, as in Petrali's time, you came to the starting line, flanked by only four to six riders. At the Minneapolis Armory, a cavernous, hangar-size space, you raced on a cement floor, the track enclosed by cement walls, which you did not want to hit. Hay bales were placed strategically around the ends of the track, but that didn't ensure safety by any means. Again, in gladiator gear, you squatted over your bike, but here when the flag came down, you dropped the clutch, the bike hurling you toward the far wall, and just as you were about to be a bug splat there, you cranked the bars to the right, put your carpet-covered left foot on the cement, and hit the throttle so hard that the rear wheel broke out from under you, turning umpteen times the speed you were moving, the whole bike sliding left, at forty-five miles per hour, sideways, over rock-hard cement, the exhaust pipe of the rider in front of you up your right nostril, the rider behind you trying to drive up and out your rear.

This sliding turn in flat-tracking is called powersliding or broadsliding. In powersliding you get your rear tire so far around that it is creating a pivot of the tracking front tire, while at the same time making it possible to spin around a smaller radius than could be two-wheel-tracked at the speed you're moving. Powersliding is scary and then some—if you crack the throttle too far open, you'll bang down on the hard concrete and possibly be hit by the riders behind you if you're a frontrunner—and it is intoxicating.

On the armory's small track, you'd come out the far side of the turn, get the bike upright again, hit the throttle full on, speed shifting up one gear, or two, the bike hurling you now at the opposite wall, and, almost there, you'd drop a gear or two, compression braking, and all over again lay the bike down in a roaring powerslide, cutting through an atmosphere blue with exhaust and smelling of burned castor oil. To this day, just the smell of burned castor oil nearly makes the hair on the back of my neck stand on end. Everything smelled of hot oil, hot metal, and burned rubber. You breathed it, simply trying on each corner—always left-handed, *counterclockwise*—to get to the *inside*, the faster line, or to hold your straight-line acceleration longer on the faster, outside line, which necessitated taking a high line in the turn, which always put you at the back of the pack again, flat-track races being won in the turns. Eight times around on the quarter mile, or sixteen full-throttle slides and sixteen full-throttle sprints. Zero to fifty in 2.5 seconds off the line, then sliding sideways, maneuvering by other riders at thirty-five, and cracking it open again. Aermacchi TTs weighed 200 pounds, put out 35 horsepower at 10,000 rpm. Engines came in Long Rod, with more torque, for short courses; or Short Rod, which were better for longer courses with higher speeds. Riders were called "hot shoes," and they still are.

And on the full-size tracks adapted from horse racing, which became the testing grounds for riders and manufacturers? At the big-money tracks?

Legends were again born. But nowhere more so in American motorcycle "dirt" racing than in Illinois, at the Springfield Mile. There, by the 1960s, riders were reaching speeds over 130 mph on the straights, were sliding at 80. Dirt tracks, by this time, were groomed. Track designers mixed clay, to hold the track together; shale; and sometimes "decomposed" granite with sand, wetting the track before races to provide the most stable surface. As was done also at Ascot, a California track famous for rider fatalities.

For the longest time, American steel, particularly Indian and Harley-Davidson, ruled, riders like Joe Leonard piloting them, until the British, particularly Triumph and BSA, gave Harley, the sole American survivor of the 1950s, competition. This, of course, was at a time when the motorcycle landscape was changing forever. The legends Gary Nixon and Gene Romero rode British, and later, when the Japanese were knocking down international racing events, Kenny Roberts rode Yamaha, going on to dominate big-money flat-tracking.

Roberts has the dubious distinction of riding *the most dangerous bike of all time:* the TZ 750 powered flat-tracker Yamaha built for him in 1974–75. Yamaha's TZ 750 engine, a transverse four-cylinder two-stroke, built for road racing, put out 125 peaky, nearly uncontrollable horsepower. Said Roberts of this bike, "You had to throw it sideways at 150 mph to get it slowed for corners." One hundred fifty miles per hour sideways on dirt? Roberts won one race with it, and switched to road racing. His last comment about the bike? "They don't pay me enough to ride that thing."

Roberts that season launched what would come to be seen as the most exciting road-racing period in history, bringing his flat-tracking skills and inventing "throttle steering." After Roberts, dirt track in the United States came to be seen as the entry ticket to the international road-racing scene, where the big money was . . . millions. And still is.

But first, in flat-tracking, class-C privateers went at professionals, riding bikes off the street. Then, as is still done now, riders like Al Burke of Richfield, Minnesota, got his start by teaching himself to do slides (in a gravel pit), then taking to the races at the Minnesota fairgrounds, where he became an eight-time state champion.

Americans love underdog stories, and flat-track racing created them by the dozens. Al, going on to race nationally in handicap/scratch races, was the typical, though unusually talented, privateer. With support from Harley-Davidson, he followed a tight race schedule, driving from track to track. Said Al, in those races "you'd go until there was only one winner. We would ride *seven* times a night, *if* you kept winning. I won the heat and final on an Iowa half mile on Sunday, seven times at the Milwaukee on Tuesday, seven times at Santa Fe on Wednesday, seven times Thursday at Flint, Michigan, seven times on Friday, and again seven times at Shererville, Indiana, taking thirty-seven first places in a single week of racing."

Flat-out endurance? Or love of the sport?

Oddly enough, Down Under a parallel development was taking place. So much so that Aussies claim dirt-track racing as their own, citing its source in New South Wales, circa 1920, though on the underside of the globe calling it "grass tracking." Whether Down Under riders were the first to develop this sort of racing, they did further refine it.

In speedway, the motorcycle has no brakes at all, runs on methanol, and uses only one gear. In my late teens, I had the pleasure of knowing a Kiwi grass racer, Reg Costigan, who told me that, yes, "track work" on a 170-pound motorcycle with no brakes, and propelled by an alcohol-fueled, 60-horsepower engine, was "rather challenging." The four-time AMA flat-track champion Chris Carr, whom I met at Bonneville, had much the same to say: "Yeah, it gets to be a handful." The real lesson here being that successful racers are *not* maniacs; they are passionate, extraordinarily focused riders. Their level of calm can seem sometimes almost preternatural.

And what were Europeans doing at this time while Americans and those Down Under were ripping up dirt ovals? The Brits were being ever so classy. Angus Scott, designer of the Scott Motorcycle, beginning in 1909, set up courses at his annual employee picnic. Crossing bogs, rocky sections, and shallow streams, observed by all and scored by judges, including Scott, the riders were given points for their ability to negotiate obstacles, but also for overall style and grace. Speed *wasn't* the point, but there was a time limit, so riders were required to move "briskly." The winner was the rider who navigated the course with the fewest errors in the least amount of time. "Observed trials" are still held everywhere in Europe, though especially so in Britain. Natty dressers with élan won the day then as they do now. It's a gentleman's form of motorcycle gymnastics, and special bikes are built for it—high steering-head angle, short wheelbase, low-revving engine. Scott's event became so prestigious that by the 1920s, Scott's Yorkshiremen boasted they were the "best and toughest" riders in all Britain.

This was laying down the glove, of course, and a southern club, in Camberly, rose to the challenge, setting down a route, but with no observed sections, the winner simply being the *fastest*. Period. To hell with style. The British motorcycle press of the time thrilled to it, while the Auto Cycle Union, Britain's governing body, argued this sort of race would not be an "observed trial." So what were they to call it? Legend has it that an Auto Union member exclaimed, "Whatever we call it, it will be a rare old *scramble!*" Meaning a form of organized bedlam, which is just about right.

Scrambles date from that very race, and became a British obsession, courses being mapped out on terrain earlier used for fox hunts and dressage. So punishing was this terrain that Brits (and the Swedes and Czechs), by 1930, had adopted plunger rear suspension, long-travel telescopic front forks, lighter-weight components, and larger front and rear wheels (roughly 20-inch in front, 19-inch in the rear), creating a bike that had greater ground clearance and was ultramaneuverable, the origin of the dirt bike as we know it today. With one exception. In Europe at this time, as in the United States, big four-stroke engines were used, but competitive "scramble" bikes were "thumpers" (four-stroke singles), the big manufacturers being Triumph, BSA, and Norton. All three produced regularly updated models for a more than enthusiastic public, which was large. Even through the thirties, tens of thousands of "scramble" bikes were sold. By contrast, in 1934, Indian and Harley-Davidson combined manufactured only six hundred motorcycles, and sales for all units were fewer than a thousand. Only wartime production saved both companies, sales picking up marginally after the war. Europeans, unlike Americans, after the advent of cheap cars and the Depression, continued to ride motorcycles, especially through the hard times of WWII.

1950s Brit bikes, for that reason, were decades ahead of their American counterparts—and there were still a good twenty-five or thirty manufacturers competing for John Q. Public's pocketbook in Britain. So popular was the Cross Country Motor Scramble, or Moto-Cross, for short, in Europe, that by 1947 the Dutch National Motorcycle Federation created an international scramble championship, a predecessor to Motocross des Nations, which was held in La Fraineuse, Belgium, thirty thousand fans turning out at competitions to cheer on their riders.

All over the Continent, and in Britain, riders went head to head in mud, dirt, and over jumps, the crowds loving it. Europeans had their legends, such as the Brits John Draper and Les Archer; the Belgians Victor Leloup; and the Swedes Bill Nilsson, Sten Lundin, and Rolf Tibblin—world champions all.

Never heard of these riders? No surprise. Or the earlier flat-trackers? For the average citizen, and especially so here in the United States, all this was as distant as the surface of the moon. Until—

## A Love Story, a Betrayal, and a KGB Murder
## That Changed All Things Motorcycle

The Sachsenring. Mean anything? To motor racing fans, the Sachsenring is now the mid-season MotoGP track. Oftentimes people confuse the Nürburgring, the track Hitler built to showcase his Nazi racing cars, with the Sachsenring, constructed much earlier and named for the Saxons, the nomadic woodland people who first occupied northern Europe. Unfortunate in its location, the Sachsenring after WWII lay in Communist-run East Germany, which is critical to this story. Put in the vernacular, East Germany was hell: bread lines, no consumer goods, and informants, KGB and otherwise, sending people to Siberia, where countless unfortunates died building the Road of Bones.

In the midst of all this suffering was a bright light for the East Germans, the international road races held at the Sachsenring. An average turnout was 350,000 to 500,000, many times the number of spectators attending the Indy 500, or even the Super Bowl today.

The "ring" was really a street-based circuit, nearly five and a half miles long, encompassing all manner of difficult turns and long stretches for speed. Spectators by the thousands could walk to barricades delineating the route, and where crossing the track became necessary, they were allowed to do so on carpet strips, which would later be removed, so they wouldn't dirty the track.

Imagine, then, hosting this event, as East Germany did, but not having so much as one competitive machine. Riders from around the globe won world-class prizes, but the prize money, of course, was good only in East Germany. Driving out of the country, riders threw race results and paper money out their windows to fans.

One such fan was Walter Kaaden, who had worked under the engineer Wernher von Braun in his V-series rocket program during WWII (both were *genuine* rocket scientists). Unlike Braun, Kaaden opted to stay in East Germany after Berlin fell, and was taken on by the motorcycle manufacturer MZ. Braun, snapped up by the West, went on to head NASA's Marshall Space Flight Center, his murder of tens of thousands used in slave labor to build the V rockets brought to light within the international community only recently.

MZ at this time had one effort in mind: to build transportation costing nearly nothing for a population having nothing. The simplest way to do it? Build a simple machine. So, the engine? The two-stroke powerplant by default became MZ's choice. It had, really, only three major moving parts: a piston, a connecting rod, and a crankshaft.

Here enters the other half of the "motor" world in motorcycling. The two-stroke. Invented by Sir Dugald Clerk in 1878, the "two-stroke" engine, instead of employing mechanical valves *external* to the combustion chamber, used the piston itself to open and close intake and exhaust ports (milled openings) machined into the cylinder wall (with a "transfer port" behind that wall for intake). This allowed for a combination of the strokes found in the four-cycle Otto engine. In the power/exhaust cycle, the air-fuel mixture is ignited and the piston is forced down, the top of the piston passing the exhaust port and the pressurized (burned) gas escaping. As the piston continues down, it compresses the air-fuel-oil mixture *in the crankcase,* so when the piston, still moving down, passes the intake/transfer port (opening it), the compressed charge in the crankcase enters the cylinder/combustion chamber, forcing the remaining burned air-fuel mixture out. All this in one stroke. Now, as the piston comes up (passing the exhaust port), it further compresses the air-fuel charge while also creating a vacuum in the crankcase, a poppet or reed valve there letting in another air-fuel charge. When the piston reaches the top of the stroke it fires yet again for another power/exhaust stroke. So there is *one power pulse for every two cycles of the engine*—as opposed to one to four in the four-stroke engine.

Theoretically, then, a two-stroke engine, per rpm, should produce twice the power of the four-stroke engine. It didn't. And wasn't even close. Not until Kaaden. The problem was, of course, that for a thousandth of a second exhaust gases were allowed to mix with the "clean" air-fuel as the exhaust port was open during the intake stroke. And almost all of these engines were "crankcase inducted," meaning the air-fuel mixture entered the engine through the crankcase, bathing the crankshaft and rod. So "wet sump" lubrication was not possible. The solution? Put the lubrication in the fuel itself. Problem solved. But others were created, in that this lubricant changed the burn characteristics of the fuel, making it potentially less explosive; caused "fouling" of the spark plugs, to the extent that they worked poorly or not at all; and the engine puked out stinky, oily, dirty exhaust.

Contrary to popular belief, these two-strokes were in use from the time of their invention. Scott Motorcycles, of the Scott Trials mentioned above, built a twin, the Flying Squirrel that was well loved by enthusiasts; and two-strokes, from the turn of the century, could be found everywhere in marine applications—until recently, nearly all outboard motors were two-strokes—and, to our detriment, two-stroke engines came to be used in power lawn mowers, chain saws, and even all manner of model airplanes. According to the EPA, a single leaf-blower engine will produce in two hours more burned hydrocarbons than a car will produce in a year.

So why use this engine? It's cheap. And, after Kaaden, it was light and powerful. Recall that the two-stroke has only three moving parts. No cams, lifters, or valves. No complex oil pump, oil lines, or heavy flywheel to counterbalance all that mass. It was a manufacturer's dream. In fact, until the fall of the Berlin Wall, East Germany's *cars* were primarily propelled by two-stroke engines.

Early on, two-strokes were not very powerful. The limitations of the design—or so it was thought—prevented much development. After all, what could you do with it?

Kaaden, our former rocket scientist, was saddled with this engine, stuck in a place where there was nothing. Kaaden's team was so poor that his star rider, Ernst Degner, rode with a helmet that had been handed down to Kaaden fifteen years earlier. Degner was not paid to race and even had to buy his own fuel and tires. Here was this old dog of an engine: simple, not very fuel efficient—you could never get as clean a burn in it as you could with a four-stroke—and dirty.

Great innovators, the Italians prior to Kaaden created a "twingle" or twin/single—a twin-cylinder engine in which both pistons had a common firing chamber, one piston opening the intake port, the other the exhaust port—to improve the "dirty" burn problem. However, in the process they also created an engine that by default had low compression, so it only produced slightly greater power. The Austrian company Puch used this engine in motorcycles for nearly two decades, selling them in the United States as the Sears Allstate.

By Kaaden's time, the simplest means of increasing engine performance (given existing four-stroke technology) was to hyperaspirate, which meant supercharging. But you can't supercharge a two-stroke, because if the air-fuel mixture is two, three times standard atmosphere, when it enters the combustion chamber with the exhaust port slightly open, the fresh air-fuel mixture will just blow out the exhaust port.

Have you ever noticed the distinct sound a two-stroke makes? *Rinnnng, ding, ding, ding, rinnnnnng, ding ding ding ding!* Hence, the nickname for them: "Ring dings." The sound is irritating as hell, unless you come to love them as I have, as all Johnny-come-lately dirt riders like myself did.

Kaaden, listening to that sound, thought, Okay, this damn thing is a noisy cuss if it is anything. It's a sound generator. Why? The exploded gas creates a shock wave as it leaves the engine. And, given there's this thousandth of a second that the exhaust port is open when the engine is taking in fuel, Kaaden thought, What if I could use that shock wave to supercharge the engine using its own exhaust gas? (This is *not* the way a turbocharger works: A turbo charger is a supercharger with its turbine for compressing intake gases, driven not by gears off the engine itself, but by the engine's *exhaust*.)

Kaaden's idea was simple. But the execution of it? A nightmare. He came up with the notion of using a divergent exhaust cone off the exhaust port to draw the exhaust gas out of the engine, and a convergent cone, after a "belly pipe," to send the sound/shock waves (and exhaust gases) back at the engine. Considering all this happens within four-thousandths of a second per cycle, the *length* of pipe from the port to the divergent cone, and then to the convergent cone, had to be in such proportion that the shock wave was reflected back into the exhaust port at the nanosecond it was open and the cylinder filling with new air-fuel. Wave pressure is 7 pounds per square inch, traveling at 1,600 to 1,700 feet per second. Realize that the sound, or shock wave, will be at the same frequency with which the engine is turning, so a pipe for low-end power, say 3,000 rpm, couldn't have the same dimensions as a pipe for an engine designed for peak horsepower, say at 8,000 rpm. A low note has a lower frequency of vibration than a high note, right? So the convergent cone had to be exactly the right angle and distance from the exhaust port to direct the shock waves back at the exhaust port.

Kaaden, experimenting with these "sound pipes" on his two-strokes, increased engine power by 25 to 40 percent while creating an engine that operated at peak efficiency within a very narrow band of rpm, say 7,000 to 9,000. Said Kaaden, "You'll know when you have the design right, because the chamber will be impossible to fit on the motorcycle." Kaaden, in addition to inventing the "expansion chamber," further improved his two-stroke engines by perfecting an earlier induction method, the rotary valve.

Together, using his sound pipe and rotary-valve induction, Kaaden created magic out of garbage: his engine was the world's first to exceed 200 horsepower per liter. That's right: 200 horsepower out of 1,000 ccs—in the 1950s. Your average Buick or Olds engine at this time produced around 20 horsepower per liter, and a hot-rodded engine, having a very short life, around 50 horsepower per liter.

Kaaden's MZ racer was tiny—125 cc—and consequently light. In this equation—low weight/high power—it was unbeatable. If it didn't explode, or foul its plugs, which two-strokes did. They were notoriously unreliable.

Kaaden's bike, with Ernst Degner aboard it, conquered the world and won the 125 cc championship. And then Degner, at a racecourse in Sweden, defected. It wasn't so much that he defected that hurt Kaaden; how could Kaaden fault Degner for it? Degner by then had tasted life outside East Germany. But what Degner did was take Kaaden's dream work and give it to Suzuki.

And that was the end of Kaaden, and the demise of MZ's racing success. Degner later returned to East Germany, where he was found in his apartment with his throat slashed—the official story of his death being suicide.

The rest is history. The Berlin Wall went up in 1961, the very year Suzuki got Kaaden's engine. Honda, which had been in the United States since 1959, had already proved there was a market for motorcycles here. Honda's mission? Said the director of sales, Kihachiro Kawashima, Honda wanted to create the image of the motorcycle anew, "a motorcycle that simply didn't seem like one." No dark dealerships, no mystery, no greasy mechanics. Their engines were, without exception, four-strokes—no dirty two-strokes for Honda.

Suzuki, seizing the opportunity to give Honda a beating, ran with it. Suzuki now had the greatest innovation of the time on their hands, Kaaden's two-stroke. It was cheap, easy to build, and produced mind-boggling power. It was also light, with lightning-fast throttle response. Kaaden's engine was stolen from Suzuki by Yamaha, and from Yamaha by Kawasaki, ushering in three decades of high-performance two-stroke motorcycles and introducing a whole generation of would-be riders to the fun of tinkering with bikes. And from the first, further modifications by the "little three" made these two-stroke engines even more reliable and powerful, employing crossflow-scavenged, loop-scavenged, and finally power-valve systems, such as Yamaha's YPVS, making for variable porting—moving the bore in relation to the piston and connecting rod—to correct the narrow power band problem.

Hot-rodding two-strokes, we found, was simple. Mill the head for better compression—you could get the damn thing off the engine in fifteen minutes—or simply pull the whole cylinder and head and install a bigger piston and aftermarket cylinder. Performance kits were available everywhere, making two-strokes a tuner's dream. Slap on an expansion chamber. Rejet, and from a docile hummer you'd get a bona fide fire-breathing brute.

All this two-stroke technology was taken to the dirt in 1963 when a Swedish company famous for its sewing machines built a 175 cc two-stroke bike for the "youth market," the Silver Pilen. By using Kaaden's "expansion chamber" exhaust, and modifying the porting, riders on factory Husqvarna Pilens were beating older four-stroke bikes *twice* their size (as is still the case today—it takes a 450 cc four-stroke to beat a 250 cc two-stroke). CZ, in Czechoslovakia, followed suit, and Greeves in England. And, given motocross was already in place in Europe, these bikes changed the landscape of dirt racing almost overnight.

Hundreds of thousands in Europe attended races, and more each year, until interest in the sport was rivaled only by that for soccer. So it was inevitable that motocross come to America, which it did, in the form of a booster named Edison Dye. A businessman and engineer, Dye witnessed the new motocross on a tour of Europe and was hooked. In the shiny Husqvarnas, with their red-and-chrome tanks, he saw a goldmine. Here was a motorcycle for the youth market in America to rival Honda's.

By that time, motocross was sanctioned by the AMA in the United States, but was practiced only in Vermont. Dye, to advertise his new bikes, hired the world champion Torsten Hallman to ride in exhibition races.

In the United States, we were still riding four-strokes, manly, meaty types piloting them: Who else could do it? They weighed nearly three hundred pounds. Dye's "Huskies" weighed two thirds of that, and put out the same, or even more horsepower, that power coming on with lightning precision. The big-bore, stump-pulling "thumpers," even with America's best on them, took a terrible beating from Hallman on his Husky.

Dye, to further drive sales, hired an East Coast distributor (Dye was in California), John Penton, who was nothing short of inspired. Penton, who'd grown up riding his father's Harley, and having ridden "scrambles" on dirt bikes of the period—in the United States really heavy four-stroke street bikes with the fenders and lights removed—conceived of something apart from what Dye was doing with Husqvarna. Penton was a ferociously tough, though compact, man. He became famous for finishing enduros even when badly injured, in one nearly decapitating himself on a cable, the cable just missing his throat but catching him on the cheek, Penton finishing partially blinded and his face so swollen his friends didn't recognize him at the finish line. So being passed by a 50 cc Kriedler in mud one afternoon, when he was riding a larger-displacement BSA, got Penton thinking about "smaller-displacement" dirt bikes.

Penton, by this time, was already known to the motorcycling world for breaking Cannonball Baker's coast-to-coast run. Very few people at the time, however, knew what had incited that run. Penton, happily married, and with three sons under five, found that his wife had progressive multiple sclerosis, from which she died, painfully, less than a year after the diagnosis. A member of a large and strong family, one owning a motorcycle dealership so the men in the family could get parts for their motorcycles, John, following his wife's death, farmed his boys out to his brothers' families, then rode himself senseless in Ohio enduros, in Dayton flat-tracks, and in the Georgia Stone Mountain enduro. When this didn't prove enough punishment to work tragedy out of his system, he got on a BMW R69S and headed for Mexico. At night he'd tip the bike on its side and toss a canvas tarp over the works to make a tent for himself.

When Penton returned home, his brother (who'd always called John "Slug"), remarked, "Well, Slug, why don't you just go out and break old Cannonball's record?" This was not the kind of thing you wanted to say to John Penton. He threw himself into preparation, training by riding on the Ohio Turnpike, cutting himself a hole in the fence so he could ride without paying tollway fees. Penton left New York City on June 8, 1959. He checked into the Los Angeles Western Union fifty-two hours, eleven minutes, and one second later, commenting that his run had been flawed by an unnecessary forty-five-minute stop in Albuquerque, New Mexico. Cannonball Baker's record, set in 1933 in a Graham-Paige Blue Streak 8 *automobile*, was fifty-three hours, thirty minutes. Said Penton of his riding into Los Angeles, "Everything got real hazy and I began to see double." His final comment on the ride? "All I want right now is some sleep"— something the indefatigable Penton seemed to need little of.

While Dye was creating motocross in America, Penton was creating a seemingly similar, though very different, variant of dirt riding: enduro, for which he was especially suited. In the United States, the big daddy of them all was the Jack Pine enduro in Lansing, Michigan, the Lansing, Michigan Motorcycle club alone feeding at events 1,200 or more participants. Penton became obsessed with the Jack Pine, which his brother Bill won in 1954, Penton competing in it first on a Harley, then a BSA B33 (a smaller displacement, lighter bike), an NSU 175 cc (on which Honda based its small-displacement vertical single-cylinder engine designs), and finally a BMW 250. Penton went on to win the Jack Pine, and the Stone Mountain, Alligator, Little Burr, and Corduroy enduros, BMW taking such an interest that they sponsored him in the International Six Day Trials (ISDT) in 1962, which he did not win.

Penton *hated* losing anything, so the ISDT was the mountain he was determined to climb, but he needed the right bike for it. Penton was perhaps the first to promote the idea that in dirt, smaller could be better—that power could be sacrificed in favor of lightness and agility. By this time, he was the distributor of Husqvarna for thirty-eight eastern states, and he went to the top brass to see if he could have a smaller-displacement, for-purpose "enduro" built around his specifications.

Husky didn't want to hear "smaller could be better." NSU had gone out of business by this time, and Penton's remaining contact was the Cleveland dealer Fritz Dengel, who was selling Hansas (named by Dengel to sound like Honda, whose motorcycles were selling at the time like those proverbial hotcakes). The Hansa was, quite bluntly, one pathetic little motorcycle. It did, however, have a Sachs (made with watch precision) engine in it. Penton met with the manufacturers of this bike, Kronreif and Trunkenpolz of Mattighofen (KTM), in Austria, arranging for the company to build from the best parts available (Ceriani forks and shocks, Sachs engine, and so on) his "enduro" for $6,000 ($60,000–$70,000 today).

"Built for Champions" was Penton's motto, and if you could get your hands on one, the rest was up to you. Penton's machines would dominate world enduro championships for ten years, including the ISDT, until rampant inflation in the United States and the Arab oil embargo made it impossible for Penton to import his bikes from KTM.

By the second year of production, Penton's bikes and riders were so competitive that *Das Motorad* wrote, "The participation of riders from the U.S. is no longer a game or a joke. They are coming!" That year, riders on Pentons won seven gold and nine silver medals. Penton, in one ISDT, rode with a broken collarbone. He went on record as saying one day of the ISDT was more brutal than the entire Jack Pine. In 1973, five of Penton's team, including his sons, would take gold medals. Overall, American riders on Pentons would take eighteen bronze, seventeen silver, and forty-four gold medals in ISDT events. While Penton would never take the gold in the ISDT (now the ISDE, the International Six Days Enduro), his sons and team members would, many times.

And the import of all this? Anyone age ten to sixty reading some motor-cycle magazine at the time couldn't help but see something about Penton and his enduros and think this form of dirt riding made sense—sure, en-duros were brutal, a test of character, but they weren't, like motocross, *insane*. Enduro was *big adventure*, a kind of re-creation of the Wild West opportunity. To go where no one has gone before—out into the middle of nowhere, over seemingly impossible terrain. And Iron Man Penton, handsome as he was, became the face of that trailbreaking rider, youthful, bright-eyed, and tough. Penton took racing off the dirt tracks in America (including motocross tracks) and into country formerly inhabited only by our mountain men of myth. What youth wouldn't want to "get out there"?

And what was Dye doing all this time? Not one to miss an opportu-nity, he realized that if one rider such as Hallman could boost his sales of motocross bikes, why not a whole team? So Dye brought over Joel Robert and Roger DeCoster, Belgians, and Dave Bickers, Britain's best. And if not a whole team, why not create the very events his riders raced in, which would be attended by tens of thousands, all of whom would be paying an entry fee? Say . . . 25,000 spectators? And thus was begun the American Inter-Am. All of this occurred by 1967.

Between Dye and Penton, a whole dirt bike revolution had been spawned. Said Dick Mann, probably America's greatest all-around rider at the time: "Nothing affected the sport [of motorcycling] so much . . . as the Europeans coming to America."

That and Dye and Penton.

## How a Monkey Lured the Unsuspecting to the Dark Side

While all this motorized mayhem was taking place, Husqvarnas and CZs and Greeves tossing gouts of mud on tracks wherever people could build them, and Pentons crossing impossible distances in enduro races, Honda was quietly lurking in the sunlight, biding its time. And exactly when the general public began to feel as if these knobby-tired noisemakers were here to stay, and so entertained some interest in dirt riding—there had to be something to it, some fun, or who would bother, right?—Honda once again dropped nothing short of a bomb. The Monkey, as Brits call it to this day. The Honda Trail 50.

The Monkey was designed to be cute. It had blue or red glossy metal-flake paint, tiny knobbed balloon tires no larger than a dinner plate, and a three-speed gearbox that didn't use a clutch. *Anyone*, and that even meant grandma, could ride it. It put out about 2.5 to 3 horsepower (as did a turn-of-the-century 1,400 cc Hildebrand and Wolfmüller), had front suspension, and was so low to the ground that, if you fell off of it at its 25 mph top speed, you'd—most likely—escape with barely a scratch.

All that ferocity of the Husky was made here in miniature—and in a four-stroke, puttering style. How *cute*! The Trail 50 was the loveable puppy of motorcycles.

Wisely, Honda went right for the jugular in America: the YMCA. That's right, Honda sent representatives around to YMCA programs all around the country, touting the clean-living, responsibility-promoting, happy motoring experience to be had on their Trail 50. The YMCA agreed, and bought thousands. So did the Shriners, Boy Scouts, and moms and dads everywhere.

A cute little Monkey was safe, right?

The minibike boom had already hit years before, but those minibikes had no suspension, were powered by lawn-mower engines, and weren't very attractive. Here was a little jewel of a machine, and it was even affordable. And, by god, it *was* fun. All the good stuff, wind in your hair, nice little puttering sound, and it even climbed hills in low gear! On top of all that, the handlebars folded down so you could stuff it in your trunk or camper. What wasn't to like?

Of course, as demand increased, Honda introduced a larger version of this bike, the CT 70, and later the CT 90, all having that signature engine—horizontal cylinder, even power, and not much of it. The company sold millions.

In retrospect, anyone could see where this was going, at least for a significant percentage of riders. You (all of ten or eleven) sold Mom or Dad on the Monkey, really, honestly, truly meaning this to be the last, the only, the best little motorbike you'd ever have. Honest, really! And, yes, you'd only ride it in the lot over by Jeremy's house.

I bought my first bike with paper-route money. I'd so badgered my father for a minibike that he'd finally relented. All right, he said, I could have it if I earned the money. I got the biggest, nastiest paper route I could find, 135 Sunday papers, each weighing pounds, and 70 evening papers. I had to have a cart to drag those papers around my route, they were so heavy, had to fight off a dog who always tried to bite me, using a baseball bat my grandfather specially prepared for me: Just give the nipper a tap on the head with this, he told me. I did, too. That dog never bit me again. In months I had the money. I'd already built my own go-cart from a plank of wood, a two-by-four, wheelbarrow wheels, and an old Briggs and Stratton motor off my grandfather's lawn mower, so—to have a factory-made machine?—nirvana! Such freedom I had never known!

All of eleven, and unsupervised, I think I lasted the better part of half an hour on that empty lot, then took to the street. It took about the same amount of time for Officer Bob Sharrett to spot me, hunched over the handlebars, zipping by his cruiser. Officer Sharrett got my Trail Horse into the trunk of his cruiser and drove me home, where he talked to my parents. But even as he was addressing the dangers of having a boy like myself riding on the street, I couldn't help notice he was trying not to grin. Sharrett's solution? Nah, don't take the bike away, he said, find the right place for him to ride. Sharrett's winking at me as he was leaving confirmed what I already knew: He was a motorcyclist also. A dirt biker.

So, off to the airport property racetrack. I could get there, conveniently enough, by pushing the Trail Horse on sidewalks to it. Which I did—at least once. And there I met the bad boys. The bad boys had real bikes, Huskies, CZs, Bultacos. By then I'd ridden all sorts of mutts like mine, Tecumseh- or Briggs-and-Stratton-powered. A pal, nicknamed Okie, had taken off the cooling shroud on his Briggs, and falling on the finned fly-wheel, had butchered his leg, narrowly missing his femoral artery and nearly killing himself. It had taken 250 stitches to patch him up.

Nothing could have prepared me for my first ride on that Bultaco, though, its engine a descendant of Kaaden's engineering, and having an enormous, black expansion chamber on it.

"Look at the little fucker," the kid with the bike said to his friend. In leathers, and motocross boots, he put his face right down in mine. "Whacha lookin' at, asshole?"

Who knows why, but all I said was, "Let me ride your motorcycle." Kind of like saying, "Take me to your leader." The kid got off the bike, held it by the handlebars for me, supremely amused.

"Be my guest," he said.

I surprised him by going around him and taking the bars. You had to start it by standing on the right side. I gave it a kick and it *pong-pong-ponged*! I threw my leg over the seat and, before I went over sideways— which that kid had thoroughly expected—I snicked the bike into gear and gave the twist grip what I thought was just enough gas to get the bike going.

In the time it took to think, Oh oh! the bike had gone through its idle range and, as they used to say in motocross, *got on the pipe*.

The rear wheel tore off at about eighty miles per hour, the front wheel came up off the ground, the bike hurtling down the track. The best I could do was hang on. Think *Star Trek*, warp factor 10.

The landscape rushed at me as if in some fast-forward movie. What my minibike had struggled to so much as navigate, the Bultaco *flew* over. (Yet another friend of mine, Billy, said, stepping off his CZ after his first moto-cross heat, "Man, as soon as I got off the line it was like I was on drugs!"). When you cracked the throttle open, the bike nearly tore out from under you—when you downshifted, the compression was so severe you were nearly bucked over the handlebars. Or you could roll on the throttle, and when the bike got on the pipe (was in its power band), it was so light and powerful that it lifted the front wheel right off the ground, while you were already traveling at thirty-five or forty on that dirt track. Shifting an engine like that is tricky, a hard downshift can cause the rear wheel to seize up, though once you get the hang of it, a joy. All that power, and so light!

They had to chase me to get me off the bike.

When I did, I sulked to my minibike. A year later I had a Hodaka Rat–powered Typhoon, then a Super Rat, and finally a Maico 250 square-barrel.

Dirt riding became an obsession, and with it dirt *bikes*. A simple ques-tion—"Do you ride?"—opened doors onto vistas never before so much as imagined. Trails into the middle of nowhere, good hills to climb, gravel roads to explore. I rode enduro on a 360 Yamaha through pitch pines; mo-tocross on a handful of bikes through mud, sand, and loam; climbed shale hills with the Maico. And all the while we were dreaming of California.

*That's* where it was really happening. Here in the United States, Cali-fornia was the epicenter of the dirt-bike revolution. Really the epicenter of *everything* new, it seemed.

We weren't greasy, fringe characters with Harleys (although, you ride dirt, you get filthy head to toe), we were athletes on bikes. Winters I skied, summers I water-skied and rode dirt bikes.

Mora, Minnesota, was the closest track, but trail riding was every-where.

Dirt biking was becoming a national obsession by 1973, a peak year, more than 1.5 million motorcycles selling in the United States alone, nearly a third of them dirt bikes. Larger and more challenging venues were springing up, such as the Barstow-to-Vegas run (the springboard for

Hunter S. Thompson's *Fear and Loathing in Las Vegas*), a demented event where, by 1975, thousands of motorcyclists roared from the starting line, having the time of their lives and kicking up six hundred tons of dust in the process (the race was so out of control by that time that it was stopped). There was the Del Webb Mint 400, which drew 375 cars and 51 motorcycles, the racing legends Bob and Al Unser, and the TV stars James Garner and Lee Majors, and the pack, all gunning for a piece of the $100,000 prize. And there was the Baja 1,000, the big daddy of them all on this side of the ocean.

Started in 1962 by American Honda to promote its new "scrambler," the CL 72 (250 cc), the course was first set by Bud Ekins (of Triumph fame) in a Cessna airplane, Tijuana to La Paz, a distance of 952 miles. Promptly after the route was run by Ekins's brother, a challenger cropped up in the form of a VW dirt-rally nut, bringing about a motorcycle-car rivalry that continues to this day. So out of control did the early Baja become that NORRA (National Off Road Racing Association) took control of it in 1967, the race then becoming the NORRA Mexican 1,000. Now it is the Baja 1,000 again, though the route varies from year to year (in 2000 it was 1,700 miles). The current champ, Steve Hengeveld, has navigated the course in twenty-four hours, fifteen minutes. Hengeveld trains for the competition by riding as much as four hundred dirt miles a day. Anna Jo Cody was the first woman to ride the Baja 1,000 solo.

So even by the early 1970s the Baja 1,000 was a widely publicized and internationally followed event.

Given the fervent public interest in all things motorcycle by that time, Bruce Brown filmed *On Any Sunday*, an all-purpose grab-bag motorcycle film, further introducing Americans to, among other things, motocross. And motocross was from the first media-friendly in America.

Still, though, into the mid-1970s, Europeans dominated the sport, riders such as Joel Robert, Sylvain Geboers, and Ake Jonsson putting American riders to shame. Gary Bailey, riding for Greeves, was the first American to best the Europeans. He has designed every Daytona Supercross track since his professional retirement. Due to this boom, more than fifty brands were available to riders, the greatest volume and diversity since the first motorcycle wave hit shortly after the turn of the century.

Yet, even given all that cheerful public interest, AMA-sanctioned races remained places where the 1%ers also congregated. Far from keeping kids away, this carnival mix of bikers, spectators, and athletes drew enormous crowds. Motocross was cheaper to sponsor than dirt/oval track and was more interesting to watch. Motocross riders shot into the air off jumps, pulled hairy wheelies over whoop-de-doos, and tumbled end over end when they fell. And unlike the comparatively staid flat-track tradition of heats, semifinals, last-chance qualifiers, and finals, motocross set the whole field of riders up, then turned them loose in a frenzy of flying mud, dirt, and exhaust.

Bands played at the events, unknowns such as the Grateful Dead, Crosby, Stills, and Nash, and Joe Walsh. Even the Rolling Stones, at Altamont, invited the bikers in (with disastrous results). This was all heady stuff, so much so that in the period 1965 to 1975, the annual number of AMA-sanctioned motocross meets in the United States grew from fifteen to fifteen hundred.

Honda, awaiting the proper moment, entered the fray with a vengeance, in the form of its Elsinore two-stroke racers, Roger DeCoster, arguably the world's finest rider, signing on with the team. And mopping up the field.

This further fueled an obsession among the top American racers (then Gary Jones, Brad Lackey, Jim Pomeroy, and Jimmy Weinert) to win both the Trophée des Nations (250 cc) and Motocross des Nations (500 cc), something American riders didn't do until 1981, in Belstein, Germany, and then not with the A team (above), but with the B team, Danny LaPorte, Donnie Hansen, Johnny O'Mara, and Chuck Sun.

When on their own soil in 1987, at Unadilla, New York, Americans won the Motocross des Nations and were invited to the White House for an audience with then President Ronald Reagan, signaling the recognition of motocross as an accepted, full-fledged sport here in the United States. For the first time we "dirt donks" weren't just wackos.

American riders won the world team championships thirteen years in a row, from 1981 through 1993, a record no other nation is likely to surpass.

This led to the creation of supercross, today's incarnation of motocross, which was no surprise, stadium racing having been popular in Europe since the late 1940s, with as many as 100,000 spectators attending. Usually soccer stadiums were used, tons of dirt tractored in to create courses. Sometimes, in these early events, unscrupulous promoters would purposely soap wooden jumps to create "spills and thrills" for spectators. In America, the first such stadium used for motocross was a baseball diamond, Miami Stadium, of the then Miami Marlins, in 1961. But it took the rock and roll promoter Mike Goodwin to stage the first "Super Bowl of Motocross" at the Los Angeles Coliseum in 1972. One detractor called the event the "salad bowl" of motocross. Promoters found Goodwin's appellation wordy and shortened it to "supercross."

Now, worldwide, televised Supercross has displaced Grand Prix racing for top billing, attendees at these races including such celebrities as William Shatner, Matt LeBlanc, Lyle Lovett, Fabio, and Pamela Anderson. Supercross's winningest rider of all time, Jeremy McGrath, has taken six AMA championships, followed by Ricky Carmichael (five), with the African American James "Bubba" Stewart, winner of the 2007 AMA Supercross, hot on their trail. Stewart is known alternately as the "Tiger Woods of Motorcross" and "the fastest man to ever get on a dirt bike." Yearly, tens of millions of dollars in dirt-bike racing prizes are awarded to top riders. In 2002, Ricky Carmichael alone, for example, earned more than $6 million.

Fast here also means *sharp*, given flat-out daring is required, but even more so a chess player's sense of strategy. Riding berms on the outside of the radius will buy you exit *speed*, for example, while riding the inside will buy you *time*—hundredths of a second, which, at motocross speeds (nearly highway speeds now) win races. If what follows a berm is a straight stretch, you want to "shoot" the outside; if it is a set of whoops, a jump, or a ditch, you want to ride the inside. You have to strategize any course, riding it to your strengths. So much as a missed shift in a tight race can cost you that trophy.

And as extreme as the new riders are, the *bikes* are even more so. The new ones have twice the front and rear suspension travel of those earlier models, which makes it possible for riders to navigate impossibly difficult courses, jumps tossing riders not ten but *twenty* feet into the air. Factory race machines cost upward of $100,000, and are kept in tune by race mechanics working out of semis, in which are untold dollars' worth of spare parts.

And "dirt" just keeps getting bigger. In 2007, in the United States alone, riders spent more than $5 billion on dirt bikes and dirt bike accessories, dirt bike sales having tripled since the 1990s.

## The Matter of Evel and Company

Somewhere in any discussion of freestyle riding there must be a mention of the man who, seemingly single-handedly, created the notion of doing truly crazy things on motorcycles, Evel Knievel.

Born Robert Craig Knievel in Butte, Montana, a hardscrabble mining town, in 1938, Knievel was abandoned by his mother and raised by his grandmother. From the first he was a daredevil, winning the Northern Rocky Mountain Ski Association Class A ski jumping championship in 1959. He was also a brawler of a hockey player, became a small-town bank robber who served time in jail, and was last a motorcycle stunt rider. Knievel made a name for himself jumping motorcycles over cars, double-decker buses, rattlesnakes, really anything that would fill up space at sports venues in the 1960s, renaming himself "Evel" and proving himself the consummate showman. Decked out in his signature white leather suit festooned with stars and stripes (Knievel essentially making himself into a glittery, Liberace-esque human flag, sporting swept-back hair, a flying cape, a walking stick, and Harley-Davidson #1 over his heart), he played to the crowds, but also performed death-defying stunts, as often as not with bone-shattering results. Knievel did this by the seat of his pants and with flat-out nerve, before crowds of thousands at baseball and football games, and on closed-circuit television, as at Caesar's Palace in 1968, where, in vivid slow motion, he crashed on the far ramp, breaking bones before our very eyes. Still, that $3 million stunt earned him a regular spot on ABC's *Wide World of Sports*, where he time and again paraded in his outrageous costume before stunning audiences with either yet another successful jump or near-fatal crash. A list of his performances on *Wide World of Sports* reads like some joke with no punch line: Los Angeles Memorial Coliseum, fifty stacked cars, success; Wembley Stadium, London, thirteen double-decker buses, crash; King's Island, Ohio, fourteen Greyhound buses, success . . .

Knievel broke some forty bones, his back seven times, while jumping. His spin-off toys earned him some $300 million. He was a relentless gambler whose favorite drink was a Montana Mary (Wild Turkey, beer, and tomato juice), but who was known as the celebrity who had "long arms": he would hand hundred-dollar bills to wait staff at hotels, or to kids in crowds. Knievel in 1974 attempted to jump the Snake River Canyon outside Twin Falls, Idaho, with a steam-rocket motorcycle built by a former NASA employee, the chute opening by accident on the launching ramp and the "cycle" safely coming down in the canyon. He once told fans he was going to jump from an airplane at 40,000 feet without a parachute and land in a haystack.

In his later years, Knievel became a golfing enthusiast. He enjoyed playing for "high stakes," sometimes as much as $100,000 a game. Once, when the man he was playing with kicked his ball back onto the fairway, Knievel pulled out a .45 revolver and had to be subdued. Knievel also went after a fawning biographer with a baseball bat, much to the chagrin of his attorneys. During his last public appearance on a motorcycle at a mall in the early 1980s, he "snapped his ankle" and there ended his career.

Knievel died in 2007, of pulmonary fibrosis (by this time he had diabetes, had suffered two strokes, and had had a liver transplant). His last comment? "I'm not sure I'm interested in heaven [unless] they've got beautiful women up there and golf courses."

All that said, crediting Knievel with single-handedly inventing stunt riding is far too much. No doubt, he was inspired by any number of earlier traveling acts which featured motorcyclists, such as Oren "Putt" Mossman's American Motorcycle Rodeo Circus and Speedway Aces. It is thought that Bobby Knievel saw Mossman's Aces perform when they passed through Butte, one stop along an international itinerary that included such far flung destinations as Paris, Ceylon, Manila, Tokyo, and London. Mossman, an Iowan, appeared to excel at nearly everything he did, playing baseball, boxing, tumbling, and, importantly in Iowa, throwing horseshoes, though Mossman came to focus his efforts on motorcycle stunt riding, which he believed would free him from farming and make him a lot of money.

Mossman, like his later incarnation, Knievel, was a consummate advertiser. Before performing, Mossman would arrive in an area where he would befriend newspaper editors, earning himself pages of coverage. Some of his tricks included riding while juggling eggs or skipping rope; riding with a sack over his head while using a broomstick to feel his way around a stadium; riding through plate glass or burning wood; and having helium-filled balloons released, which he would shoot down as he turned figure eights. A signature trick was attaching a ladder to the rear of his motorcycle and climbing down it as the motorcycle circled beneath him. Mossman, like Knievel, was injured numerous times, as when he once set himself on fire, intending to jump with his motorcycle into a lake. His Indian refused to start, and by the time it did and Mossman jumped into the lake, he was so badly burned that he was hospitalized for three weeks. Once, while jumping, he landed on his wife with his motorcycle.

Mossman did make fortunes, but he also lost them. He served in WWII in the merchant marine, and after the war did stunt work in Hollywood and small shows for birthday parties and charities. A contemporary of Mossman's, Speedy Babs, who also was a motorcycle stunt rider, in response to a journalist's asking him if he was afraid of dying, glibly replied, "Do you plan on leaving this world alive?"

Occasionally a rider becomes known for some peculiar talent, such as that of Doug Domokos, a.k.a. the Wheelie King. Domokos, a motocross rider, out of high school got a job at a motorcycle shop owned by Gene

Ritchie, who promoted the motocross national at Red Bud in Buchanan, Michigan. While riding bikes he'd repaired, Domokos "tested" them by doing long wheelies—riding on the rear wheel with the front elevated over the pavement—those wheelies becoming so long that Ritchie suggested Domokos perform stunts at his motocross races. By the 1980s Domokos was performing at national supercross events, and by the 1990s setting world records.

And it was here that the Big Bad Dog in dirt racing at the time took an interest in him. Honda hired Domokos to perform for them, building bikes that would wheelie even better than the stock machines Domokos was setting records on. Domokos traveled to Japan, Britain, France, the Netherlands, Italy, Saudi Arabia, and all over South America.

On tour he set numerous world records, some ridiculous, such as "The World's Tallest Wheelie," which he did around the observation deck of the Empire State Building, and some real, such as that for the *Guinness Book of World Records*, "pulling a wheelie" at 145 mph at the Talladega Speedway in Alabama. So popular was Domokos and his stunts that Hollywood used him in films such as *The Cannonball Run*. His most "significant" record? The world's longest wheelie (a record that stood for eight years), 145 miles.

And has the public's fascination with stunt riders gone the way of the LP and the videotape? Apparently not. In current "freestyle jumping," riders perform flips (multiple front and back); free hangs (twenty or thirty feet off the ground, riders getting off their motorcycles to dangle from the handlebars); and tricky acrobatics (such as doing a handstand on the seat while the motorcycle is arcing over the heads of spectators). Fans love it.

The current "godfather of modern stunt riding," Antonio Carlos "A.C." Farias, Jason Britton, and Anthony D'Orsi thrill tens of thousands at AMA supercross events—as does Evel Knievel's son Robby. And Hollywood recently released a drama about a Faustian stunt rider, *Ghost Rider*, starring Nicolas Cage.

When asked why they brave injury and the sometimes difficult life of the stunt rider, the new generation of riders has one thing to say: Love for the craft.

## The World's Biggest Crazy-Money Cross Country: Paris to Dakar, and Other Incomprehensibles

Known alternately as the Most Dangerous Race in the World, or the World's Toughest Motor Race, Paris to Dakar is the legacy of the motorsports enthusiast Thierry Sabine. Sabine, competing in the Abidjan–Nice rally in 1977, was stranded in the Libyan desert. Saved by locals, he so came to love the people and the area that he organized the first Paris-to-Dakar (Senegal) rally the following year. Since then it has been held annually, the route changing due to safety issues related to the politics of the area. In 2008, for example, terrorist activity caused the event to be cancelled altogether. In 2007, 525 competitors of forty-two nationalities, nearly 250 of them on motorcycles, raced across the toughest desert landscapes on earth.

Every year one or more competitors die in the outback (Mark Thatcher, Prime Minister Margaret Thatcher's son, was lost for six days during the 1982 Paris–Dakar rally), speeding vehicles killing spectators as well, so that a cap of 95 mph has been placed on vehicles outside of towns, 30 in towns. Altogether, some forty-eight deaths have been recorded since the race began, these deaths in no way limited to inexperienced riders. On his third rally in 2006, Andy Caldecott, KTM's most distinguished competitor, died from crash-inflicted injuries.

Given the difficulty of the race, manufacturers have made of Paris–Dakar the ultimate test of their machines, spending millions on riders and hardware. The entry fee per participant is $10,000, so only the serious and well-funded can attend.

All this occurs in the desert of all deserts, the Sahara—not a stretch of sand between sleepy Barstow and glitzy Vegas.

The 2007 route started in Lisbon, Portugal, ran through Spain, Morocco, and Mauretania, and ended in Dakar: 5,700 miles of potholed roads, riverbeds, rocks, and sand, in temperatures reaching 130 degrees Fahrenheit, to be ridden in two weeks.

So profound has been the influence of this rally that a further evolution of the motorcycle has taken place to accommodate it. This new machine, an extension of "dirt" bikes going all the way back to Britain's observed trials, is called the adventure tourer, such as in BMW's successful GS series. BMW's ultimate testing ground is Paris to Dakar, which the team has won numerous years. Likewise for the adventure tourer manufacturer KTM. And what is an adventure tourer? It's a dirt bike on steroids. What else could take such punishment? (Riders are so harshly hammered that they urinate blood.)

These adventure tourers have 1,000 cc engines (or larger) in racing tune, putting out well over a hundred horsepower; long travel suspension; high seat height; knobby tires; and broad, heavy handlebars with skid guards on them for those inevitable falls. These are motocross bikes weighing more than 550 pounds, a full tank and gear adding further to that weight.

Imagine riding a nearly seven-hundred-pound motorcycle at 100 mph on sand dunes and rutted, rocky roads, up mountains and down, in 130-degree heat, and you have Paris to Dakar.

One rider on a Yamaha 450 F (a four-stroke racing enduro), the Frenchman Stéphane Peterhansel, has won the competition *six times* (and there would have been a seventh, but for a crash late in the race), this accomplishment no less stellar than Lance Armstrong's in the Tour de France.

And while this race and its competitors may seem so extreme as to not be relevant to the average citizen, such is not the case. All of us are the fortunate recipients of the technology derived from such sport. A version of Peterhansel's Yamaha, for example, can be purchased from any Yamaha dealership. And the earlier, world-beating BMW GS, as well—this motorcycle alone spawning a new form of riding which is extraordinarily attractive: adventure touring. Now riders take off into the outback of Australia, the vast steppes of Mongolia (as did Ewan McGregor and Charley Boorman), or the barrens in Alaska and Canada, areas so rough and rugged that it takes a King Kong sort of bike to get through them. BMW's GS series, dubbed the "Swiss Army Knife" of motorcycles, has spawned no end of imitators, all producing machines aimed at taking riders into areas off the beaten path.

And there have been some companies here all along, winning Dakar, Baja, and others, year after year, such as KTM, which now builds the 990 Super Duke, an enduro weighing a little over 400 pounds that puts out 120 horsepower at the crankshaft (the standard Japanese sedan, Accord or Camry, puts out 140-ish ponies, to push 2,500 pounds). Insectoid in style, the KTM Orange Super Duke sells for $13,998. KTM's motto? "Ready to Race."

And KTM's Super Duke, BMW's GS, and Yamaha's 450 F are four-strokes. On the whole, this represents a new development, which is the return of the four-stroke in dirt competition, not something really seen since the late fifties. Due to EPA regulations, "dirty" two-stroke *road* bikes became a thing of the past by the early 1980s, though they continued to reign supreme in dirt riding's smaller numbers, largely due to the fact that most dirt bikes are not licensed, and so aren't required to meet the same emissions standards. In addition, new design technology has made contemporary four-strokes, such as Peterhansel's Yamaha, more powerful, free-revving, and—most important—light.

Not to let go of a good thing, engineers at the Japanese Big Four are experimenting with catalytic converters for two-stroke engines. They have found that while it is altogether possible to remove the carbon emissions, the oxidized nitrogen compounds pose problems. There is a seemingly insurmountable obstacle for engineers to solve here: With a two-stroke engine, how can the engine operate efficiently when the exhaust gases used to "supercharge" it are blocked to effect catalytic conversion? No doubt, given time, engineers will think of something. Something surprising. And when they do, we dirt riders will still be around.

Thierry Sabine's adage for his love of riding in the Sahara applies in the past, the present, and will in the future. "It's a challenge for those who go; a dream for those who stay behind."

Imagine not just heading down that long, lonesome road, but turning where a rutted, rocky trail leads off the highway, up into buttes and craggy peaks, a stream alongside the highway. In the background, as in some romantic painter's landscape, are the La Sal Mountains, snowcapped. This is Utah's Red Rock Country. Breathtaking.

I went dirt riding there last year, and, as is altogether common, our group took the wrong fork in a trail and went off into a spectacular and unknown landscape, navigating rose-colored stone canyons dotted with piñons, scaling buttes, and descending nearly impossibly steep, rutted, sandy paths. At one point the winding, rocky path narrowed to perhaps six feet. To the left was a wall of Navajo sandstone streaked with rock varnish rising hundreds of feet over our heads; to the right, three feet distant, was a 250-to-300-foot drop off into a picturesque box canyon, one so lovely a film crew was using it for a set. Anything, really, could have taken us over the edge.

Forty years of riding, and I felt new all over again. I'd never ridden on such a path, in such a place. The scenery was spectacular. I wasn't going hell bent for leather around some course, but there was the same thrill here.

For weeks after, since I'd been breaking trail, I wondered why I didn't stop, didn't turn around when we skirted that box canyon. I shuddered to think how I could have, reaching that canyon, resorted to riding behavior appropriate in the Midwest, where there are no box canyons. I saw myself and those behind me sailing out into that vast nothingness.

Into that eternal landscape.

But then, that's what dirt riding is all about. Really getting *out there*.

And for that, dirt is the ultimate.

# 5

# MCers, 1%ers, Outlaw Bikers, and Club Riders

## BRANDO, BARGER, BALLS, AND BLUSTER

Linda began to become rebellious. At the same time, she physically matured, turning seemingly overnight from a strikingly pretty girl into a tall, beautiful, and shapely young woman who drew looks wherever she went and attracted men considerably older than she. As it turned out, she was drawn to some of these older men, especially the ones that owned motorcycles.

Ted, needless to say, could not abide his teenage daughter's interest in bikers.

JOSEPH NAWINSKI, PHD
*The Tender Heart*

At least I lived.

DANNY LYON,
writer and photographer, on riding with the Outlaws for five years
*The Bikeriders*

I could kill you with my bare hands, or I could drag you behind my bike with a chain and kill you," Bart says, looming over you in his leather riding gear. He is a mountain of a man, his eyes shiny with rage.

Which will it be?

You have made the cardinal error of mistaking Bart's earlier, sly manner for camaraderie, and now are about to pay the price. He's joking, he's gotta be, you think, stifling uneasy laughter, but realize he isn't. And, anyway, you *have* earned Bart's malefic attention at this moment, an understanding that carries with it a certain shame.

But how did you come to be in this situation in the first place?

## How to Read the Scary Face of Motorcycling. (Or, a Necessary Primer for Tripping on the Dark Side)

Worldwide, probably few faces are as recognizable as that of the outlaw biker, a distinctly American creation. Bearded and in black leather, his hair wild and wind-tangled, he sits atop a rough-running Harley, ready— even eager—to meet provocation with lethal force.

So powerful is this image that it is emulated anywhere popular media has reached, sometimes with comic results. Why is a German psychopath named Helmut on a chopped Harley with ape hangers funny? Because the true-strain biker does not come out of any even vaguely European impulse, strains of Wagner, Debussy, Puccini, Chopin, or Rachmaninoff running through it. The *biker* is as American as jazz, a mythic identity so powerful and feared, characters from wealthy Wall Street to hayseed Wakarusa, Kansas, strike the biker pose.

And if there are so many posers, who are the real bikers? How can you tell? Let's get this straight from the start: only about 0.2 percent of outlaw bikers, even in the United States, are the genuine article. People you don't cut your eyes at. (And there's a reason for this, one you should know and that I'll get to later.) So, even the label given to these "real deal" outlaw bikers, *1%ers*, is inaccurate. It also happens to be apocryphal. (Something else I'll get to.)

Motorcycle clubs, of course, have existed since the creation of the motorcycle. In the United States, the first was the Yonkers Motorcycle Club in

New York, established in 1903 (the same year the Manly Life Saving Club, the world's first, was created Down Under). Club members at this time were simply enthusiasts, though even then there was public resistance to these adventurous, and sometimes noisy, riders. Still, when, as was inevitable, a rival club formed on the West Coast, the San Francisco Motorcycle Club, the nation's second, such was the social opinion of motorcycles that one of the first SFMC members was none other than the mayor of San Francisco himself. (Another member of note was Hap Jones, the first civilian to cross the Golden Gate Bridge in 1937; Hap likewise crossed the bridge in 1987—on a vintage Excelsior-Henderson—for the fiftieth-anniversary celebration.) Oakland's club, following San Francisco's lead, came in third, though by that time rider clubs were forming everywhere.

Most were good-time-Charley clubs, though some were more official, such as that created by George M. Hendee of Indian Moto-Cycles, the Federation of American Motorcyclists, or FAM. In late 1903, Hendee had 109 membership pledges, annual membership at that time being a hefty two dollars.

Never heard of Hendee's club? It is now the world's largest rider organization, the American Motorcycle Association, created out of Hendee's federation in 1924, primarily to "promote the general interest of motorcycling; to ascertain, defend, and protect the rights of motorcyclists; to facilitate touring; to assist in the good roads movement; and to advise and assist in the regulation of motorcycle racing and other competition in which motorcycles engage." Presently, the AMA has around 300,000 members.

"AMA-sanctioned" means a great deal: official, judged, properly timed, and overseen for issues of safety and fairness. The AMA made sure that, if you were racing 250 cc scramblers, for example, there wasn't some rider on a disguised 500 cc bike winning every heat and getting away with it. And there was a code of behavior, the AMA from the first eschewing the outlaw rider ethic. So riding clubs, which soon came to be called "biker clubs," sought AMA membership for legitimacy. Though some did *not*, such as the McCook Outlaws, from Cook County, Illinois—the Chicago area—which formed in 1936. You can recognize present-day Outlaws by a patch they wear on their backs, "Charlie," a skull centered over crossed pistons and connecting rods.

Oddly enough, one of the oldest of all AMA affiliates is a women's rider club started by Dot Robinson and Linda Dugeau—the Motor Maids. Both Robinson, a competitor in the endurance races that were popular at the time (see chapter 8), and Dugeau, a motorcycle courier with a reputation as being one of the best female off-road riders of her time, searched for three years to find fifty women riders, chartering the Motor Maids in 1940. Robinson became famous for riding in a pink leather suit, Dugeau for championing touring, putting some 1.5 million miles on her Harleys. Both lived into their middle eighties. Robinson is also noteworthy for being the first woman to win an AMA national competition, taking the Jack Pine in the sidecar class in 1940 and 1946.

Predictably, owner clubs sprang up everywhere: the Indian Owners' Club, the Ace Owners' Club, the Norton Owners' Club—membership in such a club almost necessary, given you (without exception) would need to repair your bike. And even if you weren't a thumb-fingered nonwrencher, what better business than to be hooked up with some guru of the breed? Someone who lived, breathed, and dreamed your particular manufacture of bike? Is this nonsense? Not at all. Every motorcycle made, and especially back then, had idiosyncratic mechanical aspects that could destroy the machine if not properly addressed. Certain years of Triumphs, for example, had inferior valve stems—the bikes blew oil after three thousand miles. You could ride with that cloud of blue behind you, or simply pull the head and install new stems—a bonehead job for a mechanic, though a nearly impossible one for the nonmechanic.

And membership in a club was essential for political/social reasons: As the AMA's slogan goes, "An Organized Minority Can Always Defeat an Unorganized Majority." The AMA has from its creation retained powerful attorneys to deal with issues critical to riders, particularly that of fair treatment and safety.

However, the AMA has also, from the first, angered riders. As with their 1940s Muffler Mike campaign. The AMA took out ads in major magazines, exhorting riders to use mufflers and not be "Boobs." This, of course, raised the ire of bikers everywhere. A common sentiment of bikers at the time was, if they (drivers of "cages," or cars) couldn't *see* you coming—drivers turning left in front of motorcyclists being the most common cause of fatalities—they damn well could *hear* you! So loud was *safe*. And the Muffler Mike campaign was seen as putting more pressure on riders who already felt a large measure of social opprobrium, at a time when it was least welcome.

As already addressed, the thirties and forties were the nadir years for motorcycling in the United States. Public opinion was that only fringe characters rode bikes, and who cared what was happening in faraway Britain and Europe, where riders were stars? Motorcycles, since the ascendance of the automobile in the twenties (when Ford sold the Model T for $545, and Harley and Indian its full-size bikes for $375), seemed to be on their way out.

World War II changed all that. Tens of thousands of GIs were introduced to Indian and Harley-Davidson motorcycles while in combat. Together, the firms delivered more than 100,000 bikes to combat units. And there were the thousands of pilots and flight crews who'd discovered motorcycles in far-flung places—from airfields in Britain (Triumph, BSA, Norton) to those in Bombay (Royal Enfield) to fields in Burma (Urals—BMW knockoffs—and little two-stroke "Corgies"). When these battle-weary men, many suffering what would later come to be known as Post-Traumatic Stress Syndrome, or PTSD, came home, they needed to blow off some steam.

Biking was the perfect outlet—and it fit. Bonds formed in combat are said to be stronger than family ties. Such bonds formed in these newly created motorcycle clubs composed primarily of veterans, clubs such as the Boozefighters and the Pissed-Off Bastards of Bloomington. These men bonded, especially the most damaged, forming families of guys who *got it*. They'd gone to hell and come back, and didn't want to explain to anyone what that meant. My uncle Bob was such a character, having served in Patton's regiment, where he fought in the worst of it. When, vacationing in sunny Fort Lauderdale, he rented a motorcycle, a then new Sportster, and with a cigarette dangling rakishly from the corner of his mouth said, "Hop on, bud!" I did just that. We roared off down the beach, the wind in our hair, the sea shining, and girls in colorful bikinis turning to look over their shoulders, giving us wary, but inviting looks.

I think that was when I became a rider, tearing up and down the beach with this (near fatally) ironic rider, who, to hell with it all, was as alive just then as you could ever be. Riding, out in the open, free.

Just six, I had to have a motorcycle. I fell hard for them, the way you can fall in love—it just happens, and you're smitten.

A good many of these returning GIs had combat manners—they drank to excess, brawled, were "womanizers," rode their machines with utter abandon and joy, not caring if death was the result. And they could give you the shirt off their backs, or lay down their lives for you, take your pick, this part of the combat "leave no soldier behind" mind-set. But if nothing else, they were wild, and coming into the Ivory Soap ethos of healing from the war with order, cleanliness, and predictability then in place, they were "outlaws." Figuratively at first, but also literally: refusing to have anything to do with the AMA (which had been battling for public favor for nearly two decades), these riders formed, technically, "outlaw rider associations."

All of this would have been just some bar brawling and noise, but for an event that thrust these GI bikers and their good-time pals into the national spotlight. And what a distorted spotlight it was.

There are really three epochs of biker notoriety, created by news media hungry for sordid biker stories, and they can be summed up in place-names: Hollister, Monterey, and Altamont. A so-called fourth "epoch," begun at a Harrah's Casino and Hotel in Laughlin, Nevada, in 2002, when Mongols and Hells Angels stabbed and shot each other, in what is now called the River Run Riot, really only served to solidify public opinion. The killers James Hannigan and Rodney Cox were sentenced to two years in prison in 2007.

Hollister, California, the first, took place on July 4, 1947. Now called the "Hollister Riot," this bit of biker bacchanal so caught public interest and media attention that a spin-off movie was made, *The Wild One*, starring none other than Marlon Brando, who in celluloid immortalized for a public starved for adventure the figure of the swaggering outlaw biker. And creating for wannabes and posers a figure to emulate.

Portrayed as an unsuspected and terrible onslaught, four thousand outlaw bikers riding into Hollister and taking over, racing in the streets, fighting, tearing the town apart, and drinking themselves blind, the reality was something else. In fact, the very photograph that is the emblem of that debauched weekend—that of an obviously drunken biker stretched out over his Harley, a beer bottle in each fist and surrounded by piles of cans and broken bottles—was staged by Barney Peterson, a photographer for the *San Francisco Chronicle*. This was the photograph splashed across the cover of *Life* magazine, along with stories about the weekend using words such as *terrorism* and *pandemonium*. Fifty to sixty bikers were treated for injuries at a local hospital, and a similar number arrested for drunk and disorderly behavior, but there were no reported incidents of violence directed toward townspeople, and there was no destruction of property, arson, or looting.

Central to the picture, though more subtly in 1947, was the loss of virtue of the women who wandered into this "den of iniquity." Elsewhere, in theaters at this time, Doris Day in her platinum bob was offering chaste kisses to a preternaturally handsome man who really didn't care much for kisses from women.

From the first, for the public the biker was a sexual figure, a kind of satyr—though on a motorcycle. A living embodiment of much that "civilized" folks suppressed.

Really, what happened was this: A few thousand "straight pipers" of the real sort (about 3,500) rode into Hollister for the Gypsy Tours AMA-sanctioned races at the track outside town. Having sponsored these races for years, Hollister threw its doors wide, particularly the more than two hundred saloon owners. Soon, bikers were riding their machines through bars and had closed off Main Street, where they performed stunts and drag raced, while the town came in to watch the fun. The bar owners even agreed, given police pressure, to close their bars two hours early (to this day, standard "run" behavior).

A modern biker "run" was what Hollister was all about, a picnic clad in black leather and swilling beer. Tavern owners weren't too concerned, as the bikers "couldn't afford the hard stuff" and get crazy. Even the local police said, later, that the bikers "did more harm to themselves than they did to the town."

The press had a field day, and even when brought to task for such distortion, suffered not at all. The public *wanted* to be thrilled and horrified by this newly minted version of the outlaw of legend, the biker. Rumor had it that the AMA, trying to retain the public's favor, which it had fought so hard to win, offered a statement claiming that 1 percent or fewer of the riders at Hollister had actually behaved as the press claimed they had.

Here, then, would seem to be the origin of the name for our true biker outlaws, 1%ers.

However, the AMA's onetime press director, Tom Lindsay, claimed, "[the AMA has] been unable to attribute . . . use [of the 1% designation to describe biker outlaws] to an AMA official or published statement." The real source is most likely to be found in a letter written by Paul Brokaw, the editor of *Motorcyclist,* in which he claimed the ruckus in Hollister was not caused alone by "the acts of 4,000 motorcyclists, but rather a small percentage of that number, aided by a much larger group of non-motorcycling hell-raisers and mercenary-minded barkeepers." The motorcyclist Keenan Wynn of Metro-Goldwyn-Mayer, trying to do some damage control for the AMA, went on record saying that the Hollister reports were not consistent with events he'd experienced while riding with his friends Clark Gable, Larry Parks, Randolph Scott, Ward Bond, Andy Devine, and Robert Stack (at the time all celebrities). No matter. The outlaw biker was here to stay, along with the 1% moniker, which has been in use now nearly fifty years. Real bikers wear it as a badge of honor.

Now Hollister is a kid's birthday party compared to the goings on at

Sturgis, South Dakota, or Laconia, New Hampshire, a meet that has been cancelled for years, due to violence.

Most of these biker guys are rough, hard living, hard-riding folks, but more often than not guys who pet, rather than kick, the dog.

I should know, I rode with them.

Still, want a piece of advice? If you see one thing on a "biker's" jacket that might say, "Don't mess with this character for any reason," this is it: A diamond with a 1% in it (or 81%—eight being in the alphabet *H*; one being *A*. *HA*. Hells Angels). Also, if the biker is wearing a sleeveless denim jacket over black leather with "colors" sewn onto it ("rockers" top and bottom) announcing, say, Stray Satans, San Berdoo (club and chapter), it's best to keep your distance. Real bikers, also, go by their adopted names. At a gas station, don't laugh at a guy who tells you his name is Vermin or Worm or Cancer, unless you're looking for an extreme and immediate cosmetic makeover.

These guys are for real, and make Brando's Wild One look like a "poofter" (no insult to that contingent, there are those Honda Rebel riders who like a feather boa now and then, each to his own, et cetera, variety is the spice of life and so on, really. Just ask a member of the Border Riders; Warriors MC; Valley Knights; or Battalion MC if they're sissy riders. Or a leather-clad member of Dykes on Bikes or the Rainbow Riders).

Hollister, as silly as it might seem now, put a face on motorcycling in the United States, that of the outlaw "biker." From that time, outlaw (non-AMA affiliated) biker clubs spread from California and major cities on the East Coast to all parts of America: in the Midwest the Outlaws and the Sons of Silence; in Texas, the Bandidos (not to be confused with that comical Lays Potato Chips character the Frito Bandito, though some say the fat Mexican bandido wielding a gun and knife on the Bandidos' colors is derived from that source); the Pagans in Pennsylvania.

Well into the sixties, to be a "bikerider," if you weren't putting daisies in your hair and riding a Honda (or some other "ricer burner piece of shit" or "Jap Crap" as they were called by 1%ers), meant, to the public, that you were a "biker," which was not close to being accurate. Bob Dylan, for example, bought himself a Harley (a flat head/side valve 45) when he was in his late teens, and in 1966 a Triumph Bonneville on which he had a serious accident, after which he disappeared for a good year and a half. No real biker, he just wanted to walk a bit on the wild side, like most of us.

Confusing the issue was this: Real *riders*, then as now, wore black leather, heavy boots, and gloves (as they had for decades in Europe). And, yes, mixed with real *bikers*.

Another patch to look out for: *MC*. This stands for *Motorcycle Club*, not to be confused with "rider clubs." MCers *are* 1%ers. Rider club members are neither. Given this distinction, it is surprising that real bikers, as I will soon enough make clear, welcome "hang around" riders (ones not cops or narcs), though to become a member of any real motorcycle club you have to go through a grueling process that can take one to two years. A "probate"—a rider on probationary status—is given the club's worst duties, and surviving that, is granted a "patch."

Most MCs (referred to by law enforcement as Outlaw Motorcycle Gangs, or OMGs) have a quasi-military form of organization. The Hells Angels, reportedly, took their name from the U.S. Air Force 303 Bombardment Group, forming around 1948 in San Bernardino and being a group of WWII veteran riders. Riders rise in the ranks from "full patch members" (perhaps the most volatile, being those in the pack needing to show their stuff) to sergeant-at-arms, road captain, secretary, treasurer, vice president, and president. A probate's initiation can run from hazing to his participation in some "act of civil disobedience or crime," which may even include killing a member of a rival gang—for which, rumor has it, you are awarded a "Filthy Few" patch.

A common "tog," or "full patch" reads: *Live to Ride / Ride to Live.* Another popular biker sentiment can be found painted stylishly on bikers' gas tanks or fenders, or emblazoned in red on leather jackets: *Born on a mountain, raised in a cave, bikin' and fuckin' is all that I crave.*

*These* are the bikers we came to know in the early 1960s, tough guys stretched out on their Harley choppers, ridin' the wind and comin' to raise hell in your town. Exciting stuff.

Again, this "more current" picture of the biker was as much a media creation as reality, one spun from a sordid incident that took place in Monterey on Labor Day weekend of 1964, reported as a "heinous" gang rape. To read the reports, one would think the Hells Angels forcibly carried off two teenage girls of spotless virtue and savaged them in a ritual blood sacrifice.

What really happened was this: Some three hundred Hells Angels had gathered in Monterey to raise funds to send the body of a member, one killed in an accident, home to his mother in North Carolina. A day later, four Angels were in jail for rape, and the media was having a field day, cooking up details that would demand thorough investigation. As Hunter S. Thompson wrote in *The Nation* at the time, these reports were so filled with "a flurry of blood, booze, and semen-flecked wordage that amounted, in the end, to supercharged hokum, [exaggerations including] 'Drug-induced stupors . . . no act too degrading . . . swap[ping] girls, drugs and motorcycles with equal abandon . . . stealing forays . . . then rid[ing] off again to seek some new nadir in sordid behavior,'" the inaccuracy of reportage so great, Thompson wrote, as to make one "wonder what newsprint is for."

And between the arrival of the Angels in Monterey and the arrests?

But first, let's not whitewash this picture: Said one Oakland Angel to a *Newsweek* reporter: "We're bastards to the world and they're bastards to us. When you walk into a place where people can see you, you want to look as repulsive and repugnant as possible. We are complete social outcasts— outsiders against society."

Certainly a pose, but one that carries with it a heavy dose of reality—real bikers, for whom the club is life, see themselves as cast-offs, and behave, at least in part, accordingly. Got things you can't afford to lose? Don't mess with these riders.

Films such as Elvis's *Roustabout* (in which he rode singing from town to town on his chrome-tanked, candy red "you meet the nicest people on a Honda" Dream 305) and *The Glass Bottom Boat* (also known as *The Spy in Lace Panties*), starring Doris Day, though now with her man's man, Rod Taylor, represented images fit for popular consumption at the time. And what did the public get at Monterey?

Even Thompson's rebuttal of bad reporting made lurid reading: ". . . all over California [newspapers] gave front-page reports of a heinous gang rape . . . [of] two girls, aged 14 and 15, [who] were allegedly taken from their dates by a gang of filthy, frenzied, boozed-up motorcycle hoodlums . . . and dragged off to be repeatedly assaulted."

Thompson, trying to get to the bottom of the incident, let one of the bikers (not identified) speak for the group:

> One girl was white and pregnant, the other was colored, and they were with five colored studs. They hung around the bar—Nick's Place on Del Monte Avenue—for about three hours Saturday night, drinking and talking with our riders, then came out to the beach with us—them and their five boyfriends. Everybody was standing around the fire, drinking wine, and some of the guys were talking to them—hustling 'em, naturally—and soon somebody asked the two chicks if they wanted to be turned on—you know, did they want to smoke some pot? They said, yeah, and then they walked off with some of the guys to the dunes. The spade went with a few guys and then she wanted to quit, but the pregnant one was really hot to trot, the first four or five guys she was really dragging into her arms, but after that, she cooled off too. By this time, though, one of their boyfriends had got scared and gone for the cops—and that's all it was.

But not really, given by then the public outcry was such that then Attorney General Thomas C. Lynch mounted an official investigation, which resulted in *The Lynch Report*, one that so flew in the face of actual events that Thompson described it as reading "like a plot synopsis of Mickey Spillane's worst dreams." Among other inaccuracies it reported was this juicy tidbit: "Any new member bring[s] a woman or a girl [called a 'sheep'] who is willing to submit to sexual intercourse with each member of the crowd." Really not even in the ballpark, bikers told the media.

Still, each bit was fodder for the bonfire the media was building in service of their story, the end of which no one much remembers.

The charges were dropped due to "questions as to whether forcible rape had been committed." When examined by a doctor, the girls exhibited no evidence to support the charges. One girl refused to testify, and the one who did, when she was given a lie-detector test, was found to be "wholly unreliable."

So the film industry testified (and Thompson, in his book, *Hell's Angels*), cranking out lurid biker films for popular consumption, such as *Wild Angels, Hells Angels on Wheels*, and *Hell's Angels '69*, thus keeping the outlaw biker, a replacement figure emerging out of the "closed frontier west," alive and kicking—and raping, killing, and doping—but also becoming the very personification of cool, as was Peter Fonda in *Easy Rider*, a film that remains, even now, a cult favorite (and which introduced us to Dennis Hopper and Jack Nicholson, both still playing outlaws to this day).

All of this fueled a morbid public fascination with bikers, so much so that they came to be officially (and unofficially) invited to events, by then AMA dirt-bike races, rallies, and open-air rock concerts attended by tens of thousands. The bikers gave the public license to push things just that bit further, making things exciting again, giving new edge to the "drugs, sex, and rock 'n' roll" spirit that needed sharpening.

Given the fever pitch that edge had taken already, sooner or later, what happened at Altamont, California, in 1969, had to happen. And it was no surprise it happened with the original bad boys of rock and roll, the Rolling Stones, who may or may not have hired the Hells Angels as security for their show (supposedly the Stones paid the Angels $50,000 for their services, but no records exist). What is indubitable is this: The Angels were at the Altamont concert in force, holding the crowd off the stage, when an eighteen-year-old named Meredith Hunter decided to pull out a pistol and wave it around, then fire a shot at one of the Angels. That Angel, as yet unidentified, stabbed Hunter to death (during the performance of "Under My Thumb," not "Sympathy for the Devil" as was widely rumored), in front of the filmmakers David and Albert Maysles, who released footage of the murder in their 1970 documentary of the Altamont concert, titled *Gimme Shelter.* Don McLean rhapsodized about the event in his tune "American Pie," this being "the day the music died." Sonny Barger, the Angels' president went on record, saying, "Meredith had shot a Hells Angel. Since the guy was a fugitive at the time, we couldn't take him to a doctor or an emergency ward." This Angel's disappearance forever barred the possibility of a witness testifying to Hunter's actions.

Again, the media had a field day with the concert itself, the Rolling Stones, and the concert promoters, though, this time, the public reached some saturation point with the outlaw bikers involved. Some too-dark, too-violent note had been struck, and the public responded.

Again, the Angels were acquitted, this time on the grounds of self-defense, the Maysles film record, in which Hunter can clearly be seen swinging his pistol, saving and condemning them at the same time. And even as public sentiment began to echo what Hunter Thompson had concluded earlier, that these bikers were not figures of romantic imagination, icons of freedom, but simply characters as "tough, mean and potentially dangerous as a pack of wild boar," the biker ranks swelled.

The whole end-of-the-sixties period has been so satirized, maligned, and joked about that it is almost impossible to write about it. Bob Dylan, later sidestepping the whole business, quipped, "If you remember bein' there, you weren't there," alluding to the intoxication of the time.

*Inferno* would possibly be a better description, fueled by the death of Dr. King and Bobby Kennedy, race riots, acid rock, and parachuting into the midst of it our Vietnam vets, some of whom were welcomed back as "baby killers" after the My Lai massacre made the reality of our "involvement" in Vietnam painfully clear. (For those interested, Michael Herr's *Dispatches* vividly, and truthfully, brings back that time perhaps better than any book since.)

By this time in black leather myself, I swam up out of suburban South Minneapolis and directly into the Vietnam veteran biker culture. Vietnam veterans would be a constant presence in my life from the early seventies to my time working with the U.S. Forest Service at the end of the decade, surveying logging roads in Montana.

These guys, let me say, were wound up. My cousin Bobby, for example, a commando in a "Lurps" outfit (Long Range Reconnaissance Patrol), was flown home in a C 131 Hercules after two years of combat. Straight into Lake Wobegon South Minneapolis, with its casseroles, lime Jell-O, and backyard barbeques. Bobby bought himself a Yamaha 305 Big Bear, which he promptly ran into the back of a truck. This sent him flying, according to the police report, 130 feet into a telephone pole, which, had he struck it straight on, instead of grazing it as he did, would have killed him. A month later he had a Harley, which he rode over to dinner with our family one Sunday afternoon.

Bobby could barely sit at the table, and when he couldn't take it any longer, he nodded me outside. We smoked in the garage, no doubt straight-from-overseas stuff that took your head off, while Bobby's and my family made small talk at the table. It seemed you couldn't say anything meaningful without getting into truly killing arguments. And what could anyone say to Bobby, anyway? You wouldn't think to ask him such a stupid question as Did you kill anyone in the jungle, or What was it like over there? or even How ya doin'? Looking at him, you knew.

We got onto his Harley and headed out on the highway (now a terrible cliché, but believe me, it wasn't then). Bobby was wearing wraparound sunglasses, his hair halfway down to his belt. He had a tattoo on his right upper arm, a parachute, under it the word *Airborne* and his division. Running straight pipes, that bike roared, and when some doofus in a Plymouth Valiant cut Bobby off, he lunged up alongside him and screamed.

"Airborne, motherfucker! You wanna make something of it?!"

It didn't matter that the doofus was in a car and could have run us off the road. The driver was terrified. This guy on the Harley was ready to leap off the saddle, through his windshield, and give him a piece of the action he'd been caught up in overseas. The perverse thing was, I was right there with him—the noise and the insanity of riding like that brought something out, what the Vikings had called the Berserker, this embodiment of primitive, destructive force.

That's what you got when you scratched through the surface of some of these veteran biker guys. One night I made the mistake of getting into an argument with a vet who'd survived the Tet Offensive, over who wrote better music, Elvis or the Beatles. I hadn't considered that this was a generational thing, and came down on the side of the Beatles. It nearly cost me my life.

So, by the time I was asked to ride with a for-real outlaw biker club, I knew, at least, to keep my mouth shut.

## Pop Goes the Cherry: I Ride with the West Bank MC

It was Jay, a guy living in the apartment complex I was painting, who invited me to be a "hang around" rider on the West Bank Motorcycle Club's Fall Beaver Run. It was late September, school had already started, and after work I'd wandered over to chat with the guy wrenching on his Harley.

This was an engineer who knew his stuff. Back in the days of AMF Harley, you either needed to be able to repair them yourself or have a mechanic handy, if you were to put in any hours on them at all. Jay was both able and knew his stuff, which I admired.

He was rebuilding the top end of his '62 Panhead, wrenched with an easy assurance, talking about bikes as he worked.

The beer didn't hurt, either.

I was nineteen, had been working on bikes myself by then for nearly four years (doing brake jobs, tune ups, and general repair), and could talk ring-and-pinion gears, tuning, and frame mods with the best of them. Jay was living with a stunningly curvy blonde, who, in her sultry, sleepy way wandered out to the garage now and then to ask when Jay would be coming in.

"All she wants to do is lie around in bed," Jay complained, glancing over the motor at me.

Jay had just turned the advanced age of thirty-six, which was this kind of Grand Canyon age difference between us—one reason, among many, I was surprised he bothered talking to me at all. He probably wouldn't have, had I not been a mechanic: "Run that blue to your rectifier," I'd told him when he held up the Pan's wiring harness, wondering which lead would go where.

"Yeah," he said. "You would think that, punk."

Still, something right there had been decided.

"Goin' on a ride," Jay said, glancing up. "Interested?"

"Sure," I replied. But there was something snarky in his invitation. A *gonna wise you up, punk!* something.

Jay told me where I should meet him, at a gas station between two highways, one running north, the other south.

"It's an overnighter," Jay said, "so bring your gear."

And with that, he set his palms on his knees, pushed himself up from beside his bike, and sauntered, rangy, tall, and handsome, toward his unit, turning to me at the last second to add, "You're on the ride I'm not playin' nursemaid to you, understand?"

I told him I did.


Driving my crappy Duster back to Lake Street, where I was living with my girlfriend Mandy, I had time to think about Jay's invitation. Nursemaid? Well, fuck him, I thought.

It was insulting, but was a warning, too—a guy as tough as Jay giving me a heads-up on what I might find on this "ride."

I thought, okay, five or six riders Jay's age, Harleys, to my hotted-up BSA Rocket. I could outmaneuver them, outspeed them, but that's about where it ended. And my Rocket was leaking badly from the crankcase, something all Brit bikes did, some worse than others. Really, what I needed to do was pull the engine out of the bike—*again*—split the cases, and put in new gaskets. The Rocket leaked so badly that, after a time, it sprayed oil onto the rear tire, making it so slick that you feared for your life when you cornered hard on it. Cornering under seventy-five was fine, or running straightline well over one hundred was safe enough, but a peg-rubbing-on-pavement sweeper at ninety was not to be done until I rebuilt the engine.

So I'd just dog it at the back of the pack, I thought, an excuse that, possibly, made the ride happen: I had a reason now for riding cautiously, for not stop-light racing or pushing blind corners—I could hang back and let it all happen.

Still, when I woke early that Saturday I was dragging my feet and knew it. I approached the ride with something akin to dread. Who were these guys I'd be riding with, and how boozed up and drugged up would this whole deal get? I mean, there is some modicum of self-preservation in even the most rabid biker. It's why we stay alive year after year—that, and of course, old Lady Luck.

Was this lucky, this ride? I had no way of telling—and that sick feeling in the pit of my stomach, what was that about?

I got my gear loaded on my bike, donned my black leather, and told Mandy I was off on a ride, an overnighter, which I'd been doing for some time, touring, and hit the highway. The Rocket was running fine, the air sharp and chill, the leaves in full color. Riding always put me in some altered state of hyperawareness, so I was edgy pulling into the gas station outside New Brighton, where the highways met.

There was no Jay anywhere, no bikers. I filled my tank, paid, and, mounting my bike again, saw a grizzly bear of a man in black leather and colors pull into the station alongside me on a dresser—a Harley with windshield, tassels on the handlebars, Maltese Cross mirrors.

"You on the Beaver Run?!" he shouted.

This I considered. And then it struck me. "You know Jay?!" I shouted over the thunder of his engine.

"Who?"

"Are you on the ride?"

"We're late!" He extended his paw, and we shook there at the pumps. "Bart!" he shouted.

He nodded to the highway and we were off. I rode comfortably behind him, Bart bringing it up to ninety for a time, then falling back to the speed limit. He doodled with some device on his handlebars—a dead-man throttle, I discovered later—and proceeded to pull a pint of what had to be whisky from his leather pouch under his windshield. He tossed back a poke, intimated that I should ride up alongside him and take the bottle, and when I declined, he got all that in order and sped off again.

We were headed south, down Highway 61 now, the Mississippi broadening, turning to our left, but always heading south. Old man river. I was looking forward to meeting up with Jay, and having the ride take some specific shape, when Bart turned off at an intersection in one of those *Legend of Sleepy Hollow* Mississippi river towns. We pulled up to a bar.

"What the hell's the rush," he said. I felt like some gunslinger from the old Wild West following Bart in, his thighs so enormous that they rubbed together, forcing him to walk with lurching steps, Frankenstein's monster meets James Arness in black leather chaps.

"Two beers," he called to the bartender, and to me, "Rack up the balls."

Pride, they say, goeth before a fall—or, here, before a murder. Or, a contemporary form of drawing and quartering involving a Harley instead of horses. Admittedly, I'd earned it, as I said before.

I let Bart run the table in the first game, suffering a mild form of teasing in a running commentary.

"If shit-for-brains here'd run the five down the rail, he'd've had this shot right here—" and, *plunk!* Bart dropped the ball I should have "—and this one!" And *plunk* again.

Bart meant nothing by any of it—but I was getting steamed anyway. He joked around so much, I took it all to be rough fun. So I ran him ball for ball on the second game.

"Now you're showin' your true colors," he shouted, and whomped me on the back with such force I was nearly thrown off my feet. "Let's see what you can do there, little buddy!"

It occurred to me to get on my bike and ride off—Bart would have followed, I know that now.

Bart was also teasing me about the advantage I had, having nursed only the one beer to his—how many had it been? Three? Four?

"Let's get it on," Bart said, now an edge in his voice. It was something you said back then before letting fly.

I ran the table. Bart did too, joking again, but there was nothing funny in any of it.

Bart left me a table-length rail shot, the eight ball at the mouth of the far pocket. All I needed to do was sink that ball and the game was mine.

"I'm gonna get me another beer," Bart said, his way of acknowledging he'd lost the game.

He wandered off to my right. I assumed he was getting his beer. I bent over the table, recalling all the tips a pro had taught me—stroke the ball, no power shots in play, only when breaking the rack—and I ran the cue ball down the rail. It grazed the eight ball, kissed the bumper, headed back out, while the eight ball rocked . . . right . . . *there*, in the pocket, me standing with the cue in both hands, raised upright, and—I admit it, I just couldn't help myself.

I cheated. I held the butt of the cue over the table, an inch, maybe, jabbed it, and—the eight ball went *plunk!* into that far pocket.

And *that* was when Bart, standing all six foot five right behind me, said, "I could kill you, or I could drag you behind my bike with a chain and kill you."

This is one of the first lessons I learned about riding in clubs: Bikers may be crazy, they may not take seriously much that so-called normal folks take seriously (the authority of the police, for example), but don't, when you're around them, for one second violate a club honor code. And cheating at pool is one thing you don't do.

Bart let me know this. "This your first ride with us?" he asked.

I told him—wondering if it were going to be a gun, a knife, or the bike—that, yes, it was, wondering all the while, "us"?

Bart paid his tab, then lumbered out of the bar and mounted his bike. I followed at a distance. It occurred to me I could turn the bike around and head home, but something wouldn't let me do that.

Bart, it turned out, was just for starters. The other riders Jay had promised, hairy, leather-clad, tattooed West Bank Motorcycle Club riders, Themadons, Phoenix Birds, Gypsy Jokers, and Outlaws, we met minutes later, at the next bar down Highway 61. All 125 of them.

It was pure bedlam in the parking lot outside that bar, though nothing compared to what was to come later when we reached Winona. There were bikers everywhere, beers in hand, roaring about on their Harleys, shouting and joking and here and there fighting, but not yet in a serious way. A blues band was playing early Allman Brothers, slide guitar, and here and there was a woman in a bikini top to look at, but in all of it a rough sort of sobriety held things together, a necessity, given we were still riding some distance that afternoon. And there was the event to distract us: drag racing on Highway 61. Hopped-up Harleys roaring and rattling and dopplering by into the distance, something almost surreal about it all, the slowly falling leaves, the lovely October light, but this tangle of explosive blood, machines, and sex on gravel, just off the highway, these racers, like medieval lancemen, charging off, and me looking for Jay in it.

"Hey, *greenhorn!*" he shouted, out of all that wild hair and leather.

I couldn't pretend I wasn't happy to see him, though showing it was not to be done. "Yeah, 'I'm not playin' nursemaid to ya!'" I called out to him, and he just shook his head, frowning.

He waved me over, introduced me to Louis, a guy with a smile crazier than Jack Nicholson's, and Tiny, a biker who, of course, weighed at least three hundred pounds.

"I see you got a little Harley there," Tiny said, over the din.

Technically that wasn't correct: "Little Harleys" were British simultaneous twins, named for the Harley-like noise they made. The Rocket was a triple, a three-cylinder motorcycle.

We were talking about that, and the shortcomings of Lucas Electrics, when a rider on a Sportster, or "sporty," roared by and crashed the bike on its side, sending out a shower of sparks, the biker tumbling from the rear and the bike flying into a guardrail where it became a metal pretzel.

"That musta hurt," Tiny said.

It shocked me to realize he meant the bike. The biker got up and dusted himself off to cheers and catcalls, and Jay spun me around, wrapping his arm across my shoulders and moving me a distance from Louis and Tiny (both of whom, already, I was tempted to cling to for the duration of whatever this madness was going to become. I must say, I wasn't wrong in my thinking, though I was happy, later, not to have jumped on the Louis and Tiny train).

"Listen," Jay said, as if some coach to a pitcher. "Hang back. Watch it all from the rear. It's safer there, and when riders go down, you have time to react. You can move up to the front later, if you want." When riders go down? And later?

"Okay?" Jay said. "Get yourself a seat and watch the races."

I told Jay I'd do that, and he wandered off, leaving me on the highway guardrail where fifty or so bikers sat watching the races. I was genuinely grateful for his concern, and wondering what I'd gotten myself into, since by this time, two Minnesota Highway Patrol cruisers were pulling into the gravel lot behind me.

Yet another pair of bikes rocketed away in a deafening roar, one that you both shrank from and thrilled to. The two patrolmen, in full uniform, even the mirrored shades, seemed to take no notice.

In the back of my mind, a more rational me was saying, Go get your bike, and when no one is watching, get the hell out of here. But, no—I sat on the guardrail, numb, one of the bikers myself now. Hair to my shoulders, in black leather, bug-spattered and dirty. I kind of enjoyed it. More than a little.

"Reese's got the fastest HD in the Cities," the biker to my right said. "Woulda won last year but for—"

"That doesn't count for shit," the biker to my left said with a disgusted snort. "He trailered the thing in."

Up until that moment, it hadn't occurred to me exactly how these bikers had turned a state highway into a drag strip. Rat, the biker on my right, told me. They'd basically blocked off the road at one end, running heats, until the cars backed up, at which point they'd let them through.

Jay, Tiny, and Louis, I could see now over my shoulder, were talking with the patrolmen. We were all pretending not to watch, to be totally engrossed in the racing, but Jay strode from the taller of the two officers, saying something to Bart, who called out something I couldn't hear, and there was this compression, as if the whole group were some ragged, sleeping lion, just awakened.

There was the cough and roar of five, now ten, now more motorcycles, the highway patrolmen easing out of the lot in their cruiser and heading away from us, a redheaded biker with a beard to his knees saying something to those at the far end of the guardrail.

The highway patrolmen had simply said the Minnesota State Police had called in the National Guard to disperse us. It hadn't been a threat. Just a statement of fact. No citations were being handed out, no action being taken. But the front-runners of the National Guard would be at this very spot in minutes. We could do what we wanted with that.

At the back of the pack, I was riding in a haze of oily exhaust and road debris, bits of rubber and dirt and insects, which stung my face.

The whole group tore along at eighty, ninety miles per hour for some fifteen to twenty minutes, gaining distance from the oncoming Guard. The pack settled into a steady sixty-five, seventy. A large percentage of these riders had been in Vietnam, right in the middle of the worst of it. It wasn't that they were afraid of the Guard. It was just time to move the party to a more convenient location—which, for the next few hours, was the road itself. Bikers carried on conversations, passed joints, laughed, roared ahead, then backed off, the single biker out ahead appearing to brake precipitously, when he was only rejoining the pack. The pack, like some complicated, roaring, mechanical scythe, passing the occasional motorist, picked up the pace, engines roaring, the motorist, keeping his eyes forward, hands on the wheel at ten and two, hoping not to be bothered.

At the tail end, I got the nasty look—which, I realized, was just another reason most bikers hate the back of the pack.

I was fast reaching what I thought was my saturation point (the Rocket, too, having leaked oil all over my rear tire) when we thundered into Winona.

The Beaver Feast, it turned out, was some barbequed sandwich, burned to a crisp and slapped into your palm, in the parking lot of yet another tavern—if you had a stamp, skull and crossbones, on your left hand.

I didn't. I'd been late, I explained to yet another Tiny, who, at the over-turned fifty-gallon drum turned into a grill, seemed to wonder if he should jam my face down into the coals there. Another biker code crossed: You don't want to so much as give the *impression* of trying to steal something from bikers, especially when they're together, but worse yet, when they've gotten to wherever it is they're going.

That's when the sport fighting starts. That other form of biker enter-tainment. Alcohol, of course, does wonders for it.

I was getting a little glassy-eyed there with close calls. I mean, how many of my nine lives did I want to burn up on this ride? Little did I know, there with Tiny towering over me with his scimitar of a grill tool, I hadn't even come close. But I was getting there, until, again—God help me—Jay appeared.

"He's with me," he said. And that was it. I got the stamp—gee, that boded well for the rest of the night—and the burger, and Tiny said, point-ing with a thick finger as if nothing at all had passed between us, "Open bar, right through the door."

I thanked Jay for intervening, and again he spun me around by my black-jacketed arm: "We'll leave for the campground in a couple hours," he told me.

I stood back from the bar, jostled by these gladiators in leather, fifty or so packed into that tiny, dark space, two of the roughest, and largest of the lot, dancing with each other to Buddy Holly's "That'll Be the Day," at deafening volume.

I hadn't known bikers would do that, if women weren't around, get up and dance, but they did, even throwing in some jitterbug moves, which I wouldn't know as such until I lived in Montana, years later. The surprise— or was it dumbfounded incomprehension—must have shown on my face.

I tried, again, to engage the services of the bartender: "WHISKY SOUR!" I shouted over the music.

"Hey, man," a biker at my side said. He was right at my ear. "You look kinda down." I wasn't down, more . . . driven into myself by the heat of it all. He held out his hand, in his palm an assortment of pills.

I tried to say something to the effect of, Thanks, and he shook his head, he wasn't asking for money.

Moments later, I had the pills in the breast pocket of my jacket, and the bartender handed over my drink—at which point I asked for two more. We weren't going anywhere, and I—almost desperately—needed to take the edge off.

It worked. Moments later I was feeling no pain, and Duane Allman, who'd died riding a Harley, run over by a truck hauling peaches, was blaring from the sound system.

Jay strode through that mass of hair and leather and caught my eye.

"We're leaving," he mouthed.

"Now?" I shouted.

But all I saw was his broad leather-clad shoulders going through the door out into the parking lot. I followed, cursing myself for having put down the three whiskies, but was, in part, amused. Now the air felt gentle, cool, inviting, and the bikers kicking about in the lot, joking, beers in hand, were compadres, and in that frame of mind I mounted the Rocket and got it started.

Jay headed out of the lot with five or so other bikers, and I, again, swung around to head up the rear. Smooth, easy, lubricated. I was look- ing forward to this ride along the Mississippi, especially—thanks to the whiskies—without the fear that had always sat like a fist in my gut when riding. Open air, freedom, all that *Then Came Bronson* stuff. I eased out the clutch to roll out of the parking lot, and a behemoth of a biker came running at me with a pool cue in his hand.

Me?

No, it couldn't be me. But no, it was me he was running at. And he was running at me with that pool cue, to brain me, I thought. Bart's revenge or something. I was too dopey to drop the clutch and roar out of there, in the second and a half that it took for this guy to reach me, but by then, anyway, what he was shouting had finally made it into the recesses of my alcohol-addled brain.

"Stop! Stop!" Not, *Die, Cheater, Die!* "Gas!"

Well, he had my handlebars now, and hit the kill switch. The bike was dead, I was dead, soon to be beaten to a pulp with a pool cue by yet another biker probably named Tiny.

"Hey, here," he said, pointing. I saw that the fuel line had come off the petcock on the gas tank, and the tank, since I'd spun the petcock open, had drenched my right leg in 91 Octane.

Had the bike spat out the tiniest spark, I'd have become a human torch—possibly at speed on the highway.

I shoved the gas line back onto the petcock and shared a handshake with the biker, thanking him, until, embarrassed at my gratitude, he merged back into that mass of wild hair and leather, Jay at that moment honking to me.

"Come on!" he called over his shoulder.


You'd have thought, at that point, I would have called myself lucky, slunk off somewhere to rent a Motel 6 room, and been quits with this ride.

But no. Mark Twain once said, "Youth is wasted on the young." I was young, and new to it all. The ride had to be finished, the summit ascended, the story told to the end. Quitting was not in my nature. So, with the gas cooling my leg, I headed out onto the highway, thinking that if there was enough gas to set me on fire, why, I'd—what would I do? Hell if I knew, but it involved rolling on the ground and putting out the flames. Maybe. Something like that. And I was feeling lucky—which, in my naïveté, I didn't know was the alcohol.

Jay was a skilled and daring rider; he liked the edge. And, up front now, away from the danger of the careless mass, he let his bike run. Ninety, in the dark, on a highway we were unfamiliar with. But they were up front, I was tying up the rear, so I had the advantage of their lights, had some modicum of margin for error. Or so I thought. We came down a long, straight section, and they let fly again, who knows how fast we were going by then—my Smith's speedometer had broken some miles back. I was snapping the speedometer's glass face, hoping the needle would pop around again, when I looked up and saw we had a very hard right turn, through trees just ahead.

I hit the brakes for all I was worth—hard on the front, feathering the rear, my brain working solutions in a glance. Nearly a decade of riding had taught me many things. Rules, if you wanted to stay alive. I'd violated most since meeting Bart at the gas station. But this was the one that could do it. Kill me.

When the Rocket leaked oil, it leaked it, for the most part, on the right side of the rear tire. That meant I had dry tire on the left, could lean the bike over on a left-hander, but was shot to shit on the right.

I was still doing seventy-five, at least, when I entered the turn. I had a few options. First, put the bike down. Take the road rash and write off the Rocket. Or? But I'd already long passed that moment. I shot off the shoulder, flew down the hillside, riding the Rocket the way I'd ridden dirt bikes my whole childhood, downshifting, standing on the pegs, countering the bike's sliding mass when it began to swerve, cranking on the throttle to squirt me around a cement culvert coming up, which would have killed me had I hit it, and—right there at the bottom, I thought, slick grass, keep moving—hit second gear and powered back up the embankment to the highway. To stop on the shoulder, where Jay and the others were just getting off their bikes.

"Jesus fucking Christ, kid!" Jay said. "What were you *thinking?*"

I didn't want to explain about the Rocket leaking oil—Jay was always giving me shit about riding a Brit bike already—or about thinking to put the bike down. I was straddling the bike on the side of the highway, miraculously in one piece.

And, as if none of it had happened, off we went, riding to the campground. In the blink of an eye, we had our tents up, and returned to the Beaver Feast, which had become a bacchanal. Loud, drunken voices, singing, glass breaking, amid the strains of blues guitar and acid rock. Patrol cars parked within sight of the bar, lurking.

Jay disappeared, and I got to talking with two newfound pals, Bernie and Al, who'd been on the ride before.

Bernie knew a coed over at the college who was a belly dancer. A short while later, from the open door of her room, she regarded us with suspicion—or maybe it was just indecision. How wild did she want to get?

"Come on," Bernie said. "Let's go dancing!"

That did it.


It had been bikes, but now at the Ratskeller, a riverfront bar, it was bikes and *sex*. Girls, and I have to say, these were pretty coeds, not the rough women who are biker regulars, came out of the woodwork from the nearby college.

But these girls definitely had that hard-living glint in their eyes. All around me, they were hooking up with my newfound road-gladiator companions. Pair after pair roared off, the bikes weaving, and the girls, long blond or brunette hair trailing, clinging to the rider.

I took to the floor a couple times, dancing as I had only once before at a Grateful Dead concert, something decidedly pagan in it. Who cared if we lived or died in that moment?

An old English poet (cited in Bede's eighth-century *History*) put it this way: Life was like a swallow darting through a mead hall, in the hall a fire blazing, and elders telling tales. But of what was outside the hall, who could say? A maelstrom, that's what it was. Deafening, sharp, overpowering.

One o'clock and the bar closed.

Bernie had gone off with his belly dancer; Al had met a woman, older (to me), who had a winning and ironic smile.

"You're a wholesome sort," she said, placing her palm on my cheek, then slipping from the barstool to take Al's hand. I took her comment as an insult. What had she meant by that? Wholesome? Like . . . Hostess Twinkies? Yellow sponge cake with that white marshmallow filling?

I wandered into the parking lot, the night cold now: it couldn't have been more than forty or so degrees. Just above freezing. I started my bike. Back on the highway bordering the Mississippi, I found I'd passed the campground, so I spun the bike around, headed in the opposite direction.

I was freezing, chilled to the bone. I had no idea how much gas I had in my tank (motorcycles of that vintage never had gas gauges, as many, even now, do not).

No Prince of Wales campground. So where was it?

Furious at being lost in the middle of the night, foggy with beer, and dope, and exhaustion, I shouted in rage at the top of my lungs. If there was anything I hated, it was being lost in such discomfiting circumstances. I mean, what was I going to do, sleep in a ditch?

I passed a pizza place, a red neon sign, TONY'S, over the roof promising, if nothing else, warmth, and went inside to ask directions to the campground. It rankled me to think that my tent was up, my Korean-issue army down bag slung over my closed-cell foam ground pad—which just then seemed a picture of nirvana. The, obviously, Italian guy at the counter, the owner, told me he hadn't the faintest idea where the camp was, but, he said, "Janice could tell you."

I approached the woman and the table, there with her three friends.

Janice, a woman of about forty, with a no-nonsense administrator's haircut and demeanor, but some . . . something else, glanced up at me.

I explained.

From the first, she could not hide her amusement. There I was in my black leather, lost, and civil as a choirboy (and an Eagle Scout, yes, there was that, too).

There was, right from the first, something between us. I don't know in what way she was lost in her life, but it made her sympathetic to my being lost—she could see right through me. She rambled off a catalogue of directions. I have never been good with directions delivered this way. After the first three local landmarks, left at Pimplewood, then straight on—don't take Mugwort, or veer off beyond the railroad tracks, but guide right where you see the walnut tree—I get lost. Useless. I have to get out pen and paper, which I did not have.

Janice rose from the table. She gave certain assurances to her friends, then told me what she would do. She would show me where the campground was, would drive me to it.

"In your car?" I said.

"I don't know why your friends chose that campground," Janice told me, alongside her car, opening her door and sliding into it, in such a way that I could only do the same. She pulled her door shut and I did likewise.

There was some kind of Mrs. Robinson thing going on here, but she wasn't going to be the one to say something, or give any indication of it. Or was I all wrong about that, I wondered.

"It's a nightmare finding that place," Janice told me. "There's no sign, and the road into it you can't see from the highway. They're as good as closed."

So, what, was this place some biker's Brigadoon?

"Oh," I said, shifting in my seat. And then I recalled the reason Jay had decided on the Prince of Wales. It was free.

We headed out into the dark, the heater disgorging great exhalations of dry, hot air. I recovered, by degrees, from my hypothermia, but I still couldn't keep all the lefts and rights and stops and whatnot clear—and that unresolved something between us was distracting me. And what kind of biker was I, anyway? Riding in this nearly middle-aged woman's Lincoln?

She took me right to the mouth of the campground. There was my tent, and a fire, and Jay and a few others around it.

"Should I honk?" Janice teased.

"I'd rather you didn't," I told her.

She sat cheerfully behind the wheel, shot me a stern but amused glance. Below us Jay and the others were trying to see who was in the car. And, kindly enough, before they could make me out through the windshield, Janice spun the car around, taking me to Tony's, and my bike.

There was a moment when neither of us moved. She was quite lovely, really, a bit of an angel. Somehow, these sorts have come out of nowhere, time and again, and have changed my life for the better, or saved it.

I hesitated, getting out of the car. Thought to get back in and didn't.

Her window down, she watched me don my helmet and gloves. I had only the foggiest notion of how I was going to get back to the campground. I couldn't think for exhaustion. I was prepared to sleep wherever—either I'd find the campground or I'd spend a few miserable hours freezing, then get to a gas station, and to a restaurant to fill myself up with something hot.

I straddled the bike and was about to give it a savage kick, to start it, when she said, "Just follow me out there," which, right then, sounded sweeter to me than a choral arrangement of "Swing Low, Sweet Chariot."

Bitter cold again. Now it was below freezing, and foggy, and the roads were glazed with slick leaves. My teeth chattered. And even given all that, I loved the feel of the Rocket. It was nimble, surged ahead when I urged it, light and surefooted around potholes.

The road peeled back around me, an endless tunnel of dark trees, the low-hanging fog lifting and dipping and running.

I sang to myself. I always did that riding distances. I smiled, even with my teeth clattering.

And then Janice swung right ahead of me and stopped, her lights cutting two bright cones through the fog. I paused, at her window, said, *Thanks!* and coasted down to the bikers around the campfire and made a smart stop. Dismounted.

Janice couldn't help herself. She beeped her horn and was gone.

I took a seat at the fire. Got my gloves off and held my palms to it.

"Who was that?" Jay said, elbowing me.

I shrugged and moved closer to the fire. Dean poked at the fire with a stick, crossed his engineer boots in front of him. "Colder'n a witch's tit," he said.

• • •

Here you crawl into your tent. You have survived an onslaught of unpredictables, and a portion of it not through your own skill, but dumb luck. There should be some cloudlike comfort here, but there isn't. You're on a biker ride. Dean and Jay and the others drink into the night, occasionally one of them rising from the fire to urinate with a loud hiss, at first into the weeds, and then, with the others protesting, into the fire. Cans rattle. Bottles clink. Rough voices jabber. You've got three eighths of an inch of pad between you and the damp, near frozen ground. Your tent is nothing but the thinnest skin between you and the crazies out there.

You toss and turn. Pull your old Korean-issue bag up around your head. Tendrils of mary jane and old man drink disrupt your sleep, and there's the morning ahead of you, and the ride home. You, thinking with something almost like dread, Do they ride as insanely getting home as they do going somewhere?

In the morning, amid the rumble and thunder of Harleys, you crawl from your tent in your leather. Greasy, sweaty, smelling of gasoline.

Jay hands you a cup of coffee. It tastes, just now, like nothing short of resurrection itself.

At the fire, Dean is making scrambled eggs in a big cast-iron skillet.

"Done in a minute," he says, grinning up at you.

The bikers who'd rolled into your camp minutes before crank it up on the road out, engines winding.

"What was that all about?" you ask.

"Business."

"Like?"

Jay gives you that blank-eyed look, then turns away. He hasn't told you this, but he's some kind of officer in this mess of leather and hard-living bikers; those who have just left, his lieutenants.

"Tiny's dead," he tells you.

Tiny? Which Tiny? You must have met three of them. "You mean of Louis and Tiny?"

"Van pulled out in front of them. Tiny center-punched it, Louis caught the rear end, lost the fingers on his hand, the little ones."

What can you say to any of this? You don't exactly feel lucky—it's larger than that. Simply standing here, breathing, the eggs in front of you, the fire warming your legs. There is that autumn smell of leaves. Smoke from the fire. And the bikes—grease, gasoline, ashy exhaust. They very nearly whinny, call to you.

The odd thing is, in some movement toward comfort, you want, right now, to get back on the Rocket, leave all this nastiness behind. Tiny and his accident, Louis and his ruined hand. And you do that, the entire West Bank Motorcycle Club riding in some collective contemplation out of Winona, and yes, pleasure, back to the Cities. No one stops. There is no chatting. Or nearly none. Just what is necessary.

At one point, you wave to Jay, peel off in the direction of home.

Park the bike in the garage.


The following morning, at the university, you take your place in line, shuffle into organic chemistry, the premed weed-out course. You're showered, shaved, but still fuzzy from the weekend.

There are more than six hundred students in the class. Professor Gugantas will fail 60 percent. (You will not be one of those failing, or even close to it; but you will, finally, wander off, into another life. One that suits you.)

But here, now everyone is—with the exception of the occasional genius—terrified. Here is the gate to the "good life," and there are too many at the door.

Eric, a lifetime hand-raiser and pleaser (a nice kid, really), who sits beside you, says, opening his notebook and clicking his pen, "Hey, I saw a great movie over the weekend, about this treasure hunter. And there's this enormous eel that almost bites off his head." He clicks his pen, makes sure it's working, and, turning to me, adds, "What'd you do?"

I get comfortable in my seat, as much as is possible. Set my pen over my notebook.

"Nothing . . . really," I tell him.

• • •

I left Minnesota for Montana two years later. In that time I went on a handful of rides with the West Bank Motorcycle Club. I rode at the rear of the pack, and in the middle, as if some crow in a roaring murder of birds, and at the head, wind in my teeth.

I never cheated at pool again. And angels, those years, as on that first ride, carried me here and there.

## As It Stands Now

Biker culture is alive and flourishing, the Angels now controlling California, Alaska, pieces of the Northwest, Midwest, and Southeast. The Outlaws own Florida and the bulk of the Midwest. The Bandidos run Texas and most of the South, with a few chapters in the Pacific Northwest. The Pagans control the mid-Atlantic. And the Sons of Silence run the Rockies and the plains.

MCs are big business now, serious "action," and to recruit new members, "hang around" riders are invited to biker clubhouses—though with far more caution than in the past, clubs giving potential riders sophisticated background checks.

The "big four" alone, the Angels, Outlaws, Bandidos, and Pagans, the FBI estimates, do nearly a billion dollars a year in methamphetamine sales alone, to say nothing of their other, now highly organized, crime businesses. Oddly enough, the Angels also sponsor a Toys for Tots Run every year, providing through this charity for thousands of kids in families too poor to afford luxuries. Go figure. This once strictly American subculture has spawned parallel developments elsewhere, such as the hyperviolent Rock Machine MC in Montreal. The Mounties hold biker gangs in Quebec responsible for as many as thirty killings between 1988 and 1992. One biker alone, "Apache," admitted to killing forty-three people between 1970 and 1985.

Interpol now counts twenty-six Hells Angels chapters in Europe, thirteen in Britain alone, with 362 members. And do these crime-figure Angels even ride? Any Angel must use as primary transportation a motorcycle, and is expected to travel on that motorcycle an average of 20,000 miles a year come rain or shine.

Now "Euro-bikers" such as the Power Dead roar through the Alps; members of the Shabby Ones and Rabies stir fear in the hearts of Norwegians; and the Mental Midgets and Bullshit rock Denmark.

One Angel from Zurich, Reinhard Lutz, is sought by international law forces for trafficking 100 kilos of cocaine with a street value of $5 million, a volume experts believe is a fraction of a percent of the yearly traffic.

And why should you especially avoid confrontations with these bikers?

The 1%ers believe that when in confrontations with those outside the gang, the gang brother is *always right*, so bring it on, and they should *always* use overwhelming force. According to government sources, police have seized from biker clubs "vast quantities of handguns, silencers, shotguns, M-16s, AK-47s, MAC-10s, and Uzis, as well as LAW rocket launchers, grenades, dynamite, bombs of all types, and C-4 and other plastic explosives"—weapons and technologies that would be a "significant addition" to any country's armory.

Said one American Angel who visited chapters in Europe, "The European Angels are just like the American ones, only ten years behind."

The title of Yves Lavigne's book on the modern-day biker scene succinctly sums up the direction they've taken—*Hell's Angels: "Three Can Keep a Secret If Two Are Dead."*

If you want to ride with these folks, or even hang with them, enough said. You've been warned.

## 99 Percenters

The truth is that if you want to get your piece of adventure with a riders club, it's waiting for you. Currently there are hundreds of riders clubs operating in the United States, a great many of them AMA-chartered. If you're looking for companionship in the dirt, there's the Dust Devils near Reno. Your love is BMWs? There's the Beehive Beemers in Salt Lake City (a club I've ridden with). Want a bite-the-wire, sport-riding experience? How about going for a spin with the Crazed Ducati Riders of Massachusetts? Need a women's group? Try Women in the Wind, or the Towanda Tours Group. There are Christian groups, such as the nationwide Christian Motorcycle Club ("a biker Brotherhood with Jesus"), and Jewish rider clubs, such as the King David Bikers in South Florida, Montreal, and Philadelphia (Rabbi Zig Zag is there to answer questions), and the Jewish Motorcycle Alliance. The Dharma Bums Motorcycle Club (with a nod to Jack Kerouac), you guessed it, is for Buddhist riders, and the Temple Riders, in Salt Lake City, for Latter-day Saints.

There are nearly a hundred clubs for Army and Marine bikers alone.

There's HOG, the Harley Owners Group, which has chapters in every state, clubs for Ural owners, Honda Gold Wing owners, British bike owners, and antique bike owners. There are clubs for owners of all manufactures of bikes, including scooters, vintage and contemporary, Vespa, Lambretta, and Piaggio.

Are there riders enough to fill the ranks of these clubs? Motorcycling is currently enjoying a worldwide renaissance, its ranks here in America, according to U.S. Department of Transportation statistics, having swelled from just under 5 million licensed riders in 1990, to nearly 9 million at present (though some studies that include dirt bikes and ATVs put the number of riders closer to 25 million). A significant group when taken in itself, though a minuscule one when compared to that of automobile users, 196 million licensed drivers operating some 247.5 million registered cars and trucks in the United States alone. Motorcycles, in this picture, account for a mere 2.37 percent of all passenger vehicles in the United States.

And the demographics are changing, too. According to the Motorcycle Industry Council, in 1980 half of our riders were twenty-four or younger. Now, riders under eighteen years of age constitute less than 4 percent of the biker population; around half are over forty, and a good quarter of riders are over fifty. The average Harley rider is forty-seven.

These statistics prompted the *New York Times Magazine* writer Christopher Caldwell to comment in his "The Way We Live Now" column, "To keep wearing Levi's, you have to maintain the physique you had when you were 20, which is a tricky proposition. To keep riding a Harley, all you have to hang on to is the ideas you had when you were 20. Anyone can do that."

No one rides for ideas. Nor, as Caldwell claims, do bikers simplistically believe that motorcycles "embody certain spiritual properties." What motorcycles do is take us places. They are not just vehicles of convenience, or conveyance, or even comfort, necessarily, but machines created for specific uses, each machine a kind of ticket, if you will, giving the rider a right to enter.

For the longest time the only ticket for the outlaw biker was the rough-running, iconic, and altogether American Harley. Though Brit bikes, such as the Triumph that Brando rode in *The Wild One*, Bonnevilles, and Thunderbirds would suffice.

A KTM Duke will take you through desert in which no Harley would last five minutes. A Ducati Desmosedici, if you were good enough, could make you the kind of money in world GP events that Valentino Rossi makes. But it is the very smaller number of riders in relation to drivers of cars that makes the rider a noteworthy figure. That and the freedom any rider buys at the price of serious risk.

Real adventure can carry you into the sphere of the ordeal, which, only on reflection, can be amusing. It can kill you.

And there is this: Despite our espoused American rugged individualism (about which many writers, such as Alexis de Tocqueville, have had much to say), we don't much want people in the main to "get out there." Riders of motorcycles do exactly that, and outlaw bikers more than the rest of us. Take, for example, a list of noteworthy riders, not a wallflower in the bunch: Robert Hughes, historian; Roald Dahl, Hurricane pilot in WWII and author; George Orwell, author of 1984, among other books; James Dean; Malcolm Forbes, magazine magnate and adventurer; Charles Lindbergh; Roy Rogers; George Bernard Shaw; Elvis Presley; Steve McQueen; T. E. Lawrence; Michael Jordan; Che Guevara; Buddy Holly; Ann Margret; Bessie Stringfield; Jay Leno; Arnold Schwarzenegger; Queen Latifah; Wynonna Judd; Sammy Davis, Jr.; Jeremy Irons; Mark Knopfler; Liam Neeson; Keanu Reeves; Sting; Oliver Sachs; Enzo Ferrari; Hermann Maier; Brad Pitt; Tom Cruise; and Dwight D. Eisenhower. The former board and flat-track acer Freddie Marsh was still riding at one hundred, making seventy-five laps a day in the lot of a Moto Guzzi dealer on an "Indian badged" moped, claiming it was what kept him alive. Stringfield is particularly worthy of mention here: Bessie, as an African-American orphan from Jamaica, was raised by an Irish Catholic woman in Boston. When she was sixteen Bessie decided she wanted a motorcycle, a 1928 Indian Scout, and got it. She rode through the Deep South in the 1930s and 1940s, fearless, making friends wherever she went. Asked by a journalist what made it possible for her to ride solo in the South, she quipped, simply, "The Man Upstairs." Bessie was married five times. In all, she rode for more than sixty years. At the end of her life, when people expressed surprise at her earlier audacity, she'd reply, simply, "I was somethin'!"

Bikers put it out there—living to ride, riding to live. It shakes us out of our socialized (and sometimes personal) narcosis of safety, comfort, and predictability.

Bikers are alive, and to some frighteningly so, and to hell with who doesn't much like it (a very large number of people). Everywhere, non-riders strike the biker pose, such as my dear friend Meredith, a woman with terrible eyesight, an art school graduate who has never so much as sat on a motorcycle, who, nonetheless, went online and bought a vintage Schott Brothers black leather jacket, just like Brando wore in *The Wild One*, which she wears to art galleries and around town. The artist outlaw. Look around New York, New Jersey, Boston, any big East Coast city, any city at all, where people everywhere are striking the biker pose, none of them having so much as filled the tank of a motorcycle, much less having ridden one, or if they have, for any distance.

Another friend, living in Geneva, who works in an office, dreams of buying a Harley and touring the United States with her husband. I have warned her, repeatedly, that she has no conception, whatsoever, what such a trip would *really* be like. At this she always laughs. After all, what do I know?

Wannabe outlaws in biker garb are everywhere, and they amuse those of us who do ride. I have a Schott Brothers motorcycle jacket, one with countless thousands of miles on it, so many I've had to have leather workers bring it back to life. I've had my biker jacket thirty-five years. When I put it on, it means something. It's a talisman, a good luck charm, a tie with the past, and a guard against road rash. But more than anything, it always means, instantly, that I'm a part of a club, the *real rider* club. So I wear my jacket—out on the highway, or in town, or to road races or hill climbs, which have been dominated by Indian and Harley-Davidson for fifty years, being true biker gathering places—with, sometimes, a certain trepidation.

But more so this: Thrill. At the prospect of coming alive again, astride some fire-breathing, heartbeat-thumping bike.

# 6

# Widowmaker

## Hill-Climbing Killer
## Extraordinaire

**C**roydon, Utah, is a sleepy little town tucked in a fold of the Wasatch mountains northeast of Salt Lake City. Approaching Croydon on Interstate 84, if you blinked at the wrong time, you'd miss the sign. Towns like Croydon are everywhere in Utah. A central thoroughfare named, appropriately, Main, runs the length of it. There is a bar, for the non-Mormons, a small nineteenth-century temple, and everywhere are the remnants of former mining dreams—oxide red implements, buckets and cables and cranes, broken shovels, engines of all sorts, and mining cars on narrow-gauge rails going nowhere.

There's a tempting vacuity to it, the ocher sand of the Navajo strata filling in the corners, a grit over nearly everything. You could set yourself down here and never try to be shiny again. But you aren't here for that. All this quaint and seductive Utah oblivion is not for you.

A sharp right takes you alongside century-old irrigation, where a line of poplars have majestically planted themselves. As you move south, the tiny Croydon valley narrows, the foothills of the Wasatch Range rising up around you.

You bump off the road onto a rutted track, your bike chuttering and lunging over potholes, a truck behind you, and behind it ten more like it, all towing trailers, lurching and screeching on their springs.

There's a woman who doesn't diet at a ticket booth, and you get yours, sixteen dollars, and, forging ahead, you swing into the parking lot and kill your engine, kick down the stand, and hop off. You remove your helmet and get out of your leathers—it's already pushing eighty and only late morning—then head into the ebullient insanity of it.

Hill climbs are always family events, but, as already noted, they are also the traditional home of bikers (albeit well-behaved), creating a kind of social three-ring circus, and Widowmaker is no exception.

Knee-high kids in bright clothes run everywhere, some with dogs, or parents, in hot pursuit. Sullen teenagers eye one another warily, but with interest. From makeshift towers surrounded by hot dog, soda, beer, and sweets vendors, George Thorogood's "Bad to the Bone" blares. There are, easily, already five hundred people here, many relatives of the pee-wee event competitors making runs on the small hill now. And more folks are packing in, all lugging coolers, setting up tentlike sun canopies. Biker upon biker in black leather a-sparkle with badges and medals, and in avuncular good cheer, swagger into the grassy area set back from this ocher cusp of Wasatch foothills.

*Hill* is a misnomer in Croydon. This "hill" is a ragged, stone-strewn bowl rising 1,200 feet. The northernmost end, the face of it, a 35-to-50-degree slope where the main event, Open Exhibition Hillclimb, will be held, is nearly all sand. *Sand.* Feet deep, and rutted, and littered with rocks, from the size of softballs to sofas.

You take this in, thinking: That's *crazy!* Who could get up *that?*

Off to your left on the smaller hill, the pee-wee class competitors are having a go at it. Decked out in leathers, and on tweaked-out little bikes sporting leaf-blower-size to 125 cc engines, these kids rush, bikes zinging, at the hill, hit the bottom, and, rear tire kicking out yards of dirt and the little riders bent over their handlebars, they ride higher, then higher yet, and in the middle, at the 150-foot mark, almost without exception, they begin to weave, then violently bump, jerk, and toss side to side in a gulley.

And there they crash—hurling themselves away from their bikes, men catching both. From start to finish, the "handlers" are positioned right alongside these pint-sized gladiators, sprinting with them in intervals up the hillside in the heat.

It's mesmerizing, watching.

You know it is no small thing climbing a 250-foot hill. There is, even on a slope like this, the simple fear of falling to complicate matters—and worse, the fear of having your bike with all sorts of pointy steel things sticking out of it fall on top of you and, maybe, poke out your eye or break your nose, eh? Falls hurt, and in hill climbing they're pretty much inevitable. Hill-climb and you're going to go down, and hard.

Nowhere in motocross, or observed trials riding, is there a hill as large as even this one—the "pee-wee" hill at Widowmaker.

So, watching—each kid taking off like a rocket, then wrestling his bike to that seemingly inevitable fall—you admire these little daredevils.

To get to the top, the average adult street rider with a stripped 650 cc bike would be in for a white-knuckle, full-on-throttle run that would last a good heart-pounding four or five seconds—if that rider didn't fall, which he would, because a stock street bike could never negotiate the rocks, sand, and gully.

For these kids, a bike half the size of a standard motorcycle is just right, and so the 10 to 20 horsepower their little bikes put out make it *just* possible for one or two to make it to the top.

In the space of half an hour, while you've been watching these little competitors run ragged at the hill, the grassy field has filled in around you. It's a full-on rag-tag crowd now, even the trophy girls present in short-shorts and revealing tops, strutting and flashing their capped teeth.

All is cheerful anticipation.

Louder now, the music hammers down from those towers, Talking Heads' "Burning Down the House," the Stones' "Rip this Joint," Tom

Petty's "Damn the Torpedoes." And the ever present ZZ Top's "Tube Steak Boogie," punctuated by a D.J. announcing the riders on the pee-wee hill.

All of which this jocular crowd pays little or no attention to. We're all waiting for the full-out, big-bore mayhem.

There's a chain-link fence set a good two hundred feet back from the base of the real Widowmaker, and between the base of the hill and the fence, riders are lining up with their support crews. The mess of machines and men in fancy, colorful leathers is like so much bright confetti until you approach, where, unless you address yourself to a specific rider, you don't so much as exist.

The riders' leathers are in themselves fascinating, and embody, in gladiator fashion, the spirit of Widowmaker. Emblazoned across one rider's chest is *BIG COCK RACING*. And the rider behind him? *SEXY FAST*. There's *FOX RACING, FLY RACING*, and on one joker's leathers, *BEER RACING*.

A rider too hot to have his leathers on is nearly head to toe in tattoos—the largest and most prominent on his right shoulder, which is, in its entirety, a skull, under that skull a banner reading simply: *DEATH*.

Everywhere, on every inch of free surface of these bikes and riders, too, are advertisements for sponsors and their parts: Waseco Pistons. Big Sky Racers Edge. Dominator Tire. Hayward Engineering.

All of this would be so much Britney Spears, pomp and flashing lights and nonsense, but for the bikes. These are *not* toys. These bikes are instruments of contained explosion, to be translated into torque sufficient to mount a 1,200-foot-high "hill": Widowmaker.

Recall the dirt bikes used for motocross: ultralightweight and ultra-powerful, delivering lightning-fast throttle response, and nimble and sure-footed as cheetahs; geared low, and weighing around 200 to 220 pounds. A 60-horsepower KTM, for example, is scary fast, a bike that can easily overwhelm an inexperienced rider. Power-to-weight ratio? Around 1 horsepower per 3.7 pounds. These hill climbers use this same sort of bike (granted certain frame modifications), but bolt into it a made-for-drag-racing street-bike engine nearly three times that of box-stock displacement. Kawasaki, Honda, and Harley engines are favorites.

Big deal, right? You've seen tame-enough Kawasakis and Hondas. And Harleys, aren't they those blubber bikes with footboards and saddlebags?

I'll admit something. Having cut my teeth on highly tuned, lightweight Brit bikes, I'd always thought of Harleys as a great many of their riders refer to them: hogs (or, sometimes, scooters). Low-revving, low-horsepower, heavy V-twins. But imagine now that *irritating*, Marilyn Manson–playing kid's little dirt bike, that *ring-ding* you've wanted to vaporize with a laser beam (isn't there always at least one per neighborhood?), and shoehorn an insanely modified and lightened 1,600 cc hog engine into it.

The rider of this bike? You guessed it, the guy with the skull tattooed on his shoulder. Gene. He tells you about his bike, a thing of pride.

First, it's got piston-melting, piston-shattering compression. High compression is ten to one and requires aviation gas. This engine's got *fourteen-to-one* compression. The crankshaft has been balanced and blueprinted, the connecting rods lightened. The cam is such that the bike won't run under 1,500 rpm. There's a fuel injector on it from a car, and an optical spark system, putting out voltage hot enough to melt holes in aluminum alloy.

And the fuel? *Nitro methane.* Nitro, as in that stuff they use in, what else, explosives—for mining, or removing trees, or . . .

This bike, Gene tells you, burns that nitro benzene at ten times the rate of a gasoline burning engine. Or, roughly one gallon of nitro (which must be purchased from a racing-fuel company) in less than ten seconds. A single run, such as at Widowmaker, will cost *eighty dollars* in nitro alone. And nitro makes an engine such as this one explode easily.

Even with that monster Harley engine in it, the bike weighs 300 pounds. But what you want to know is this: After all that fussing around, all that painstaking modification, all that effort, what kind of flat-out horsepower does this thing have?

It has 225. To push 300 pounds. Up a craggy, boulder-strewn slope you wouldn't hike up on your best day.

And the power-to-weight ratio?—1 horsepower to move 1.3 pounds.

Recall that the power-to-weight ratio of a Camry or Accord is, at best, 1:20, or, 1 horsepower to move 20 pounds. The world's most powerful stock production car, the Bugatti Veyron, with 1001 horsepower, has a roughly 1:5 power-to-weight ratio. A power-to-weight ratio of 1 horsepower to every 6 pounds, such as that of the once white-knuckle Norton Commando, is sufficient to propel a street motorcycle from a standing start to around 110 mph in about twelve seconds. Zero to 110 in three blocks.

At one time that was fast (and, honestly, it still is).

So this monster Gene is riding has a power-to-weight ratio six times greater than that of your vintage tear-your-scalp-off road bike. *Twenty* times more power than your family sedan.

Mufflers? You've got to be kidding. Massive exhaust pipes run straight to the back of the bike, where they are cut at ninety degrees. Brutal. This thing is a hill-climbing motorcycle version of the Stealth Bomber, and the rider's got the tattoo to prove it. But, you notice now, this thing has no electric start, and no kick starter. So how do you even fire this two-wheeled killer up?

The only thing that comes to mind is bump starting, the rider pushing the bike in gear and dropping the clutch to turn the engine over, but the last time you saw someone do that was at a . . . *vintage* hill climb. It's a connection you've never made before, but now you do.

Here, under the ultrabright Utah sun, in this so-called high desert, you study the bikes in line front to rear, easily thirty of them ready to go, and right here, oddly enough, amid all this explosive *potential*—because the riders haven't yet started these things—is the very *beginning* of motorcycle competition.

Here is where it all started.

## Pedal Pushers and Hill Climbers

The first motorcycle competitions were *hill climbs*.

Back at the turn of the last century, and for some time after, when tinkerers and inventors were experimenting with powered bicycles, motorcycles could not climb so much as a 20-degree slope. This meant that, on the average, your motorcyclist—decked out in snazzy jodhpurs and boots formerly used for riding horses—had to *pedal* up hills, assisting the machinery to scale inclines of any size.

Imagine, if you will, wearing all that gear: the heavy boots, the Belstaff waxed cotton riding jacket, gloves up to your elbows, and the requisite jaunty leather hat and goggles. You are puttering along on an open road, most likely gravel, if even that, but free, outside, the trees flashing by, doing all of thirty or so, which, really, is a lovely speed.

*Intoxicating.*

No one has radio. There are no cars on this road. No one can afford cars. The population of the United States is roughly 92 million, less than a third of what it is today, and much of that concentrated in major cities.

You wing by pastures, the old hayburners in their fields chomping away, in this bridge period when the machine hasn't yet become demon: polluter, destroyer, irritant.

Let's say we're riding a Pope Big 4. World War I, the War to End All Wars, is barely a rumor in far-off Europe. The sun is shining. An expression is popular: "Every day I'm getting better and better." You believe it. Your Big 4 is proof of it. Winging between trees, the sun aflash in your eyes, you hum a popular tune: "Fascination." Your well-to-do aunt Gert played it for you on her Edison spool recorder. Electrification is taking place (but for very few areas outside major cities). Bell telephone is extending service, and soon—within the next decade—every home will be connected.

Such *magic*, and nowhere to go but . . . up!

Which brings you to the inevitable slope, winding invitingly through a stand of majestic oaks ahead of you. On the other side is Eugenia Speers, the spitting image of those Gibson girls you've been eyeing in the Sears catalogue. All your other invitations, to the hay ride, the square dance, the ice cream social, she has refused. But when you asked her, with great trepidation, "Would you *possibly* be interested in a ride on my new motor-bike?" she smiled, and to your heart-thumping surprise, said yes, and wanted to know *when?*

(Or, for the not-at-all-rare woman rider of the time, some version of a fin-de-siècle Fabio was waiting on the other side of that hill.)

You crank open the throttle, advance the spark, give the hand oiler a few hard jabs (engines at this time, remember, had total loss lubrication), and lean over the handlebars. Your engine straining, thirty miles per hour becomes twenty, and twenty becomes ten, and you are ascending the hill now more as a result of momentum than power, and—smack in the middle—the engine putters away uselessly, puking out gobs of black, oily exhaust, and you hit the pedals.

Imagine pedaling a three-hundred-pound bicycle.

Did you ever ride a Schwinn Varsity, probably the most popular bike of all time in the United States? Fifty pounds, even without Schwinn's doodads fixed to it. And, remember, Schwinn manufactured motorcycles at this time, under the name Excelsior—the spitting image of the Pope you're on.

I don't think even Arnold Schwarzenegger could pedal a three-hundred-pound bicycle up the kind of incline found on roads during this period, and—given there was no standardized road grade—far greater than 20 percent grades were common for short distances.

Don't forget, either, that you're wearing those heavy boots, that waxed jacket, and the natty leather hat and goggles.

Ten or twenty heaves on those pedals and your heart is working away fit to burst (and many sedentary types did die pedaling those first motorcycles up hills), and now, too, you're sweating something awful. Your arms are shaking, your legs are rubber under you, and this is only for starters. I know, having pushed far too many dead bikes up slopes such as this, dirt bikes *and* road bikes. So, cursing the motorcycle, God, your flat feet, piles, and the fact that you so loved riding that you skipped your oatmeal, you dismount.

And thank God that you didn't take the main road as you thought you might, picking up Eugenia and coming at this hill with her on the back. No, some little voice warned you to give the hill a go solo first.

Now the real work begins. Grasping the bars, feet on the ground, you thrust the bike up the hill, foot by miserable foot, the bike threatening to fall on top of you, every heavy iron inch of it, or to fall on its (fragile) side away from you. Money's tight, and you've spent your last dime on this @#$*! motorcycle, and you have more than half yet to pay off (payment plans for motorcycles were typical at the time, which ministers and the like swore was the devil's work, the motorcycle itself being the devil's machine).

And at this point, it is all uphill. Fury. Disgust. Revulsion. Why, a colicky, splay-footed, out-to-pasture nag could get you up this hill faster than you're moving now, and in some degree of comfort.

Not even close to the top, you quit, shouting, GODDAMN POPE MOTORCYCLE! And you mean it.

You eye the crown of the hill. No way are you getting this boat anchor of a motorcycle over it.

And, in all circumstances, the rider maneuvered the bike around 180 degrees, and, supremely defeated (all Science, all popular Positive Thinking of the time and Love itself included in that defeat), coasted down the length of that slope that had been ascended largely by momentum. And when gravity had done her work, Nature (and pessimism, disease, and death) triumphant, the rider engaged the engine and puttered home, yet again enjoying, though now in a bittersweet way, the ride.

The *hill*, as you can see here, was *the* enemy. Singular, identifiable, towering over the rider and boasting superiority. The hill *begged* to be knocked down.

All early motorcycle advertising addressed hill-climbing ability. Whole societies of motorcyclists sprang up around hill climbing. There were, at this time, hundreds of them. And not just in the United States, but all over Europe as well. They had names like the Dungannon Club, of Dungannon, Ireland; the Bushkill Valley Club, of Centersville, Pennsylvania; and the Laconia Hillclimb Club of Laconia, New Hampshire. These clubs catered to a broad range of individuals, from the hobbyist well-to-do banker (by 1911, the San Francisco Motorcycle Club had swollen to more than five hundred members and included Mayor P. H. McCarthy in its ranks) to the high-mile postal worker who put in day after day on his Excelsior or Indian or Ace, which required Herculean effort, due to the bikes themselves.

All bikes at this time suffered two problems, which engineers were hard-pressed to remedy. First, a simple lack of power. The Pope Big 4, mentioned above, was so called because its engine was rated at four horsepower—which could have been (marginally) adequate but for a second problem: transmitting that power to the rear wheel in some effective manner. Automobiles of the time used devices incorporating complex bands to engage in succession gears in incremental ratios (exactly the design Henry Ford adopted, a decade or so later, with his profoundly successful and affordable Model T). These devices were called transmissions (they transmitted power).

So, given transmissions existed, what was the problem in adapting them to motorcycles? Realize that at this time Sturmey-Archer had not yet invented the multiple-speed bicycle hub, nor was the derailleur so much as a spark in some inventor's mind.

The problem, first of all, was in *materials*. Metallurgy and the present understanding of fluid dynamics prevented the design of more efficient engines, or lightweight transmissions suitable to smaller, cycle-sized machines. Ford's transmission worked as well as it did with the alloys he was using because, in his Model A, the transmission could be the size of a small suitcase, and there was no problem that it weighed 375 pounds.

Given the power that early motorcycle engines generated (the Pope Big 4 was a fire-breather for its time), any motorcycle had to be lightweight *and* of a size suitable to human use.

So most early motorcycles relied on a single leather drive belt, tightened with a pulley and lever. If coupled with a variable (centrifugal) drive hub at the crankshaft, this *could* have worked, *if* you could have tightened the belt sufficiently. But you could tighten leather only so much before it broke. So? Rubber cracked. And nylon and the light synthetics we take for granted today hadn't been invented (they didn't exist until the thirties), and, the simplest solution, a drive chain such as that used on a bicycle, or direct drive, made the motorcycle a machine from hell—every gulp, back-fire, and revolution of its engine was transmitted directly to the ground, also making the use of brakes while the machine was under power impossible.

Chain-driven motorcycles you could stop only by killing the engine, which, if they were moving, would cause the rear wheel to lock up, so the motorcycle skidded onto its side, along with the rider.

So these early hill climbers were stuck with machines that were, by their very design, the poorest climbers of hills, which made hills a quintessential challenge, one never to be experienced by us again in the same way again. (As with Hillary's ascent of Mount Everest. Since the introduction of lightweight and superior climbing equipment, scores of men and women have scaled Everest.)

It was the most archetypal of problems, *getting to the top*, and one of the easiest to measure. It happened or it didn't, which made good press. Manufacturers were desperate to mow down competition with proven superior performance, given, as mentioned earlier, at this time in the United States alone there were well over one hundred manufacturers of *motocycles* (Indian would continue to call its bikes *moto*-cycles until their demise). So manufacturers, desperate to sell their machines, were sending their bikes to hill-climbing competitions to set records.

One of these early competitions in the United States was the Pike's Peak International Hill Climb, the second oldest officially run major motorsports event in the United States, second only to the Indianapolis 500. An early record, set around 1916, got the rider and bike to the top in twenty minutes, fifty-five seconds, on a course with half the turns on it now. This year's fastest rider, Gary Trachy of Orange, California, got to the top in eleven minutes, forty-six seconds. To do this, Trachy reached speeds of 130 miles per hour, navigating 156 gravel turns on a course with 2,000-foot drop offs and no guardrails.

The first recorded *official* motorcycle hill climb took place at La Turbie, near Nice, France, on January 31, 1897. And the world's oldest continually staged motorsports event, the Shelsley Walsh, was held just years later in 1905, in Worcestershire, England, and is—you guessed it—a hill climb.

Given that successes in hill-climbing competitions guaranteed sales of motorcycles, manufacturers such as Indian, Harley-Davidson, Cyclone, and Flying Merkel had stables of paid riders. Some of these early hill climbers became legends, such as Smokin' Joe Petrali, Willard "Red" Bryan, and Orie "Irons" Steele. Steele competed from the earliest period, at the turn of the century, to become Indian's poster rider and advertisement during its golden years. In 1922, he won the nationals for Indian in Egypt, New York, and was so successful that Indian built, for the public, an Orie Steele Special. In 1926, Steele competed in forty-nine events and set twenty-two hill-climbing records.

By this time such advances had been made in metallurgy and engineering that Steele's factory hill climbers, running on methane, put out 70 horsepower at 9,000 rpm. So powerful were these bikes that all riders were required to have a "kill button" on their handlebars, a peg jammed into place by a small spring, the peg connected to the rider's wrist by a cord. If—or, more accurately, *when*—the rider was thrown from the machine, the cord pulled the peg and disconnected the ignition, cutting the engine. Experience had shown that these riderless bikes could, and did on earlier occasions, charge into the staging areas, causing fatalities among spectators.

Then, as now, this only fueled more interest in these motorcycles, and in the venue that showed them at their most brutish and refined—a thrilling combination in a culture obsessed with gadgets and technology.

So, from the inception of the motorcycle, hill climbing was a singular and popular (even family) form of event—you could always picnic, and still can, in the open area back of the "hill." And, as always, the riders—but the ride, too—were the stars, each generation of competitors employing current technology to build more ferocious bikes.

Early on, bikes and riders were inseparable, but by the 1950s the riders themselves took on the project of building better climbers. Shade-tree engineers, these climbers started with motorcycles built for street use (there were no dirt bikes as we know them now, and street bikes had the largest engines) and adapted them to tackle hills chosen to be *nearly* impossible to scale.

And in this way, the current, de rigueur design was arrived at by the late sixties, through Earl Bowlby, a Hall of Fame climber.

Bowlby, a dealer of British bikes, began experimenting with BSA motorcycles in 1967, but it wasn't until 1976 that, frustrated, he decided to get radical with a BSA 650. First, Bowlby extended the rear subframe, giving the bike an unprecedented eighty-four-inch wheelbase, making the bike nearly *ten feet* long. This was to prevent the motorcycle from flipping over backward. He then removed all the gears from the transmission with the exception of fourth, using the cavity as an oil reservoir. He gave the engine oversize, high-compression pistons (which he designed and had Venolia forge, bringing the displacement to 782 cc). The bike also had oversize carburetors, and the like, and in one last weight-saving gamble, Bowlby removed the rear brake and hub and installed, on the front wheel, a tiny brake to meet the rule that the bike have one at all. Bowlby's brake wouldn't have stopped a moped, much less this monster.

Running on nitro methane, the bike put out a good 120 or more horsepower, weighed 300 pounds, had one gear, the top gear, as do most open-class hill climbers now—and no (in any way effective) operating brake.

Earl Bowlby took his "rocket" to the nationals in Muskegon, Michigan, and on a near vertical slope that was as much mud as dirt, beat them all.

And with this same bike, he won races into the eighties, when the rocket exploded and Bowlby went looking for another machine to modify. It was, no surprise, another BSA.

After twenty-five years of competition, Bowlby retired in 1991—at the age of fifty-seven, that year the champion of the 800 cc pro class, and a legend, in his years of hill climbing having won ten national championships, a feat still unmatched.

And, over this century of competition, the hills themselves have become legends as much as the riders, their names alone intimations of the challenges riders face on them, hills such as the Devil's Staircase, in Oregonia, Ohio, or Poag's Hole, in Danville, New York, which is only 525 feet high, but with the top 200 at a 75-degree incline. You need climbing gear to get up Poag's Hole on foot. Or there is the hill outside Billings, Montana, where the Great American Championship Motorcycle Hill Climb is staged on the Rim, a 420-foot shale face that is actually vertical in some spots, so steep the competition pays "catchers" to tackle the bikes and riders when they fall, sometimes in midair.

But it is Utah's Widowmaker that has drawn the most attention as the singular monster hillclimb. Most AMA hills are 350 to 500 feet high and take six to eight seconds to climb. Widowmaker is 1,200 feet high, and a successful run to the top takes over forty seconds of full-on, breakneck climbing.

Originally held at Point of the Mountain south of Salt Lake City, on land owned by Skip Christiansen, the hill was so dangerous, only insurance coverage provided by the media giant ABC (*Wide World of Sports*) made the competition possible. One referee for the North American Hillclimbers Association, James Wenner, went on record saying, "It's a nightmare to get through the legalities of setting competitions up." Still, when ABC pulled out, another, even more daunting site was found on old mining property, and since then Widowmaker has been held in Croydon.

Where we are now, at the chain-link fence, talking to Gene. He's got a diffident, distracted air about him. And why shouldn't he? He's about to attempt to scale a forty- and sometimes sixty-degree slope nearly a half mile long through knee-deep sand and rocks on a two-wheeled berserker that has no rational reason to exist. Hill climbing *doesn't* sell motorcycles anymore, and manufacturers have withdrawn from any intentional involvement (or legal liability). The sport as it exists now is purely privateer—only manufacturers of performance parts sponsor riders, if they are sponsored at all.

Hill climbers simply love the sport. Says Robert, who has traveled from Washington to compete, "My next-door neighbor got me into it, and I just fell for it. I like how it gets your adrenaline rushing, big time."

Gene tugs at the plastic spine protector under his jacket, adjusts his likewise padded gloves and Thor (yes, a real brand) boots. Behind him a couple of hill climbers are joking: "How do you finish marriage," the first says. The second knows this joke and grins. "Death," he says, and the two toss back their heads and laugh.

Everywhere in the line bikers check fuel lines, talk of compression ratios and cams and carburetors, check rear tires—the *rear* tires on these bikes are "paddle tires," have hard rubber scoops on them, each the size of a cupped hand and spaced three or four inches apart around the circumference of the tire, or they're wrapped in chains like those used in snow.

Yet there are two things they *don't* talk about: No one mentions the *holy grail* of the climb, which is the *best line* to take (all riders by this time have quietly chosen the route, or line, they think will beat the hill). And no one mentions the *purse*: $38,000 is up for grabs today, in thirty different classes, for some 320 riders, the top, highest-paying classes being 540 cc, 800 cc, and "open." And even for those making it to the top of Widowmaker, granted any two riders do, only the fastest will walk away with the top purse, well over $10,000. The irony being that this $10,000 will only cover a small portion of what it costs to *maintain* bikes such as the ones these riders are on, much less buy or modify them for competition. So here, in hill climbing, the love of the sport and pride in winning carry the day.

For the last hour, riders have been attacking Widowmaker with bikes from 125 cc to 500 cc, but not one has gotten beyond the lowermost skirt of sand and rocks, and now, finally, the judges have given the signal for the open competition to begin and the crowd gravitates toward the fence.

A cadre of gear-wielding pit crew steps to the bikes and there is a commotion at the front of the line, preparations to get things under way. Gene, Mr. Death, is ten or so riders back.

There's time, which you spend talking to Laura, the Weber-Morgan (Croydon is in Morgan County) public health inspector. She's here to make sure that the fence will prevent dangerous boulders from tumbling down Widowmaker and crushing the spectators, that children aren't wandering around with cans of Budweiser, and that the public loos are in working order. Laura's son, just ten and brought along for the event, has, instead of being frightened by the mayhem, taken an alarming interest in it. He's all big eyes and points to his favorite rider, a guy in screaming white and neon pink, on his vest, *California Racers Edge*.

"It's just so—" and here Laura has to raise her voice over the roar of the bikes being started at the head of the line, a good two hundred feet distant "—*NOISY!*" She tussles her son's hair with an affection that is touching.

"I wanna do that," he shouts.

"I think I've created a monster," Laura says, and, turning her back to the bikes, cocking her head as if something has just occurred to her, she adds, "*You* haven't done this, have you?"

Yes, you tell her, you have.

What you don't tell her is that you and your pals found a site that served the dual purpose of both hill climb and jump—having as a distinctly unwise landing the asphalt parking lot of the Richfield, Minnesota, water purification plant. You discovered early on that if you hit the base of the hill at fifty, instead of climbing it from a standstill, you could not only "climb" the hill but also sail through the air where the hill ended. Nor do you tell her about your friend, just about her son's age, who made that jump exactly at the moment some irritated citizen decided to drive over and see if he could stop all the f'ing racket.

That's when my friend Paul came flying off the jump on his crappy little Honda 70. Sailing over Norm Vegan's green Plymouth Fury, he inspired Norm's full and total attention. Paul landed on his front wheel, bottomed out his (highly inadequate) front suspension, and was pitched over his handlebars to slide, for the most part on his head, across that asphalt, the bike skidding along behind him.

Paul's Kmart Easy Rider helmet saved his life, as did his springing up and getting on that awful motorcycle and roaring back to us, all of us at the top of the hill struck dumb and watching slackjawed, until Old Man Vegan, in an apoplectic fury, took a few steps in our direction.

Off we went, Paul (who needed only sixteen stitches to patch up his cheek) a hero of the order of Evel Knievel, each of us planning his legend-winning-to-be assault on the water-plant hill, which, of course, was just one of many hills in my dirt riding days. Little "Widowmakers" are every-where; give any normal kid a motorcycle and turn him loose and he'll find it in no time at all.

So, as to Laura's question about letting her son have a little dirt bike, asking if it would be "safe," you have to answer, with a raised eyebrow, "Only if you go riding with him."

And now the first open-class bike roars away from the starting line, the rider hunched Quasimodo-like over the handlebars. There'd be something cartoonish about it all, but the bike makes a percussive rap so earsplitting it strikes you like artillery fire, which makes you want to duck, even at a distance. When the rider hits the bottom of the hill, he makes for the gulley, because, at least initially, it has a shallow inclination, his strategy, we can all see, to gain speed, and where the gulley ends, at the three-hundred-foot mark (elevation, not distance), leap the gulley's shallow berm onto the right side of the hill.

This rider's line makes perfect sense, and there is an almost delectable delight in it, as in watching fireworks: *fuuuut!* goes the launch charge, and you follow the sizzling trail (here, the rear tire throwing out a plume of sand easily a block long), up, and up, and up they go, you wondering all the while what it will be, the coming explosion, and right where you'd have a star burst, or crackling daisy, or a simple *kaboom!* the rider hits the berm and, launched into the air, sails a good distance to land off balance, the bike contacting the hill with its rear tire, shooting forward so violently the rider is thrown off, the bike kicking and tumbling and roaring on the slope like something altogether insane—exactly the way each of us feels at certain times during the work week. But while we just smile, this thing lets it all out.

That's what hill climbing is all about. Letting it *rip*. There's a stone sober ferociousness about it. The biggest f'ing hill to be found, the mean-est motorcycle man can build and ride, all in a concoction *shaken*, not stirred.

The "catchers" get to the bike, which, due to the rider's having come off it, has stopped and now lies on a steep section of the hill. The rider is up, dusting himself off, first his knees (the fear is breaking your legs—if you can brush your legs with your hands, see, you already have your upper body covered). Then he has the bike, and—even granted this is one tough hombre—you can see he is wonky-legged from his fall. The adrenaline, when you've blown through the rush, leaves you limp all over, your heart galumping.

The height this first rider reached is about exactly that of the largest hill I ever made it up—the Burnsville Pit in Minneapolis. A—maybe—three hundred footer. My bike at the time? A 250 cc Maico knockoff (a Cooper, manufactured in Mexico). Tuned to the breaking point, 40 horsepower, coming on at the pipe around 4,000 rpm. A screamer.

Here is what hill climbing *feels* like.

You've got your full-coverage helmet on, which gives you the sense of being, marginally, protected, though a bit disconnected from your surroundings. If you use your peripheral vision, turn your head to either side, or glance back, there is a cavelike darkness in a full-face helmet. Still, your attention is so hyperfocused on the hill and your motorcycle that only a part of you is aware of the helmet anyway—or the gladiator gear you have on: motocross boots that go up to your knees, leather pants, leather jacket, leather gloves.

As explained earlier, highly modified engines put out peak horsepower in a narrow range of rpm. And two-stroke bikes (ring-dings), like the Cooper, are even more so that way. So you have a challenge. A big one. But it isn't as simple as sitting on the damn bike, cracking the throttle open, and aiming yourself at the hill.

First, there's the fear factor. If you were even hiking on this hill, you'd be very careful not to stumble, because if you did, you might fall all the way to the bottom going end over end. Now add to that the fear that, if you screw up (and I'll get to the averages of successful rides on sanctioned hills), you will have a two-hundred-pound-plus metal object falling on you at anywhere from fifteen to forty miles per hour.

Sound like fun?

So your only recourse is to tell yourself that *before* the bike falls on top of you, you will leap *backward, down the hill.*

Still sound like fun?

Now, here's the strategy part. Your engine makes peak horsepower only in a (for a two-stroke) very narrow band of rpm. With a bike like the Cooper, 4,000 to 6,000 rpm. If you let the revs drop, your bike's a lead sled, puts out about ten horsepower. And if you overrev, it will misfire and run erratically. Also no good.

You have, leading up to the foot of the hill, one hundred feet or so. To gain maximum momentum advantage approaching the hill, you want to work up as much speed as possible. So you want to shift (as you would in a car) in succession to the highest gear you can in that distance, right?

Dead wrong.

More important than anything is having both the momentum *and* the engine in its peak rpm range at *precisely the moment you reach the foot of the hill.* Once on the hill, you can *never* let the rpm drop below 4,000 or go above 6,000, which is hard to do because as soon as you are on the incline you have traction problems.

Sometimes, when you don't get it right, you're dead in the first fifty feet, all sound and fury and spinning rear tire (or bogged and powerless engine if you aren't "on the pipe"—turning "bread-and-butter" rpm). You have to ride the portion of the hill that will give you the best traction, but it must also allow you to maintain momentum. So, a *high-angle traverse* is best on the longest hills. Straight up, berserk on the short. On a surface that is sand, rocks, gravel, and sometimes mud.

So, hill climbing, you are always, in an intuitive way, aware of that old conundrum, one especially critical with motorcycles: *static or sliding friction?*

Which to employ?

If you opt for sliding friction, which provides infinitesimally less traction, you can get the revs up right from the start. At the starting line, you simply pop the clutch with the bike in a high gear—say, third—and propel yourself to the base of the hill with screaming power-band revs—the rear wheel spinning crazily under you. Even if this works (and sometimes it won't, the rider going over on his side before even reaching the hill), you have to time this sort of start perfectly, so the motorcycle is propelled (at peak rpm) by the spinning rear wheel (sliding friction) toward the hill, accelerating so that when you reach the bottom leg of the hill there is again a near one-to-one relation between the tire and hill surface and revolutions of the engine—and the bike in the gear ideally suited for climbing. The rider will, if he/she is lucky, stay in this gear the entire, screaming ride up the hill (granted sufficient power).

It's a tricky start, but all sorts of riders use it, especially those with smaller-displacement bikes. Tricky and effective.

The static friction method, unlike the high-gear start, necessitates up-shifting to the hill (keeping the rear wheel in a one-to-one relation to the dirt), and on the first part of the incline, *downshifting* to keep the rpm in the engine's peak power band. The problem here is this: As the bike loses momentum and the engine propels the bike up the hill, each fraction of a second used in shifting—even when the rider "speed shifts," shifts without the clutch—creates not only a gap in the delivery of power, but also a concomitant jolt of sufficient force to break a usable ratio of tire-to-hill surface traction (rarely is it one-to-one with dirt bikes). Or, in biker's language: The tire breaks loose from the hill and the engine revs are all over the place.

In this sort of situation the run is finished, the rider and bike flopping over onto the steep slope and, sometimes, tumbling down a good distance.

But, again, here is what it *feels* like—at the starting line, blood thumping in your head and neck, you sit high on your bike, gripping the handlebars, which are roughly a yard wide, waiting for the nod from the flagman. When he gives the signal, you press sharply *down* on the shift lever with the toe of your left boot (all motorcycles now have this "down for slow, up for go" pattern) until you're in first (at the "bottom" of the pattern), then, with your toe under the lever, "pull smartly up," as the Brits put it, once through neutral, and again into second, then third. You're after a high-gear start. A sliding friction start. You're in third gear now, and ready to rock and roll. This bike, set up as it is, will do zero to forty in two seconds. You'll be doing thirty when you get to the hill.

The hill rises up in front of you like a pitted yellow wall—it's that steep. You're going to hit it as hard as you can. You blip the throttle, and when the flag is raised, you crack open the throttle, the engine, right there between your legs, roaring like some monstrous chain saw that could blow your balls off. When the flag comes down you drop the clutch, and the engine, turning at 6,000 rpm, tears the rear wheel loose, so it is spinning at fifty miles per hour, propelling the bike toward the hill as if you were shot out of a cannon. When you reach the hill, the force of that forward motion is translated into upward motion and slams you down on top of the bike, but you're braced for it. If you weren't, your head would bang into the cross-piece of your handlebars, splitting open like a melon.

On the hill, the bike is pitched so steeply under you that you hang from the handlebars for dear life, trying to maintain your weight somewhere front of center. The engine roars, you clinging to the bike while you are pounded, rodeo-rider-like—in this mind-altered state, time, now, longer and cavernous—steering around rocks, avoiding deep sand, but always aware of the engine. If the revs drop, you'll have to make a last-save shift into second gear.

The bike wants to jet out from under you, and you press yourself to it, punish it for all you're worth, keeping the engine right on the pipe no matter how much the bike bangs up under you, jerks from side to side, or crow hops. At times the bike so pounds you that your vision is blurred and you ride entirely by feel.

The top of the hill is usually the steepest portion, the worst, and you're aiming for it like something you'd pull yourself over, chin-up style. You're almost there, knees pressed to the tank, the machine throbbing with this explosive vibration, and then, just when you think you've got it, you catch a rock (or hit a soft spot, a gulley, anything) and the bike is jerked out from under you, and even as you're coming off it, you throw yourself in the opposite direction to land hard, knocked absolutely silly.

In a second, and it is one very long second, you cock your head (neck's all right), huck your shoulders, test your hands, then jump to your feet. A handler has your bike and is walking it across the steep slope to pass it off to you.

And like that, your legs Jell-O under you (nearly collapsing from adrenaline deficit), you get your bike, and while you are working it down through the brush, another rider has a go at the hill. At the bottom you get a score card: 250 feet (of elevation), in . . . beginning to end, six seconds.

What's remarkable about this is: For 99.99 percent of riders, a hill climb such as just described would be *more* than plenty.

These days, most nonpro riders hill climbing (give-it-a-rip hill climbers such as I was) will be on bikes with equivalent to double the displacement of my Cooper. *Stock bikes* with forty to sixty horsepower, more than enough to overpower any unseasoned rider. However, when compared to machines such as these pro open-class hill climbers are riding?

It not only boggles the mind but makes one wonder just how nuts do you have to be to do this? But then, of course, these riders started smaller too.

Now, here at Widowmaker, ten open-class riders have hurled themselves at the hill, these climbers trying new and untracked lines up the sandy, rocky mountainside, each roaring from the starting line, then climbing under traction, but soon riding on a plume of ocher sand to crash, flying, a little above the three-hundred-foot mark. These riders use the high-gear start (their bikes have only that one high gear), jet out of a starting box filled with sand.

Gene, soon to run, nods for his pit crew. They step in with a car starter and batteries on a dolly, such as you'd use to move a refrigerator. The starter has a socket on the end, and the crew fit it to the left side of Gene's modified Harley engine. With a grinding *whir whir whir*, Gene astride the bike, the Harley comes alive with an earsplitting roar. The sound it makes is nothing short of *magnificent*—a hollow, throaty bellow with a crackle in it, each combustion so powerful that even standing yards from the bike, you feel the whole range of revolutions like little fingers palpating your body head to toe. And this Harley engine runs the rpm range almost spontaneously.

And *if* that little voice in you wondered when you were at the starting line whether your Cooper might blow your gonads off, here there is no doubt. This thing is such contained ferocity, something tells you, that if it came apart, it'd blow the rider, you, and the spectators to bits. Which, given the forged con rods and such that modifiers use in building these engines, never happens. Not the explosion. Rather, the counterbalanced and catastrophic cracking and shearing of engine internals. But it *feels—* absolutely—as if this thing *might* explode. You intuitively fear something this . . . volcanic.

It's a scary piece of work, but you, being the motorcyclist you are, wonder: Hmmm, could *I* handle that?

This bike's a bit like that atomic bomb Slim Pickens straddles out of the B-52 in *Dr. Strangelove*, riding it like a bronco down into old Russia, and the end of the world, hollering, "Yeeeeeehaaaaaaa!"

*That* is the spirit of hill climbing.

Gene, with a blunt nod, heads out. At the starting line he's given the raised flag, and when it comes down he's off in a roar so loud it echoes the length of Croydon's little valley. Up he goes, taking the gulley, that characteristic plume of ocher sand behind him, twenty feet high and a block long. Then Gene's over the lip and making S turns around boulders, passing the four-hundred-foot mark, then the five hundred, and just like that—*whump!*

Down he goes into a shallow gulley, the bike so powerful that, obstructed, it tosses out gouts of sand, the wind blowing the sand back onto the hill so the rider and bike can't be seen—not until the dust clears. To the crowd's disappointment, the hill climber stopped right there. Still, he has climbed the highest yet. Five hundred feet. But given the height of the hill, it is at most disappointing. Is that *all* the distance anyone's going to make it up this thing? Less than *halfway?*

There's a peculiar aspect to a hill climb that makes it unlike other motorcycle competition events: as mentioned before, a hill climb really is a *family* event. And now everyone at this point catches up on gossip, the kids throw Frisbees, adults throw balls to dogs, the bikers joke and cackle, but everyone is aware of each rider throwing himself at Widowmaker and *failing.*

Up, up, up they go—Gee, did you hear about Candy's divorce? Old Bobby was stepping out on her . . . There is a crowd-wide, sideways attention. It's just fun, a hill climb, people watching (exactly as they watch fireworks), having a drink, and there is conjecture now, too, among the officials, and the crowd in general, that maybe the face of Widowmaker is too sandy to be scaled. Perhaps earlier hill climbs here have softened it too deeply. Maybe it *is* just truly impossible today?

Still, all eyes turn to the hill if a rider nears the five-hundred-foot mark. And there is this group wishing for, wanting, hoping the rider will make it beyond that, or even to the top. It's odd, really, but it's the classic underdog situation:

Damn Widowmaker is beating the shit out of the riders, and, by god, we want to see somebody give it back.

The crowd's looking for a hero.

It's as if the impossible dream has manifested itself in the form of this towering hill, a giant each and every one of us knows.

Goddamn fucking hill. Said an acquaintance of mine, Dag Aabaye: "When there are no mountains to climb, you may as well hang it up." He wasn't talking about physical mountains.

Getting to the top here becomes the materialization of the whole human problem: We can't *truly* live without challenges. But true challenges, by their very nature, are life-threatening, or status-quo-threatening, or ego-threatening. (Friedrich Nietzsche, the philosopher, claimed we define ourselves through opposition—through challenge.) This is why the hill chosen for the competition is so *nearly* impossible. It has to be, or climbing it would be insignificant.

Still, in the sun, and with an unhappy lassitude beginning to settle over the crowd, the rider that the health inspector's son noticed earlier, in white and neon pink, the *California Racers Edge* rider, pushes his bike toward the front.

You've lost count of the number of hill climbers who have fallen, easily fifty or sixty, as the average run to the three-hundred-foot mark takes all of six seconds or so. Only two have made it to five hundred. All, without exception, have fallen less than halfway up.

So who cares about this rider? He's on a solid-enough-looking dirt bike, with those enormous sand scoops on the rear tire.

The engine in it is a Kawasaki 1000, bored out to 1,428 cc (you can read this on his gas tank) and modified to the breaking point. You'd be afraid to ride this thing if it were a street bike: it would do the quarter mile in, maybe, nine seconds. Zero to 150 in three blocks. It must put out around 220 to 230 horsepower.

Unlike the Harley, it's not pretty, this engine. It's spray-painted matte black, square as a breadbox. A transverse four-cylinder. Here, this hill climber's home engineering is nearly the match of that employed by world-class speed racers, such as those you meet at, say, Black Rock or the Bonneville Salt Flats, where shade-tree engineers squeeze explosive performance from otherwise everyday machines.

When the pit crew starts the bike, it makes a harsh, almost gnashing sound—*ugly*, but awesome—which sets your teeth on edge.

Still, if people are watching now, they're watching with distraction. It's a bit like that scene in Breugel's painting *Landscape with the Fall of Icarus*, with Icarus falling, as the poet Auden put it in his poem "Musée des Beaux Arts," out of the sky, and the ship, having "somewhere to get to," sailing "calmly on."

At the starting line, revving, the bike sounds like some four-stroke version of a Texas Chainsaw Massacre McCullough.

Then the flag is down.

Away this hill climber goes, kicking out a rooster tail of dirt, navigating to the right of the gulley. Then he is around it, passing the three-hundred-foot marker, then the four hundred, the bike not slowing one iota. Then he's past the five hundred, and the whole crowd begins to rise, and there are hundreds of thrilled voices, "Hey, hey, will you *look* at that!" they say, this rider now on a high traverse of the steepest section, seven hundred feet, eight hundred, the bike roaring like some dragon, the rider hard put over it, nine hundred feet, the plume of sand it's spitting out nearly the length of the hill, one thousand feet, eleven hundred, and there is this horrible lip there . . . he couldn't *possibly* get over that—here the wind blows into the hill, the bike obscured by dust for what seems an eternity, the crowd wondering, Will this end as it did with the Harley? This bike buried up to its rear axle and stuck?

And, just then, a rooster tail of ocher dust jets off the top to the right and the crowd roars. There, on the top, the rider makes a show of it, fist raised, victorious.

All in forty-two seconds. Thrilling. What was impossible is now possible.

And here the crowd settles into itself, supremely happy, and the hillclimbing competition goes on.

Up, and up, and up and *crash*!

By the time you leave Widowmaker (they're still riding when you do), nearly three hundred competitors have had at the "hill."

Only *two* have been successful.

Which, in fact, is just . . . *perfect*. There is no doubting that you've seen something extraordinary here.

And riding home, a sense of possibility lifts your spirits like a song. Your bike burbles reassuringly, and when you reach a steep section of I-84, an all of 6 percent grade, you downshift and roll on the throttle. The bike surges, climbing, in it a sweet, elastic burst of power, but you're already thinking: What would a junkyard Kawasaki 1000 engine cost? And a 250 cc dirt bike with a blown motor? A little elbow grease, some wrenching and welding, and a whole lotta crazy . . .

Widowmaker could be yours, too.

# 7

# At the Last, Fastest Place on Earth

## SALT FEVER

**E**ven Hollywood couldn't create a place like this.

The light as you step from your truck is blinding. In every direction you turn, the salt, a shocking white, stretches without blemish, so far into the distance that you can discern the curvature of the planet.

You've come here to this seeming end of the earth place to see men do end-of-the-earth things.

You kick your feet under you. The salt is coarsely crystalline and porous. With the toe of your boot you can jam up ridges of the salt and, stepping squarely on it, compress it again to a surprising rock hardness. The salt is wet underneath, hard on top.

At the sound of what appears to be an airplane, you lift your head, but all you can see is a jumble of colorful spots on the distant horizon, red, blue, yellow, shimmering in the heat haze. Off to the left floats a ridge of craggy ocher mountains. Just after eight in the morning, it is already ninety degrees. Perfect conditions, you've been told.

Surreal, but real.

"Well," your friend Bill says, "you ready?"

Out on the salt are the anointed world-class motorcycle speed crazies you've come to meet. And this year, the big dogs are duking it out for the top spot. That's the buzz. History is going to be made here, on the salt. Today, tomorrow, the next day.

On motorcycles.

That is what you heard: not an airplane, but a motorcycle making a run out on the flats. They're right in front of you, at it already. Nonstop.

You hesitate a moment, taking in the flats one last time. There is something breathtakingly austere about the place. Spectral. Awesome. Beautifully barren and, oddly, inspiring.

Here is *the* Bonneville of legend. The place makes you feel a little crazy, all right. But in a good way. It is a place you have to either pass through, or, staying, however briefly, fill with something.

Crazy, obsessed people seem just the right thing for that. People with Salt Fever.


Mile after mile you rumble in on the salt, the tabletop-flat stretch on which the racing is done.

At the entrance, you show your press passes. Here there's a complex security system, timing towers three stories tall, pennants flying from them, and even a private radio station, Radio Free BUB, that covers each ride.

At no point do the racers let up. They roar by on either side, slung over their machines like melted glass.

You've got your radio tuned to hear the results. The announcer sounds a bit like an auctioneer, rambling off numbers and names and statistics. The big dogs are going to run last. But who they might be, of all these enthusiasts in front of you, two or three hundred of them parked in the salt median, you can't tell. It's a jumble of colorful machines and people.

You'd expected to find a collection of nuts like you met at Widowmaker here at the BUB International Speed Trials, but driving into the parking area, you don't seem to see any. No Gene with a skull tattooed on his shoulder. No one wearing a Big Cock racing suit. No Beer Racing decals.

The whole setting, rather, strikes you as being akin to a medieval jousting tournament. Everywhere, around and under tents with professionally made banners flying over them, the banners reading *Gates Engineering, Red Line Oil,* or *Western Biodiesel, Inc.,* crews of mechanics and engineers, and financiers, and owners, riders, and designers are bent over machines. There's a range of them—from the homemade and cobbled-together ugly 666 special to your left, to the silver-gray BSA Rocket on a trailer behind a '53 Rolls-Royce Phantom. In the very air is the tang of burned oil, scorched metal, and melted plastics and fiberglass and neoprene.

Still, it all looks like money. Even the oddball motorcycles. Big money. Or barring that, serious hours of labor, thousands of man hours.

No family outing, this is a class affair of obsessed individuals, and their obsession is speed, which you can see already translates into Buy It, or Make It, or both. There's a joke out on the salt flats. How fast do you want to go? And the answer? How much money do you have?

*Brrrrrrrooooooooooommmmmm!* Another bike dopplers by to your left, what looks like a box-stock UJM (Universal Japanese Motorcycle).

"A hundred thirty?" you say.

"We'll see," Bill says, both of you listening to the radio.

Kawasaki Ninja: 149.65.

"Wow," you say.

Bill stops the truck. You've left the camper at an intersection of two roads onto the flats, so you're free to park and meet these folks (without looking like Billy Bob and his cross-eyed cousin). Though, in the crush of it now, you notice the preponderance of straw cowboy hats, broken down, oil-stained, cockeyed from use. You wonder where that salt tradition came from. Racers, crew, and owners wear them. Most are staying in West Wendover, on the Nevada side, where gambling is legal and anything goes.

You've designated Bill as your official photographer, so you can talk freely with the nuts, the first of which you meet being a ghost (very nearly).

Two men pull short of you, towing a trailer with a tricked-out Harley Sportster on it. While the bikes at intervals minutes apart roar by to your left, there's the usual how-you-doin' talk, where'd you come from, and an exchange of names. Terry and Mike, from Reno. By this time Bill and I have stepped out of our truck to look at the Harley, which, at a glance, is badly damaged.

"What happened?" Bill asks, a jovial humor in his voice. His warm, down-home drawl makes it possible to get away with asking just about anything.

It's pretty obvious what happened. The bike is a pretzel, the front-wheel hub is bent back to the bike's left footpeg and the paint has been scoured off one side. What is surprising is how the salt has caked around the engine. Prior to coming here, you were assuming the salt would have the texture of sand near the waterline (Daytona Beach was the choice for speed racing before Bonneville), but it doesn't. At all. Nor is this salt like that in your salt shaker. These crystals pack together, having the hardness of new cement. It takes a two-handled drill and a half-inch bit to penetrate this surface, which is anywhere from six inches to six feet thick. It's coarse, rough stuff. When you force a piece of it over the back of your hand, it takes the skin right off. Nice. It's a little scary, actually, because it begins to dawn on you what this surface would do to your body if you fell on it at speed, even wearing leathers. So the most striking image in your mind of motorcycle speed racing at Bonneville, that of Rollie Free setting the motorcycle speed record, naked but for a pair of tight-fitting swimming shorts and tennis shoes, takes on new significance. That guy, you think now, was bona fide *crazy* to do that.

Bill gives Terry that querulous look of his. "So, how fast was he goin'?" he says.

There is a certain cheerful animation in Terry's lashing the ruined Sportster to the trailer.

"Crashed at one twenty-six."

This is something you immediately encounter on the salt flats: no confusion or uncertainty about speed. An international, American Motorcycle Association–approved contingent of timing fiends measures speeds here, down to a thousandth of a second. So it's not a little over 100, or 120, or even 125. It's 126. And if you asked, Terry would give the remainder of the figure he surely knows.

"What happened?" you ask. You're fairly certain the friend riding the bike isn't dead, given Terry's grin, nor permanently injured—so this is all becoming the stuff of an entertaining story.

"Well," Terry says, "we trailered the bike in with some others, and Al flew in last night. Made a party of it, and Al was taking Benadryl or something for allergies. Something out here just got to him. And he wasn't used to the heat, either, riding to the flats, and he was over there at the Run What You Brung, waiting an hour or so in the sun, and—"

"Run What You Brung?" Bill says. Somehow, nearly everything he says is an amusement, though, being a geologist and engineer, he's no slow study.

"You ride it in, run it as it is." Terry nods to himself. "A Suzuki did nearly one seventy this morning. A woman. Pretty, too."

"That's somebody I want to meet," I tell him.

"Just head down the fairway," Terry says with a wave of his arm, "you can't miss her. Or her competition. They're right there with the big three."

"The big three?" you ask.

"Bub-lucky-ack-attack-eezee-hook," Terry says, grinning. Or at least you think that's what he said. You know BUB is the . . . is it a name for the organization running the show here? Is BUB like, Hey, Bub! as in . . . Friend? Amigo? Compadre? Or is it an acronym? But then, for what? Best? Better? Universal? . . . And there you think, Forget it. You can't think of anything remotely to do with engineering or motorcycles that could come out of BUB. Yo, BUB, your mother wears army . . .

Again, a bike flies by, though this time to the right, in the world-record lane, louder, and at a speed that turns heads, the gist of that story passed up the line of spectators in seconds.

"V-rod," Terry says. "Through the timing mile at 170.7 miles per hour. That's Bud Schmidt. A guy that's almost . . ." What did Terry say, *eighty* years old?

And did Terry really say "Bubluckyackattackeasyhook"? Or was it something else? And at that you grin, for Terry. Whatever!

Terry smiles, aware of just how not-of-the-salt you are at this moment. How little you know! his smile says, and, possibly: Clueless, outsider, and maybe even—and most important—moron! Which prevents you from asking him to elaborate. About Bud Schmidt or the Bub-yacka-hook-what-chamacallit. Like hell, you'll ask. You'll find out elsewhere, that's for damn sure.

Bill nods at the bike and Terry gets back to it.

"So," he says, "Al heads down the track on the bike, seems to be doing fine, only, when he went by you could see he was anything but, his head hanging off to one side. Passed out right about the four-mile mark, took a wobble, and went over. Slid over a quarter of a mile."

That, considering what I've just discovered about the salt, is a sobering thought. Here, in this Sportster, is the embodiment of what a crash can do to cast iron and forged steel, much less flesh and bone.

"How'd he do?"

"Only went through his leathers in a few places. Graft some skin off his rear end, get him hydrated, let him rest off a pretty severe concussion, and he should be fine. Get right back to it next year." Terry shows us his teeth. He's not kidding. "Salt fever," he says. "You know."

And already you do *sort of* know—

On the way in, you counted off the mile markers where the racing is done. The motorcycles are timed from mile marker four to five. The racecourse is eleven miles long, the whole area covering about 160 square miles, adjacent to Interstate 80. This spectacularly barren area is the flattest length of hard surface on earth. Just looking at it makes you itch to crack the throttle open, whether it might kill you or not.

From the time you got on your first motorcycle, you've taken each and every bike you've gotten your hands on to its very limit. Some rides have been particularly memorable, you lying over the gas tank, teeth chattering, the engine threatening to explode and throw metal parts through your heart—like that tweaked Tecumseh powered mini bike, which, maybe, did 50 mph, but then you were ten at the time and riding in sand. Then the Suzuki Duster 125, which, if you really tucked in on it, would do 75 or 80 out on Highway 62, but that in the middle of the night, since you were only fourteen and had no driver's license and no training. At fifteen, the Kawasaki 750, which your friend and you rolled out of his garage in the middle of the night, your friend's brother's bike, which he'd stolen the keys to, and which you had no business riding, the bike doing 130 out on I-35. There was the BSA Rocket A-75 you rebuilt, which, roaring like some otherworldly monster on Highway 61, did 140. And finally, the Ducatis you rode and owned, those Ducatis taking you just short of 150, but feeling so good at speed they had you navigating 30-mile-per-hour clovers at 80, then cracking the throttle and weaving through traffic at 90 or 100, this "bite the wire" intoxication in the hammering pulse of the L-twin engine. But always, the bike was the built-in limitation, and you are, privately, thankful that machines like the Ducati 1098 or Suzuki Hayabusa didn't exist when you were in your teens and early twenties. You wouldn't be here, at Bonneville, if they had been.

Still, running at speed over miles of terrain is not like running up to speed and backing off. And on highways, you just never have enough space to roll it on and hold it there. So you wonder. Just what would that be like? To ride ten miles at flat-out, gut-wrenching top speed?

"One twenty-six," you say.

"One twenty-six," Terry replies, and with a nod, away you and Bill wander, to the border of the Run What You Brung track, which is laid out parallel to, and about two blocks distant from, the World Record track. Here friends, family, and nervous significant others watch riders attempt to set new records just out from the line of cars and trucks bordering mile four.

After asking around about the Run What You Brung class, you find that a version of the bike you were riding last fall, a Ducati ST4, did 168 mph earlier this morning. Now some little voice in you says, Think what *you* could do with that ST4 here! Which is what you start doing after having spent any time on the salt flats. You think speed. Imagine speed. You get the salt fever.

It's in the very air. At Bonneville, late August to early September, the racing never stops. But then, that's how it's been here for well over a century.

## Salt Movers and Shakers

It was W. D. Rishel, engineering a racing course for bicycles from New York to San Francisco in 1896, who first saw the potential for speed racing at the Bonneville Salt Flats.

Native Americans as early as ten thousand years ago occupied the Great Basin area, adapting to its harsh climate and inhospitable soil and topography. Jim Bridger and others bushwhacking trails to the Pacific coast recorded exploring the salt flats as early as 1824. And Captain B. L. E. Bonneville's expedition mapped the Salt Lake basin in the 1830s, his chief lieutenant on that expedition, Joseph Walker, naming the flats after his boss, even though, curiously enough, Bonneville himself never set foot anywhere near them. Also of interest: Thomas Paine, famous for his War of Independence patriotism, but more so for his rousing rhetoric of the time, had been Bonneville's mother's paramour and was rumored to be Bonneville's father. Washington Irving, remembered for his stories "The Legend of Sleepy Hollow" and "Rip Van Winkle," chronicled Bonneville's expedition to the salt flats in *The Adventures of Captain Bonneville*.

Others, too, whose names went down in history, visited. Kit Carson was one of the first to actually cross the salt flats, with Captain John C. Fremont's survey party. Soon after, Lansford Hastings retraced the Fremont route, and against the advice of Fremont, Carson, and Walker convinced a westward-bound group of settlers to take what had come to be known as the "Hastings Cutoff" through the flats. The Donner Party, as it came to be called, did not have sufficient water for the crossing, and after losing necessary oxen, they were delayed. Even abandoning four of their wagons couldn't sufficiently speed them. Entering the Sierra Nevada mountains weeks later than they'd anticipated, they were caught in an early snowstorm that stranded them in the Sierras without sufficient supplies. When those supplies were gone, they "fell upon themselves," as one historian put it. (The meat between them ribs is good eatin', Cal! Try a bite, won'cha?)

So inhospitable were the salt flats thought to be that it wasn't until the Southern Pacific Railroad was built in 1910, linking Salt Lake City and San Francisco, that "motor enthusiasts" considered the area for speed racing. And even given rail development, crossing the flats was problematic. First of all, a good part of every year they flooded, as they do today. Each winter nearly a foot of water covers the entire surface. Around the last ice age, Lake Bonneville was the size of Lake Michigan and covered nearly one third of what is now Utah. In places the water was a thousand feet deep. When on the salt flats, you can still make out the high-water marks in the surrounding mountains. Here, the encompassing land formation has been likened to a colossal bathtub, the eons-old marks the grubby rings left by bathing giants.

This water was a problem for the Southern Pacific. While Salt Lake City had been chosen to be the railroad's Rocky Mountain hub, engineers found that it was nearly impossible to keep the tracks from sinking. As a result, the hub in Salt Lake City was not developed as had been planned, and a new one was established in Denver.

But what was a problem for the railroad, the water, now makes the Bonneville Salt Flats *the* location for world speed attempts over all others, particularly El Mirage in California, Black Rock in Nevada, and Lake Gairdner in Australia. Sure, due to the water, the flats are usable only a few months of the year, at the close of the blistering Utah summer when the temperatures hover around one hundred. Still, it is the water that floods this vast surface every winter, and evaporating, leaves a billiard-table-smooth, inches-thick crust of salt that makes the flats a perfect surface for racing. Think of that water as nature's Zamboni. In years when the water evaporates early, and there is little rainfall late in summer, the flats are ideal.

Yet, even given this, the salt flats can be treacherous. As already mentioned, the heat can knock you senseless. Imagine wearing, neck to toe, a leather suit in blinding sunshine, in hundred-degree heat, with your head encased in a padded helmet and your hands in padded gloves, your feet and lower legs in heavy motorcycle boots that rise to—or over—your knees. Then consider straddling some version of a two-wheeled heat-seeking missile powered by a radically tuned internal-combustion engine. Remember, the average internal-combustion engine converts about 30 percent of the fuel it burns into mechanical energy; the remainder becomes heat. An average peak-performance engine running on nitro methane burns fuel at ten times the rate of a gasoline-powered engine. Ever popped the hood of your car when it's hot? Multiply that times ten, and put that engine in some low-riding motorcycle. Hop on! Straddle that engine! Take a ride!

But to return to W. D. Rishel and his discovery of the flats for racing—*bicycle* racing. You might be wondering, given the water, the heat, the (early) inaccessibility of the salt flats, What was anyone doing out there, much less a bicycle racer?! Was he simply out of his mind?

And why did Rishel choose Bonneville, and not Daytona Beach, given that by this time Daytona had been developed as a resort area and offered miles of hard sand for speed racing? Why? And in 1894?

The answer? William Randolph Hearst. Hearst, wanting to improve the circulation of his newspapers, engineered a publicity stunt wherein a message would be sent by bicycle courier from his office at the *New York Journal* to his office at the *San Francisco Examiner*. It would be a race with an enormous purse and publicity for the winner.

Recall that bicycles were the rage in the Gay Nineties. (And recall that motorcycles were an outgrowth of that rage.) Bicycle racers were stars. Hearst hired two well-known riders of the time, Rishel and Charles A. Emise, to plot the route for his race across the west. Rishel, who'd gotten hold of an old prospector's map, chose to cross the Rocky Mountains and Continental Divide at the Bonneville Salt Flats. To avoid the terrible heat of that portion of their route, Rishel and Emise left on their crossing at two a.m., traveling at the very brisk rate of twenty miles per hour—until they hit the mud, on the periphery, and were forced to carry their bikes, the salt crossing taking Rishel and Emise twenty-two torturous hours—which, oddly enough, became the story Hearst used to sell his newspapers. The results of the later contest, and the message the winning rider delivered? All lost to time.

Strange? Not in Salt Flats history.

An equally unlikely motivation propelled the first motorcyclist (and motorist, for that matter) to cross the salt. When abstemious lawmakers ruled that a fight between the boxers James Jeffries and Jack Johnson, scheduled to take place in Salt Lake, would be illegal, the promoters simply moved the fight to Reno. The now-famous David Abbott "Ab" Jenkins, not about to miss out on the match, took his motorcycle to the flats, a large part of which he crossed (the mud in particular) by riding on the railroad ties of the new Southern Pacific line. Jenkins later said riding those ties was like being a "bronco-busting cowboy."

A decade and some years later, Jenkins would go on to set a world speed record on the salt flats in his car, the *Mormon Meteor*, which, in turn, would bring out world-class challengers, such as Sir Malcolm Campbell, inaugurating the high-dollar duels that continue on the flats to this day.

But, it was Rishel, the bicycle racer, who became the first promoter of the salt flats as a motor-racing site. In 1910 he returned, convincing his friend Ferg Johnson to take his Packard onto the salt, where they "let her rip," Rishel later saying of his and Johnson's white-knuckle experience, " . . . the velocity of the car was fantastic. When we reached the horizon it seemed as though we would topple off into nothingness."

Two years later, Rishel brought A. L. Westgard of the National Highways Association to Bonneville for a few fast rides on the salt, and Westgard responded by declaring Bonneville "the greatest speedway on Earth."

And there was the birth of true salt fever.

## True Grit: Bona Fide Salty Dogs

While, understandably, a number of aristocratic figures are best remembered for their exploits at Bonneville—particularly the Brits Sir Malcolm Campbell and Captain George Eyston—others, through ingenuity and drive and obsession, have made their mark, especially in motorcycling.

One such was Glenn Curtiss, who founded the Curtiss Aeroplane and Motor Company. Long before he was known for his interest in airplanes, Curtiss was an avid motorcyclist and speed enthusiast. In 1907 he decided to break the world speed record, so bolted a V8 blimp engine of his own design and manufacture into a motorcycle. Curtiss, stretched out over the engine, set a record on his first run. That record, 136.36 mph, would not be beaten by a motorcycle for twenty-three years.

Many riders set records in the decades after Curtiss, but none so notably as Rollie Free, who, arguably, to this day has been the most visible of any—literally (and figuratively, pun intended). Somehow, of all the photos taken of riders attempting to break the world motorcycle speed record, it is that of Free, naked but for a pair of "swim trunks" and beach shoes, lying on a Vincent HRD Black Shadow while crossing the salt flats, that has captured for the public the Bonneville spirit.

Invariably, a caption puts the event in even sharper focus: "Rollie Free, Setting World Motorcycle Speed Record, 1948. 150.313 miles per hour." Or some such.

And what kind of nut would do something like that?

Free, who got his first motorcycle when he was twelve, grew up around bikes, going on to sell Ace motorcycles for the O.K. agency in Kansas City, and later Indians at Al Crocker's. Much to the consternation of rival Harley-Davidson, while at Crocker's, Free earned the reputation as the fastest street racer on two wheels, which, of course, sold more than a few Indians over Harleys. Free later raced long-distance events, such as the two-hundred-mile in Jacksonville, Florida, and he competed in the inaugural Daytona 200 in 1937. During World War II, Free enlisted in the air force and was stationed at Hill Field in Utah, a hundred miles from the Bonneville Salt Flats, which he visited. So when, after the war, the Hollywood sportsman John Edgar asked Free to come out to Bonneville to make a speed-record attempt on a Vincent, Free was more than enthusiastic. On his first run, he beat the eleven-year-record held by Joe Petrali (of hill-climbing fame), turning in a speed of 148.6 mph.

For most people, that would have been enough, but Free, thinking his leather suit was creating wind resistance, decided to strip down to swim trunks and shoes and lie on the bike with his head down to create less resistance to break the 150 mph barrier. Steering by following the black stripe on the salt under his bike, Free was clocked by recording equipment at 150.131 mph, riding into motorcycling history.

Free joked later: "I stole the swimming trunks idea from Ed Kretz, who used to do the same on Southern California dry lakes. Incidentally, Ed looks much nicer in a swim suit than I do."

Some "salt" characters have garnered no place in public history, as did Curtiss and Free, but are—deservedly—known to fellow racers with the fever. One such character was R. L. "Bud" Schmitt. A drag racer from Indiana, Schmitt took his dual-engined "Monster" to the salt in 1955 and hit a one-way speed of 157.2 mph, breaking Free's 1950 record, which had stood for five years. On that run Schmitt burned a piston, so he couldn't make the return (opposite direction) run for the record.

Schmitt, just short of eighty, has come to the salt to celebrate the fiftieth anniversary of his "unofficial" record, but even more so to surpass that former record, which he'll try to do on a tweaked V-Rod, supplied by his friend Dan Bell, owner of Eagle Harley in Lafayette, Indiana.

Bud, you discover talking to him, is an incredible character. His first motorcycle, he tells you, was a Hawthorne balloon-tired bicycle with an Iron Horse washing machine engine (needed in rural areas before electrification) bolted to the back. The motor drove a propeller, carved by Bud from a two-by-four. Says Bud, "If you had a tail wind you didn't have to pedal at all!" Asked about safety, he replies: "Sure, if you'd fallen off the back I suppose it would've made sliced bacon out of you, but what the hell!" And how did the "Monster" come into being? Bud, back from WWII and riding a Harley, and not satisfied with the power of his stroked and bored bike, welded up a special frame and set two eighty-inch "stroker" engines in it, called it the Monster, and went drag racing.

In 1953, Bud ran at 130 mph in the quarter mile (or, 0 to 130 in three blocks). It was this very bike he took to the salt in 1955. Says Bud, "I had one more higher gear and with the extra power nitro produces we should have clocked 165 or 170. I guess we'll never know."

While unknown salt heroes such as Bud are more the rule than the exception, some riders at Bonneville have spawned decades-long associations between the records they set there and manufacturers' models. Johnny Allen, for example, piloting Triumph-engined streamliners, broke two world records (194 mph and 215 mph), both in 1956, and was responsible for the Triumph Motorcycle Company naming its all-time bestselling model the "Bonneville." The irony here being that although a malfunction of timing equipment made Allen's record an "unofficial" one, Triumph decided to use the name for advertising purposes anyway, which caused a major flap with the FIM.

In 1965, the Detroit Triumph dealer Bob Leppan built a streamliner powered by two Bonneville 650s, and went 245.66 mph on the salt. Afterward, Triumph applied a gold transfer decal to the tank of every motorcycle leaving the factory, reading: *T120R World's Fastest Motorcycle.* Sexy? You'd better believe it. Just looking at that decal made you feel like you were going over a hundred.

A more recently heralded salt curmudgeon and hero is Burt Munro, who attracted the attention of the filmmaker Roger Donaldson, who chronicled Munro's life first in a documentary made before his death (*Burt Munro: Offerings to the God of Speed*), and later in a popular film titled *The World's Fastest Indian.* Munro, who, prior to this, was not unknown on the salt, became, due to Donaldson's full-length feature, an inspiration to the rider and nonrider alike—and for very good reasons.

Munro, from the tiny town of Invercargill, New Zealand, loved motorcycles from an early age. Beginning in his middle twenties, he competed in hill climbs, trials, road racing, flat track, and drag racing. But what made

Munro so unusual was this: He did it all (primarily) on one motorcycle, a 1920 Indian Scout, which he modified by hand in his shop. Munro even made it to Bonneville on this bike, where he set the record for under 1,000 cc streamlined—183.58 mph. On his qualifying run, he made the fastest ever officially recorded speed record on an Indian, 190.07 mph.

In his own words, here's what Munro wrote about modifying the Indian: "For 10 years I have worked 16 hours a day in the shed and was told to slow up a few years ago and now I only work 7 days and about 70 hours a week." And the parts he hand crafted? He spent eight hundred hours in 1963 making the Indian's engine into a four-cam setup (the stock machine is a side-valve flathead). Nearly everything in his engine was handmade, replacing the original parts. Munro filed 1916 Indian Power Plus gears to fit into his much newer gearbox. He made the cylinders from old cast-iron gasworks pipes and lined them with bores made from pistons that had "failed" (of seventeen beach test runs he recorded one year, eleven resulted in catastrophic "explosions"). Munro hand-filed his own cams; cast and forged his own pistons from scrap; reworked the bike's original 1927 Schebler De Luxe carburetors (he made six for his machine); and cut connecting rods from truck axles, and later a DC 6 propeller.

The first aluminum streamliner shell took him five years to hammer out, which he did between beach tests. When he finally got the bike up and running at speed, using the shell, the new aerodynamics made the rear wheel spin at over 160 mph. To stop rear wheel spin, he built a sixty-pound lead brick which he bolted in front of the rear wheel. The brick caused the bike to swerve so badly that Munro was nearly killed riding the Indian on his first test run. When his crew got to him, they found him laughing. Why? Munro replied, "I was happy to still be alive!" (He found that mounting the brick in front of the front wheel did the trick.)

And what is it, really, that we love in such a character? Nothing, absolutely nothing, stopped this man from living the life he wanted to live.

"If you don't follow through on your dreams, you might as well be a vegetable," he liked to say.

Follow through he did. And won!

As did also Don Vesco, who was the first to break the 300-mph barrier. Vesco was modifying model airplane engines by the time he was eight, making them faster, something he did with bicycles, skateboards—anything mechanical. "Racing was always a part of my life," he said. Don's father owned a body shop, and as a hobby ran hot rods on California dry lake beds, his son with him. As a teenager Vesco borrowed friends' parents' cars to trailer his motorcycle to an old military airport outside San Diego, where he taught himself to ride at speed. Road racing that Triumph in Southern California later, he was so successful the then-fledgling Honda hired him to pilot its 250 cc RC 161. Given that Southern California was the epicenter of what would become the Japanese Motorcycle Invasion, Don was at the heart of the heart of it, at a time when Honda placed its machines in bank lobbies and swanky auto dealerships, changing the very image of motorcycling for all time. Don, a clean-looking racer, became the poster boy of the movement at a time when British bikes, in particular Norton, Triumph, and BSA, did their business out of shops in the lower-rent parts of cities. So attractive was Don that he was hired away from Honda by Yamaha to run a shop designing and machining speed parts that became sought after, first in California, then throughout the United States, and finally internationally. The famed racers Gene Romero, David Aldana, and Yvon Duhamel rode Vesco-prepared Yamahas. When he was told he had to quit racing to devote all his time to the business of manufacturing speed parts, Don quit his day job.

He built a streamliner powered by two 350 cc Yamaha engines, and on September 17, 1970, set the world motorcycle speed record at 251.66 mph at Bonneville—a record his good friend Cal Rayborn surpassed just one month later on a machine designed and built by the up-and-coming rider-designer Denis Manning. (Yes, *the* Manning of BUB Speed Trials, which you are now attending.) Vesco continued racing, winning five world's-fastest-motorcycle racing titles over nearly ten years, even continuing to compete at Bonneville after he lost an eye to a flying stone at a dirt-track event.

True grit? Or true salt?

From a distance, the accomplishments of these men on the salt might seem at best misdirected deeds, or worse, the product of some not-so-benign dementia, but such is not the case. Being there, *you* get the salt fever.

And, maybe, it's salt fever for life itself.

Filling that vast, blisteringly white space by racing through it comes to make sense. It's that space between birth and death, right in front of you. And who, after all, hasn't been on a particularly long and lonely stretch of highway and thought, "I wonder how fast I could go if—" If no cops were around. If there weren't any turns. If the road was flat. If there weren't any ups or downs to the road. If there weren't those . . . trees, shoulders, drop-offs, cliffs to the side, sand, gravel, et cetera.

Well, that's Bonneville—up to about two hundred miles per hour. Because what that billiard-table-smooth salt surface *looks* like is not at all what it really *is* at ultrahigh speed.

You'd think, for example, that to improve your power-to-weight ratio, you could simply make your speed racer lighter, but given the porousness of the salt, a light machine, due to the force necessary to propel it to competitive speeds, meets with traction problems. Specifically, traction necessary to force the speed racer forward via a rear wheel.

We are talking motorcycles here: To be a motorcycle, for the purposes of the two major governing bodies of world motorcycle speed racing, the FIM (Fédération Internationale de Motocyclisme) and the AMA (American Motorcycle Association), the vehicle must run on two wheels, be steered by the front wheel, and be powered by the rear wheel. That eliminates two-wheeled rockets, tricycles of all sorts, and so on, yet leaves a lot of room for invention.

So, given we've removed the cops, hills, turns, and other usual road hazards, what challenges remain for both the 200-mph-club wannabes and the bona fide contenders for the world motorcycle record?

First, the salt itself is complex, tricky, and greatly variable. Some years, even by the end of summer, the water from the winter months hasn't entirely evaporated under the surface, and, with significant force, can be "broken through," the salt then much like heavy crystalline, not entirely set cement. It is highly unstable at high speed. Imagine making a fast run on a highway, and while you are doing well over 100 mph, the very surface under your wheels taking on the consistency of hardening molasses. Also, given the salt is porous, at velocity air compresses into the salt under the motorcycle, so the designers cannot use air dams or other air-routing devices to hold the motorcycle on the surface to improve stability and traction.

So why not use a drive tire with significant tread (studs) to obviate the traction problem? At over 150 mph, the tread, due to the centripetal force generated by such high-velocity rotation, would be thrown off. Bikes making significant speed require specially manufactured high-speed tires—which cost nearly their weight in gold. If, as we'll see soon enough, they can even be had at any price.

So the traction problem is dealt with how? Through alchemy: a delicate balance of engine pulsation, weight ratio, aerodynamics, and rider finesse (at ultrahigh speeds, for example, all motorcycles countersteer—to move left, you turn the front wheel to the *right* while leaning *left*).

There's no sure formula, and each team works its own version of what it hopes will be the winning combination. That's what makes the salt so wonderful. Sure, competitors can create monster machines in California, or Nevada, or New York, but they won't necessarily be the fastest on the salt, and won't set world records. There's engineering, engineering, and more engineering, and then there's the art of speed racing at Bonneville. Racing there, competitors, by trial and error, come upon discoveries that at first make no sense from an engineering standpoint. They play flat-out lucky hunches, tweak systems to produce winning results.

And even when all that's in place, your motorcycle a contender in its class, the salt will eat your machine—it's highly corrosive. You discover this when you set your pack (cameras, notebooks, pens, and such inside), hat, shirt, or rear end on the salt. The salt, by osmosis, will always move from an area of higher to lower concentration, until concentrations are equivalent, so the salt will creep into anything that is in any way porous.

Add to that salt's abrasiveness, which we've already noted. You've got to wear that protective gear to ride on it. There are the variations in the salt surface, which are hard to see. Salt ripples (even ones yards apart) remain from that water evaporating under windy conditions; at high speeds these ripples can cause intense vibration in competitors' machines—these ripples being nearly invisible, too, since they are uniformly white, like the salt itself. There is a salt "tide," the water rising under the salt toward the end of the day, which changes its character.

And, most important, the very air must be dealt with. For anyone wanting to move quickly, atmosphere is their nemesis. At speed, air builds up around any vehicle like snow in front of a snowplow. The resistance this bunched air creates is squared with each mile per hour. At low speeds there is very little effect. For that reason, a car (and the surface area here is greater than that of a motorcycle, so there is more resistance) needs only about 100 horsepower to reach 100 mph. To propel this same car at 200 mph will require about 400 horsepower. But to propel it at 300 mph will require in the range of 2,000 horsepower.

Already you can see some of the challenges this presents for motorcyclists trying to set speed records. Even given that a motorcycle has a fraction of the surface area of an automobile—let's even say somewhere around a third or less—that means to reach speeds over 300 mph you're going to need, at a minimum, around 600 horsepower. But the motorcycle can't be too heavy, or displace too much air, or it will negatively affect the salt surface.

The answer? Aerodynamics. The world's fastest motorcycles are handmade "streamliners" engineered for the Bonneville Salt Flats—end-of-the-bell-curve engineering projects having two wheels, though not much more in common with those machines we generally think of as motorcycles.

And here is where the bone fide fun of Bonneville happens, especially at the BUB International Motorcycle Speed Trials. All competitors race in distinct classes. Given the advantages of streamliner bodies on motorcycles, there's the streamliner class—which also breaks down into engine displacements, 50 cc to open-class streamliner. (Denis Manning, the owner of the BUB *Lucky Seven*, has, for fun, offered a $5,000 prize for the world speed record under 50 cc, which has spawned some strange little motorbikes indeed.) There's a fairing class, which allows fiberglass or sheet metal wind cheaters, some of which are also found on many street motorcycles, particularly those used for touring. And a bare bikes class.

In fact, there's a class for nearly any and every motorcycle ever built. AMA designations read like this: S, PBG, 2, and so on, which would describe the streamlined, supercharged dual-push-rod-engined, gasoline-fueled Vincent owned by "Mad Max" Lambky. These classes follow the evolution of the motorcycle.

There's side valve/flat head class (bikes common from the 1920s up and into the 1950s). The push-rod class. The gasoline class and the nitromethane class. There's vintage class (and vintage streamliner) and scooter class, naturally aspirated and turbocharged/supercharged class. And to put the whole mess in perspective, there is, as already mentioned, the Run What You Brung class—bikes coming in off the highway, all in a variety of engine displacements.

So—yes, you, too, can be a world champion at the Bonneville Salt Flats! That's the thrill of it. If you want, you can take a box-stock, boring-as-dirt Honda 350 to the salt and try to set an unmodified record. There are only two qualifications for doing this: You have to beat the old record by a minimum of 1 percent; and you have to do it making two runs (which are averaged) within two hours. One run going west, the other going east, which cancels out the effect of the ever-present winds.

It's democratic. And egalitarian. Sure, those boys in the streamliner class are multimillionaires, but you, with your hopped-up-to-within-an-inch-of-its-very-life Vespa, can be king of the world, rider of the world's fastest modified 150 Wasp—if you're crazy enough to pursue that. Or, stranger yet, the rider of the world's fastest vintage Cushman Eagle! There are many of them out on the flats, the cheesy old Cushman having a very dedicated following.

All it takes is some cash, and that salt fever—which is the second thing that really strikes you about Salt Flats culture. Once you are out amid the three to five hundred folks racing, stretched alongside the course for a good quarter mile or so, the bikes flying by on both sides (to the south, the world-class racers, and to the north, the Run What You Brung riders), you find a surprisingly cheerful camaraderie. These guys are fun!

Everywhere is a kind of "Hey, this might do the trick" sort of play, and the eternal Us versus Them competition, which here is gentlemanly. Classy. There are no boom boxes playing any sort of music. No one is drinking on the salt; it just isn't done. There are no BUDWEISER KING OF BEER banners, bikers in leathers staggering around, no carnies and cheap plate games. Everyone out here is either banded together in small groups around bikes about to run the salt, or hunched over disassembled machines making adjustments—some of them major, such as getting new pistons in an engine or a supercharger installed.

The classes run from just-after-turn-of-the-century flathead Indians to the weird and esoteric. The latter are on the approach side of the flats, on the west. So, fresh in off the highway and the pretzel Harley that went down at 126, you start with the odd and the modified. Either by default, or by design, the machines farthest from the entrance onto the flats are also the costliest—world-class, open-competition streamliners. So, here at Bonneville, the weird, furry, and friendly is a good place to start.

For example, there's an electric motorcycle class. Here the Keepers of the Blue Flame team are battling it out with team Electrobike, even while supercharged, doubled-engine Harleys are roaring by a stone's throw away. Far from following the same strategies, these two teams have utterly divergent approaches to winning and different goals. The Keepers of the Blue Flame have taken an old Suzuki bullet bike and put a Ward Nine electric motor, for industrial applications, in it. That electric motor, Mark, the team engineer, tells you, is so "thirsty" that to get the bike up to speed and run through miles four and five for the record requires eight truck batteries. So the batteries alone, without the motorcycle, weigh nearly two hundred pounds. Can you imagine using two hundred pounds of gas to fuel a small-displacement standard motorcycle? And how do you get eight truck batteries on a sleek Suzuki motorcycle? If you're this guy, you hang them off the sides like low-slung saddlebags.

"Got three fifty amps, ninety-six volts," Mark tells you. "We run the whole thing in series, not parallel." So the voltage is cumulative: 8 x 12 = 96.

There are bare terminals and thumb-thickness power lines snaking all over the darn bike. It looks cobbled together and dangerous.

"Touch the wrong thing, you'd get a hell of a shock," you joke.

"You're not careful, amperage like this will kill you stone dead," Mark replies, standing with a wrench and grinning. He's a big guy, wearing a Hawaiian shirt and white baseball cap with a blue visor. He's got the boomer-age California surfer look. Mark's eyes glow with that blue flame. You talk about electric motors, cycles, number of poles, battery technology, problems with heat—the enemy of electric motors, Mark tells you. It kills the power. There's something having to do with current and sine waves—and somewhere in there you begin to ease away from the bike.

"The X, Y, Z of PL percent of Q at maximum recovery . . ." Mark is saying, or something like that, the chest-rattling roar of a fueler going by drowning out his engineeringese, even as you inch farther from him and the bike, desperate for a gentlemanly way to escape. And there it occurs to you. Your parachute. Your escape hatch on the flats. Your way out. You already used it on the pretzel Harley guy. And this guy, with his thick, hairy wrists, is not the one to ask about *bubluckyackattackeezeehook*. So you'll cut this short.

You simply have to ask the ultimate, the *only* question. Which, with an electric bike, has got to be deflating.

"How fast will it go?"

"Seventy-some miles per hour," Mark tells you without a moment's hesitation. "With more juice our motor could put out as much as forty-five horsepower, which would put us over one hundred, but we haven't figured that out—*yet*."

And away you go, right to the competition: Marcus Hays, in stylish black T-shirt, mop of curly black hair, soul-patch beard, and the Electrobike, their motto on Marcus's shirt: "Innovation/Comradery/Creativity". Team Electrobike has designed an ultralight, ultrasophisticated two-wheeler. It's a beautiful, spare, downfacing semicircle of bead-welded four-inch-diameter aluminum tubing, the front articulated so the handlebars will turn the front quarter of that single-spine frame and the wheel attached to it. There's a tiny, maybe three cubic inch, gasoline engine to bring the motorcycle up to the timing traps, and an electric motor to pull it through those traps. One battery not much larger than a cigar box "fuels" the motor. That way, unlike Keeper of the Blue Flame's bike, Electrobike doesn't need as much electrical "juice" to propel the machine, given it weighs very little. So, in turn, it doesn't carry as much weight in batteries, and consequently can be much lighter overall. In fact, Electrobike uses ultralightweight bicycle tires, wheels, and disk brakes.

"It weighs not much more than an old balloon-tired bicycle," Marcus tells you. "And this year we have ten times the power we had last year."

Unlike the Blue Flame team, Electrobike is aiming at future production of this thing for everyday riders. It's a cockeyed hybrid of sorts, built for the environmentally minded. The production version even has a solar charger and will be marketed . . . in the San Francisco Bay area. Having lived in the Bay Area, you don't mention that, hey, it rains a bit much there for a solar charger, doesn't it?

"We're aiming," Mark says, "at one hundred miles per hour, and three hundred miles per gallon."

"Wow," you say, eyeing Electrobike's ribbon-thin tires. Then you slip in "Bubluckyackattackeasyhook," trying not to look as though suffering from heat prostration or brain damage.

"They're out there," Marcus says, dismissing the whole lot of it with a sweep of his arm, pointing to the end of the column. This must be where journalists asking too many questions are run through a wood chipper, you think, as was the Steve Buscemi character in *Fargo*. There's talk, again, of battery technology, recovery rates, motors (not engines), heat . . .

And you have to ask that last, essential question to escape:

"How fast did it go last year?"

Marcus, gathering himself, replies, "Last year we went through mile four and five at forty-eight point five miles per hour. We're hoping to do over eighty this year."

After all that, 48.5 miles per hour? But then, this thing does look like some Flash Gordon bicycle with an electric motor in it.

"Who's got the world record out here?" you ask, wanting to get to the bottom of the *Bubluckyackattackeasyhook* business, and, seeing the punctured look in Marcus's eyes—Electrobike isn't even the winning machine in its class—you add, "For the big gas guzzlers?"

"Easyriders," Marcus says.

Again, there's confusion. "You mean, as in that . . . chopper magazine?" This brings to mind Peter Fonda and Dennis Hopper astride (now) goofy-looking, raked-out Harleys, with beards, beer bellies, and hobnailed boots. Easyriders, you discover later, financed construction of their streamliner through selling twenty-five-dollar shares to the public, ten thousand people signing on, each having his or her name printed on the shell of the bike.

Marcus shrugs. Who's to be bothered with all that?

And with that thought, you move over to the diesel class. Here the flashiest bike in the pack belongs to, of all organizations, the U.S. Marines. Right there beside the sparkling, arrest-me-red motorcycle is Fred Hayes in his equally snazzy leathers. The bike has a cylinder and head that are almost comically tall, which makes it look like some—painstakingly—reengineered four-stroke dual-purpose dirt/street bike. The trick with this class is that the bike must run on the lowest grade of fuel possible, biodiesel. Years ago, some nut arranged to take the oil from McDonald's French fry traps and ran his experimental biodiesel engine with it. Here is the same concept. The engine in this bike is in the multifuel class, which means it will run on aviation kerosene, diesel, and biodiesel.

Among fuels, biodiesel is the most challenging, most problematic: it has an extremely high flash point, temperature at which it explodes under compression, which makes for a less powerful engine. Go Perkins Bacon Fat! (Just kidding.)

Fred's bike is both a serious attempt at building a biodiesel motorcycle, for a world record in that class, and a recruiting stunt. You, too, could be a top-notch engineer/mechanic in the Marines, the project says without saying a word. Sign up right here, we'll cover your education—granted we get from you a little labor out in the field (currently desert) in return.

Their best speed to date? "One hundred and eight miles per hour," Fred tells you. Which just beats the—pathetic—previous standing record of 105 mph. But then, the street version of this bike will get one hundred miles per gallon. (Compare this to the gallon every ten seconds a nitromethane engine will use.) So, not at all shabby. And, it almost goes without saying, Fred is not the guy to ask about the Bub-whatchamacallit. So, maybe the guys next door?

In almost comic fashion, the competition is none other than the Crucible, which calls itself "the world's fastest arts organization." You'd almost expect some antipathy between team Crucible's Birkenstock-wearing, bearded art/engineering school types and the Marine team's . . . well, *marines,* but there isn't any of that. People don't talk politics on the salt, or religion, or much of anything but racing and salt history.

The Crucible's entry is a modified BMW R1150RT touring bike with a BMW automobile 320 diesel stuffed into it. As a result, the bike is massive. It weighs 1,100 pounds.

In motorcycle speed-racing circles, transplanting engines from sources other than motorcycles has a long and storied history. Recall Curtiss and his blimp-engined bike; another such tinkerer was Fred Luther, an employee of Chrysler, who, in 1934, persuaded management to provide him with an Indy Speed Shop–prepared PF-6. Luther shoehorned this engine into a Henderson X cycle. The finished bike weighed 1,500 pounds and was over eleven feet long. Officially, Luther did 140 at Bonneville riding this bike. Rumor had it that he was doing nearly 180 on his second, return run when the bike threw a connecting rod.

The Crucible's bike, likewise, has these sorts of dimensions. When you sit astride it, the injector manifold, a big, cast-aluminum affair, forces your knees apart as would some enormous bongo drum. On it is stamped, in two-inch letters, *Die Moto*—short for *Diesel Motorcycle.* The entire bike, built by the Crucible's "Diesel Dozen," is like that. Massive. It even sports what was once called a "dustbin" fairing (or a three-quarter fairing), which is wrapped around the front of the motorcycle, giving it the look of an aluminum, decal-covered shark—the bike's got to be well over ten feet long, with a little sheet-metal tail over the rear wheel.

Michael Sturtz, team leader and rider, tells you the bike will generate 78 percent fewer emissions than a standard diesel engine and will run on SVO.

"SVO?"

"Straight Vegetable Oil."

"And what's the Crucible?" you ask.

"The Crucible," Michael says, "is a consumer group founded by people engaged in the work of personal and global transformation. Our goal is to foster the collaboration of arts, industry, and community." This guy, you decide, is not the one to ask about the *Bubeezeeattackluckyhook*. You'd be here until next week, or even later, getting the story in all of its gory, sociopolitical context.

And there are the bikes roaring by on both sides, providing believable and convenient distraction—particularly a woman on a Harley, her red suit so tight and form-fitting it screams WOMAN! Even at 150 mph.

"That's something," you tell Michael, wary, meaning both this rider and what he's just said. You're getting very close here to politics *and* religion.

"The point here," Michael tells you, "is to break the diesel record, but the real story is that environmental responsibility and alternative technology can result in a high-performance vehicle." He pats the bike. "This is the proof. No bullshit."

Wonderful! Now we're back to English!

"How fast will it go?" you ask.

"We'll see," Michael tells you.

And that said, away you go, headed for a motley group of racers under a sun canopy waiting to take a run.

Standard bikes. Oh, what a relief! Bikes you've ridden and seen on the street. In short, real motorcycles. The kind you yourself have owned. Or ones like them, but not so modified. The salt is getting to you—it makes you want to just take . . . any damn old thing and *go*. This is what each of these crazies under the sun canopy has in his or her brain, behind their sometimes overactive, glittering eyes.

Seeing people excited about something, though, is wonderful. Especially here, where, when one of the racers goes by on the world-record track, as one does now, there is recognition and discussion.

"Tom Hailey on his double-engined Vincent."

Heads turn like tracking devices. The motorcycle, flying by at an astonishing rate of speed, makes a beautiful noise.

"What's your guess?"

"He'll be pissed. Not over one seventy."

"Like hell."

"You wait."

And then there is the announcement on Radio BUB (that damn BUB business again!), in the announcer's flat voice: "Tom Hailey. Supercharged class. Double engine. 171.788 miles per hour."

"I was right. Over one seventy."

"But not one percent over the record."

The two, civilly, argue on. Everyone under the sun canopy listens in, waiting for their turn on the salt. One is Bill Warner, sitting astride a modified Yamaha V-Max. The two are the picture of battle. The bike is covered in salt, decals, and dirt. It's been lowered, the faux gas tank removed, on the frame a thin pad of neoprene for Bill to lie on. The knees of Bill's riding suit are black and shiny with multiple layers of electrical tape.

You're getting the hang of it, talking to these people.

"What's it put out," you ask.

"Two hundred nine rear-wheel horsepower," Bill replies. "That's good for two fifty or two sixty at the crankshaft."

"How fast's it go?"

"One ninety-seven even."

"Wow," says the guy to your left. He's wearing one of those olive green wide-brimmed hats with a little feather in the band.

"What are you riding?" you ask him, and when he opens his mouth, out comes this . . . yodeling-area accent. German? Swiss? Plattdeutsch. So?

"Buell, in the Run What You Brung. I'll do better this year with my Ducati."

You shake hands. "Robert," he tells you.

He's more talkative, excitable than the others you've spoken with.

"What's that like?"

"What?"

"Out there—having at it." There, you've done it. Asked the big question. Why would you do it?

"Out there?" Robert smiles. "It's like . . . *shooting heroin*," he says, nothing short of rapture on his face. This is amusing to you, since, from the first, you've seen him in lederhosen and hoisting a beer stein, even though he's wearing a black leather suit.

It must be the hat . . .

Robert—from Austria, it turns out—is a recent convert to the religion of speed. He'd been training as a chef in Europe, when his father, who'd been footing the school bill, died suddenly (suicide), which left Robert to fend for himself. An opportunity to come to the United States presented itself, and here he did all sorts of jobs, was a cabbie in Los Angeles, a warehouseman, a salesman, and ultimately trained to be an electrician. He was, as he put it, stuck in L.A. "wiring all sorts of stupid things," living in a tiny apartment with white walls, his life going nowhere.

And then, one night, he saw *The World's Fastest Indian*. Robert was transformed on the spot. He bought a bike, a Harley-powered Buell, painstakingly modified it, and made the trip to Bonneville.

"It was nothing short of a love-match obsession," he says. "You get out there on the salt and the whole world just opens up. You'll see," he says, nodding. "You have it, I can tell."

To deflect this bit of revelation you're not too happy to recognize, you ask the usual: "How fast you go last year?"

"One hundred seventy-two, even." Robert nods.

One hundred seventy-two on a bike you ride to an event is nothing to sneeze at.

And then he arches an eyebrow, and says, in all seriousness, "Do you know what BUB stands for?"

You have to tell him you don't. "Do you?"

"No," he says, with a shrug. "I have no idea." He asks the others under the canopy. There's a general consensus. No one seems to know. So you're not an idiot after all. Here are these guys draped over bikes they've spent tens of thousands of dollars on, having filled out forms relieving the sponsor, BUB Racing, of liabilities, having paid fees, and having waited here, now two hours, says Bill Warner, and they don't know.

"I'm just here to go," a comic-looking guy straddling a yellow bike chimes in. This gets a belly laugh from the group.

Now here is another character: Tom Liberatore. He's a member of what's called Team Cooked Goose, a joke related to his bike, a 1973 Moto Guzzi V7 Sport. A "*Gootsee*," as it is pronounced in Italian. Goose. But then you see that everything Tom's wearing is a sort of joke about his bike, or Italian made, or . . . spaghetti. On the tank of his Guzzi is *Pepperoni Bros. Racing.* He's wearing wide black suspenders, on them, in yellow lettering, *John Deere.* (De-tractors, pun intended, of the joke that Guzzi engines have been derived from Italian farm machinery.) There's a decal on Tom's rear fender that reads, *Boom Boom # 1.*

"What's that all about?"

"Old expression in Vietnam." Tom winks. "Second only to being out here."

Right. Over more bikes roaring by, you talk tech: Tom's bike has Carillo con rods, domed pistons for 11.7-to-1 compression, a Mega Cycle cam. The bike, like so many things Italian, is beautiful, a work of art. Every last detail is harmonious with the overall design, the Guzzi a low, sleek bike with an enormous and voluptuous gas tank, the artfully sculpted cylinders jutting out just-so underneath it, sand-cast alloy.

Again, when it's time to move on, one simply says (you guessed it):

"How fast ya go?"

"133.233," Tom says, "trying to beat Harley this year for the push-rod world record."

"Good luck," you tell him, and you and Bill, your photographer, make for a cluster of men and motorcycles, but the cloud that's been threatening to let loose rain does now, which causes all parties on the salt to scatter for shelter. If there is lightning, anything higher than a salt ripple can act as a lightning rod here. A motorcycle would be a prime target, so the racing is shut down.

And there's the wind. It sweeps the clouds, magisterial and trailing curtains of droplets fat as cherries, across this stretch of white salt.

The smell that comes with the rain here is like nothing you'll find anywhere else. There's an oceanlike salt smell in it, and the scent of brine shrimp, which live farther out, on the Great Salt Lake itself. But most surprising are the almost mintlike smells of sage, Mormon tea, four-winged saltbush, and rabbit brush. It's palate-cleansing. Invigorating. Surprising.

After all those smells of burned oil, scorched metal, and melted plastics and fiberglass and neoprene, those overheated engine/machine smells, this desert perfume seems almost . . . *holy.* If you weren't standing, feet set firmly on the salt, you imagine you might just float off. And it occurs to you again—there's something magnificent and almost obscene about racing across this spectral land, on it, not over it, and at the highest speed possible. Something extraordinary.

As is usual in the desert, the rain passes quickly, the sun bears down again, and you and Bill make a quick tour of the wannabes camp, three quarters of the distance from the entrance. Here are Mad Max's double-engined Vincent streamliner (you can only imagine what that cost), that supercharged Norton streamliner 666, on the fiberglass front of which someone has comically drawn a large, Halloween-like, toothy grin. There are Ducatis, MVs, V-Rods, and streamliner two-strokes. A Gates Harley, bored and stroked to 2,600 cc, so loud that when the mechanic, Marvin Teobrin, starts it, you instantly cup your ears to prevent the exhaust rap from—literally—shattering your eardrums. There's a Confederate Wraith, also Harley-powered, highly tuned, and for sale to the public, at only

$70,000. A bike, the owners tell us, now prized by stars such as Tom Cruise and Brad Pitt. All this you take in, chatting with owners, each obsessed with the technical challenge of making his or her bike competitive. Three quarters of the distance down the strip this means one thing, and one thing only: joining the Two Hundred Miles Per Hour Club. Nearly all riders in this class are sponsored by major manufacturers or well-heeled businesses.

All, when asked that grail of questions, "Bub-easy-ack-lucky-hook-attack?" simply point to the end of the line. Guys like Billy Epps, the "world's fastest school board member," riding a 1,400 cc Kawasaki, on his bare biceps the only tattoo to be seen here: a skull and crossbones, and under it, *Live Fast.* And Crazy Super Kaz, wanting to go 250 on his turbo-charged V-Rod.

And . . . two gorgeous women. Curvy, with silken blond hair cascading over their shoulders—you had just decided, Okay, to hell with all this almost-to-the-end stuff, let's jump Boardwalk to the end of the end of all things salt racing, when you spotted them. Two hotties in black leather. Gatekeepers. Desert mirage, right?

No. You've just run into Valerie Thompson, of Hacienda Harley, and Leslie Porterfield, of High Five Cycles. Both have entire crews wrenching on their bikes, elaborate tent set-ups, and trailers half a block long, painted in Hollywood glam style, vivid and glossy. Valerie, on her trailer, is up close and personal, ten feet high, her smile a few feet across, her teeth as white as newly cast porcelain.

So talking with Valerie, who sits on the gate of her truck swinging her legs, is at first intimidating. But she's a personable, likeable sort, you discover. It's the ethos of this place, and Valerie carries it well. Including her not mentioning her competitor, pacing over at her trailer.

"I'm here to go over two hundred," she tells you, and smiles. When you ask her how she got into this . . . business, she says, "I was out of control on the streets, so I started drag racing. Once I got there, I was hooked. I was running V-Rods, for 9.16 quarters." That's 0 to 146 mph in a little over nine seconds. Squinting, glancing up at you, she adds, "Did one fifty-three on a nitrous Panhead last year, which is a world record, but we're trying to improve that by half."

As is Leslie—who, likewise, doesn't address Valerie. Leslie, you find, is a tangle of surprises. A woman who once bottle-fed dogs for the Humane Society, she's been racing since she was sixteen, used to own a construction company, and swung a hammer there. She also ran a Yamaha dealership and, later, a used-bike outfit in Dallas. Leslie's aim?

"I'm pushing for two twenty," she tells you. "The Hayabusa with a turbocharger should do that."

Her Suzuki is red and black (sex and death), and when she poses beside it for a photo, she grins, almost impishly.

The thing no one is saying here is this: Any fall at over 200 mph, in the partial streamliner class, would probably be fatal.

You address this in a look, to which Leslie responds: "That's not so fast, if you compare it to the world record."

"And that is?"

"Three twenty-two. Set sixteen years ago by Easyriders. Conditions like this, though, I'll bet one of the big three take it."

And they are, you ask? (Again.)

"BUB *Lucky Seven*, *Ack Attack*, and *E-Z-Hook*," Leslie replies. You are tempted to cock your head at, once again, not quite getting it. "Thanks!" you say with a smile. Right. Of course.

Leslie nods, motioning up the column. "They're up there. Check 'em out." And as you head off, Leslie calls to you, "Do you know what BUB stands for?"

"What?" you call back.

Leslie only smiles.

But you don't make it to the end of the end of all things salt racing. There's a furor on the salt, all color and motion, a scrabble and run to the world-class side of the salt.

"What's up?" you ask a guy in one of those crushed-up straw cowboy hats.

"*Ack Attack*'s gonna run," he tells you.

That, you discover while you're waiting alongside the course with the others, is Mike Akatiff's machine, a dual Suzuki Hayabusa–engined streamliner.

Blinding white salt. Soft banter. Where-you-from talk. Sweden, Australia, Venezuela. Texas. Right here in Utah. Beaver, Pennsylvania. That seeming expanse of endless Utah blue sky expands, and into it, making a muscular, almost churning sound, comes the blue-and-yellow *Ack Attack*, at first barely visible, then pencil thin on the rim of the salt, and in a flash *Ack Attack* is broadside to the crowd at mile four and, as if sucked into some white void, gone.

There's a moment of silence. And then a universal, crowdwide, "Wow! What was *that?*"

Seconds later, a cheer starts at the entrance end of the salt, comes at you at the speed of rumor.

"344.637!" someone says.

"Woah! That's a world record!"

And amid the exclamations, the excitement, and the grumbling that no, it's not a record yet—Akatiff and crew have to turn *Ack Attack* around and run it again, successfully, and in the opposite direction, within two hours, for a combined average over 322 mph, or there is no record—heads turn to the end of the end of all things salt, the BUB trailer and tent, the largest and most elaborate, where the supposed speed wizard Denis Manning resides.

The *BUB* of BUB International Speed Trials. It is there, the Aussie tells you, that you'll find the only machine capable of besting *Ack Attack*.

So that's where you head now. To the Manning camp and *Lucky Seven*. And, by a process of deduction, you now know, also, that somewhere out here on the salt flats, in some under-the-radar camp, must be E-Z-Hook, the possible spoiler. The third of the world-champion triumvirate. BUB *Lucky Seven*, *Ack Attack*, and *E-Z-Hook*. But under the Manning camp canopy, and in the blessed shade, you don't find Denis Manning. Though you do find *Lucky Seven*—a cherry red, two-wheeled land missile over twenty feet long.

If there is such a substance as unobtanium, this bike is built from it. The body is vertically ovaloid, a shape taken from fish Manning studied, and composed of carbon fiber and Kevlar—*Lucky Seven* has no metal frame. For gawkers, like yourself (and you are gawking, albeit quietly), the side panels have been removed, so the bike's internals can be seen. Here is no Suzuki Hayabusa engine, no modified Harley machinery. In fact you don't recognize one bit of this hardware, which is like some symphony of high-tech magic, every cast part (aluminum cylinder block, cylinders, heads, turbochargers), machined or welded or formed bit (cooling and oil lines, carburetors, distributor, and unidentifiable bits of motor jewelry) exquisitely hand wrought.

"Joe Harralson," says a lean, gray-haired fellow, and you take his offered hand. "Scratch-built. The only thing off the shelf is the K and N oil filter. Purpose-built three thousand cc V-four. Sixteen valves, double overhead cam, turbocharged. Runs on methane. As is, it'll put out around six hundred horsepower."

"Six hundred horsepower," you reply.

John Jans, the machinist, steps in. The whole crew is here in the shade, minus Manning, who is out taking core samples of the salt. There's the team machinist, electrician, engine development expert, and wives, girl-friends, and children.

"*Ack Attack*," Jans tells you, "has more horsepower, but this engine has a pulse that gives better traction on the salt. We could easily get more power, but not all of it would be usable."

You look into the cockpit.

"So," you say, "the rider—"

"The pilot," says a small man sitting in a lawn chair at the nose. Chris Carr is a seven-time AMA National Flat Track champion. At five foot three, he's able to fit into the cockpit. "The controls," he tells you, "are out of an F4 Phantom fighter jet."

When I mention *Ack Attack*'s record, there are just grins and cheerful nods, which is something I want to get to the bottom of—there's some-thing . . . unusual there.

"It's cool," Chris says of the new record. "For them to bump it up twenty miles per hour is impressive."

You ask when Manning, the owner, will be back.

"Thirty-five . . . forty minutes?" says Chris, and then adds, with a wink, "Do you know what BUB stands for?"

"No," you tell him, thinking you're about to get that same runaround. Even here, at the end of it all.

There's an amused silence.

"Big Ugly Bastard," Chris says.

You laugh. It really is funny.

Chris nods. "No, *really.*" He eyes the others there, amusement wrinkling the corners of his eyes.

You've come all the way out here, as have characters from all corners of the globe. You can't imagine what all this machinery on the flats is worth. Tens of millions of dollars?

"Who?"

"Manning."

"Right," you reply. "This is the joke. I circle back around here, and say, 'Hey, you're Big Ugly Bastard,' and he pops me in the nose. You guys have a little free theater."

"You gotta meet 'im," Chris says. "All these damn hats?"

You tell him you did sort of notice the salt look.

"Come back," Chris warns you, giving advice to the writer and fellow motorcyclist. "You don't wanna miss this guy, okay?"

In the *Ack Attack* camp, the pilot, Rocky Robinson, is ecstatic. "I'm still walking on air; this is the happiest day of my life," he tells the assembled journalists. Then, laughing, he adds, "So far."

It is a prescient sentiment.

Asking around, you discover that Rocky was Manning's pilot until they came to a difference of opinion, Robinson even being instrumental in the development of Manning's *Lucky Seven*. Manning, you're told, recommended Rocky to Mike Akatiff, the designer and owner of Ack Attack, when his former pilot left.

Still, when you circle back to the *Lucky Seven* camp—no Manning. Then, minutes later, the "blue monster" comes roaring along the salt from the opposite direction, *fwaaaaaaaaaaaaaahp!*—crossing the entirety of mile four in just seconds. A slow turn of the head, and it's gone. Again. And like that, with a second run of 340.922 mph, *Ack Attack* becomes the world's fastest motorcycle and Rocky Robinson the world's fastest rider. The average of the two runs is the new standing record: 342.797 mph.

Manning, it comes down the line, won't bring out *Lucky Seven* this late, is unhappy with the wind, or the slant of the sun, or something, and Bill, your Appalachian photographer, and you head in to Sin City (West Wendover). Inside some casino, done up with mirrors so you can't tell once you're inside where the walls begin and end, machines chinging and talking and spitting out coins and bells going off, Bill gives you his take on these salt folks.

"What a bunch of nuts!" he says, with near glee.

You couldn't agree more. But interesting nuts! You spend the evening swapping motorcycling horror stories, like the time you were set on fire by your bike, and so on, and bike bits—"Jesus," Bill says, "I think for every hour I rode that damn Harley of mine I spent two hours repairing it."

Still, waking bleary-eyed, and worse for wear the following morning, you can't wait to get out to the salt.

There's a sunrise to match any painted by Constable or Turner or Bierstadt. Breathtaking. Coffee, on the flats, tastes like ambrosia, granola like manna. And like that you're off, with three things in mind: Manning. Manning. And Manning.

In your head is chiming, You're off to see the wizard, the wonderful . . . And, glory be to God, at the Manning camp, Chris Carr nods to his right, and here's the Man himself. In his trademark crushed wide-brimmed straw hat, suspenders, and enormous, low-slung belly, Manning is all American, all cowboy.

At first glance, it occurs to you, *this* is where the salt look comes from.

"Heard you were lookin' for me," says Manning, offering his hand.

"So, what's it all about?" you ask. At six two, maybe 285 pounds, he's not going to be squeezing into any streamliner soon.

Manning grins. "I'd have to take my clothes off to have any more fun!" he says, winking. "That's what it's about!"

"Why *Lucky Seven?*"

"Six of the fastest motorcycles in history are mine. *Seven* because this is the seventh."

There are the usual questions. When did he get his start? In 1968 he ran his first streamliner, though '57 was his first time at Bonneville, when he got salt fever. I know about salt fever, right? I tell him I do. In 1970 was the Cal Rayborn bike. In '72 a double-engined Triumph-Norton. In 1984, *Tenacious* and *Tramp.*

"*Tenacious,*" he tells you, "is still the world's fastest production single-engine bike."

"And what about *Lucky Seven,* how long did it take you to build it?"

"Took three years to build. Thousands of man-hours, I couldn't even say how many and wouldn't want to know."

"And cost?"

Manning only laughs. You've been indiscreet, asking. Millions, is the answer, and no one has to say it. Five? Ten? Still, Manning's got the deep pockets for the project—he owns a motorcycle exhaust-pipe business in Grass Valley, California, having grown up in L.A., his father a carpenter for the *L.A. Times.* So, winning world's-fastest titles sells pipes, and then some. BUB Enterprises pipes. Yup, Big Ugly Bastard Pipes. It takes some balls to carry that off, and Manning's got them. Still, in American fashion, his reputation does all the talking, Manning, like everybody out on the salt, is just another guy.

He's got an infectious grin—God, isn't it just great to be alive? it says, and you have to agree.

"Just another day at the Church of the Immaculate Motorcycle," he jokes.

"So what drives you?" you ask.

"What really makes it happen," Manning replies, suddenly all serious-ness, no kidding here, "what really makes it for me, with *everybody* here—especially with Chris Carr—is desire." He pats his bike. "This is a rocket ship named *desire*. Unless you really, really want it, there's no reason to do this."

Well, there it is. At its most elemental. And you understand—it's the damn salt fever. You're besotted now too. Manning has just finished you off.

"Getting out here is all I can think for the last fifty-three years," Manning says.

There's some commotion behind him now, and he lifts his head, in-dicating he'll return in a moment. His immense back to you, Manning confers with a guy who's got some instrument in his hands.

Manning nods, and the whole crew is mobilized. Just out from the awning, you're standing there in the middle of this sudden beehive of ac-tivity.

"Let's go, folks!" Manning calls to his chief engineer.

No less than fifteen support crew, engineers, and Chris Carr are throw-ing together their equipment.

"Sorry," Manning says, this pure excitement in it. Even joy. "Wind's down! Everybody, let's get to it!"

They roll *Lucky Seven* to the starting line, fueled, and Chris shoehorned inside in his fire-retardant suit. The conditions are perfect: the salt is flat and dry, the sun is out, and there is little or no wind.

Again, hundreds of spectators and racers stand back of the mile-four strip of salt where *Lucky Seven* will pass. Again, it's a pleasure. It's not so hot now, and there's this breeze, and small talk, that dome of endless blue overhead. Anything is possible here. You're in the land of dreams come true, and it is inspiring. So what if they're crazy dreams?

This is, after all, the end of it all. We're all just gentlemen here, witness-ing something . . . unnecessary in a practical sense, but necessary for the spirit. In the midst of all else that is serious, that has an expected, inevi-table end, this has no end at all. We do it for engagement, for our amusement, because in it, the everyday impossible becomes possible for all of us. If this can be done, what else can be done?

Out of that expanse of white salt and blue-sky nothingness, here comes *Lucky Seven*.

Along mile four, we could be watching the Wright Brothers, or Lucky Lindy taking off in his Curtiss monoplane. But it is *Lucky Seven* that approaches, thousands of man-hours of intense concentration applied to some all-too-apparent problem, attention to the smallest detail, the loss of the pilot to the competitor, and a new pilot found, tuning, and more tuning, and tinkering, and thinking, but most of all, applied imagination. Imagination conceived this bike. Imagination saw it running. Imagination dared to see it win. And will it?

*Lucky Seven* roars by, this engine, unlike *Ack Attack*'s, making a lower, growling *raaaaaaaaaaaaw!*

In a short swing of our heads, we see it go by, first a dot, then lengthwise, a missile, and a dot again. As if, we, too, have imagined it into existence.

Minutes later a cheer, again, runs the length of the line: 354.832 mph. A new world record! Shortly, there's a follow-up run, 346.947, for a combined average of 350.884 (which is what my black T-shirt, hastily printed up right here on the flats, reads).

While the light is changing, going into that blistering desert white, and while you and Bill, sure you've seen the end of it, motor out of all that Bonneville brightness and space, the *Ack Attack* boys have another go at it, try to break Manning's new record.

Which means they would have to average 355 on the salt. And given that the magic number here is 400 mph, why not?

At the exit onto the highway, BMW has set up a trailer and canopy. The sign reads: "Free Demo Rides."

Of course there is a complex knot of paperwork to get through, need for proof that you're no first-timer. Still, you just happen to have your helmet and leather jacket, so won't be deterred. Somehow, you knew someone would let you throw your leg over his or her fire-breathing monster out here. You just knew it.

"Here," Bill says, handing you your helmet. And in the same breath, he tells you that *Lucky Seven*'s record stands. Even though Sam Wheeler, with his machine, *E-Z-Hook*, has just set the fastest one-run time of the day, at 355.303—shredding his one and only front tire, preventing him from making his return run.

So, three world records.

The BMW rep spins out onto the highway, which parallels the World Record Class salt, you behind him on the new sport bike: 160-plus horsepower, to push 400 pounds. You see all those folks there, tinkering, inventing, refining, and there, just now, someone going for it, streaking away.

You let the rep get some distance ahead of you. Blinding white light on all sides, you crack the throttle open. The bike shudders with some violent internal combustion.

It's a work of art, this bike.

90. 100. 120.

Out here you ride in a bubble. A friend, not long after you return from the salt, comments, "Well, after one hundred I'm pretty sure it's all the same, you can't tell how fast you're going."

*No.* Not true at all. And as terrifying as this kind of well-over-one hundred-miles-per-hour speed is, the world sort-of-just-in-that-moment turning inside out, it is, for some people, thrilling. But even more so, intoxicating. And for some, even addictive. As the Kiwi Burt Monroe said, "At speed, you live whole lifetimes."

Just short of 130 the bike shuts down, the electronic rev counter engaging, you approaching the rep, the salt coming back into everyday proportion. Of course, the folks at BMW thought of this. You agreed not to pass the rep, so lagged behind. They also knew that after you'd been on the salt, you wouldn't be able to help yourself. You'd fall back, then drop the hammer—which, predictably, you did.

This bike, with a sport fairing, will do 170, the literature says.

And even back in the truck, later, with Bill narrating the geology of the area, telling charming-as-hell stories, there's this nagging something in the back of your mind, and what it's telling you is this: You'll never know, until you come out here yourself, ready to run.

Is this you?

How fast could *you* go?


Keeper of the Blue Flame's bike managed 88.221 miles per hour, Electro-bike 68.848.

Valerie Thompson set a new record in her class at 156.717.

The Crucible's Die Moto is now the world's fastest diesel cycle, having made two runs for an average of 130.614.

Eighty-year-old "Marty" ran at 149.095.

An off-the-street MV Brutale did 189.

# 8

# The Ultimate Freedom Machine

## (Just) Getting Out There

**H**eaded toward Wolf Creek Pass east of Salt Lake City, Highway 40 unwinds beneath you, your engine turning over at a comfortable 6,000 rpm, your bike pulling eighty miles per hour effortlessly. To the east, the Uintas rise to thirteen thousand feet, the Wasatch, encircling you, twelve thousand. The flat area you are crossing is Heber Valley, small ranches to both sides of the highway, in corralled pens picturesque spotted cattle.

Your heart trips a little, the valley narrowing, here the road rising and winding. Ahead of you in black leather, on a professionally modified Ducati 900 SS, is your friend Rick, a pilot.

Rick cracks the throttle open and jets ahead, cutting through the first sweeper like a fighter jet, picking up the pace.

Ninety now. A hundred. You, even here, where there's a left hairpin, are wondering if you could pass him on the inside.

You are riding a Ducati ST4, a miracle of a bike, a sport tourer. A bike new to you, really the first you've ridden since you sold your Ducati 750 two years earlier. The new one is smoother, handles and brakes better than your old bike did, but most significantly, this bike makes half again the horsepower, 117 to push 450 pounds. Not a Kawasaki Ninja, or a Ducati 1098 S, but, by even current standards, a handful. Crack the throttle open and you veer up behind Rick, the speedo swinging well over the century mark, the engine not missing a beat, and once again, you perform a high-speed near stop, let the bike fade to the left, so it falls toward the apex of the turn, and just beyond it, you screw on the throttle, the bike pulling hard, trees tearing by you, ragged green silk.

You enter Wolf Creek Pass, and the road winds right, then left, and with a nod, Rick is off, and you behind him. Racing. Hot engine smells, exhaust roaring to a crescendo, the bike rocketing over pavement that is a blur, and your heart kicking fistfuls of blood into your head, canyon chasing. All those years of riding are with you, dirt riding, flat-tracking, road racing, and touring, but the two years away hasn't helped your timing. Once a ski racer, you still take the occasional slope at sixty, did this last winter, but this is something else.

And this Ducati is higher in the saddle than your last, which makes hanging off it to the inside seem not quite right. That, and the road now switchbacks, here guardrails at last, a thigh-high barrier, the only thing between you and a drop into the canyon itself. The speed limit is fifty-five, tight-radius turns thirty-five, and you're averaging eighty.

Your hands work the controls, this hyperawareness monitoring your every move.

Somewhere, you're still riding that old BSA Rocket, Peter's Ducati 900 bevel racer, that lovely but awful Yamaha 750, layers upon layers of bikes. Right shift, down-up for the Brit bikes; right shift, up-down for the Italian bikes; left shift, down-up, for all those Japanese bikes and now this ST4 (all bikes finally having been standardized to this pattern). Still, when you begin to really ride hard, now as much by instinct as by intention, you jab at the brake with your left foot (getting the shift lever on the ST4), or pull up with your right to downshift (getting the ST4's brake)—the ghosts of the machines you came to know still there, until you let all that go, as you must, and begin to settle into this machine, coming up now on a hard right-hander, and nervous, aim for the inside, rolling on the throttle,

engine roaring and the needle on the speedometer swinging around over
one hundred again, the bike righting itself, as it should, but since you've
come at the apex too early you're shot out of the turn at the oncoming
lane.

A bad move, and not a confidence-inspiring one, the Ducati so powerful that you are carried over the line, a car coming at you in the distance,
and you jump on those Brembos, your heart in your throat, then back off
the throttle, the engine and brakes pulling you into your lane, the car
shuddering by.

You think, Had I been riding my old bike, I wouldn't have made it. But
would you be riding this fast on the old bike?

The ST4 is so intoxicating that you work at feeling your way into it—so
the bike at best becomes an extension of your body, and you do as Peter
taught you to nearly thirty years ago: keep your eyes up, locate the apex of
the turn, brake hard going in, roll on the throttle just past the apex, lead
with your chin. At double the speed limit. That Ducati V is howling, up
and down the range of the scale.

It feels spectacular, the ST4 flying, and now you are hard on Rick's tail.
He's a superb rider, and canyon chasing with him is a challenge. The two
of you plunge down one slope, roar up another, now three, four, even five
times, the bike's brakes saving you, but you are on the edge, in love again,
hanging from the tank to the inside, the guardrail to your left, a blur, that
big, 1,000 cc V-twin pulling hard, roaring again, both of you passing cars
as if they are standing still, left hard, hanging from your right knee, then
fading opposite, hanging to the inside, your head down, and the pavement
brushing your knee. And when the road opens up, Rick jetting ahead, and
there's a left-hand sweeper around a solid mass of mountain, you think,
Now I'll take him.

You've been waiting for this, to finally sit the bike, to become a part of
it, and all of that racing has come back, here on this road, such as you saw
those riders on in Italy. You have it back, really, and you glance down at
your speedometer: it reads 130 mph on a road designed to be driven at 60.
You think, in that nanosecond, that quiet that is pure concentration, If I

run it up to 150 I can get around him, stand on the brakes in that space before the sweeper, throw the bike over onto its side and—

You can't see around the mountain, and just as you're about to crack the throttle wide, you think, No. Stupid. What was I thinking. And, Christ! What's wrong with you, it's too late now.

But no, that is exactly what it is *not*—too late.

## What Motorcycles Are Really About

In the end, it's not about the bike. Given all that we've looked at—road racing, dirt riding, hill climbing, outlaw bikers and their mounts, motorcycle engines, in all their peculiar engineer-inspired variety, frame technology, clubs for riders of all types, and over a century and a quarter of invention and manufacture of these two-wheeled dream machines—the truth remains we ride because the *experience of riding* does something for us. Ask the three riders who put nearly sixteen thousand miles on Honda Cub 50s in one week in the Maudes Trophy endurance test in England in 1962, a record that stood for eleven years.

Riding teases us out of the prison of our thoughts, carrying us into some, as Keats called it, "Cold Pastoral." As Matthew Biberman explained in his piece "Cold Pastoral: Notes on Becoming a Vincent Owner" (*Int'l Journal of Motorcycle Studies*, Spring 2008): "Our vivid consciousness of the artifice [of life] makes us vividly, radiantly conscious of our experience of its meanings." That is, we are always divided in our waking lives—we are moving through life, but removed from it all the while by being aware of doing so. The dream of the pastoral arises out of the desire to un-self-consciously reenter that edenic landscape that so moves us. Of course, it's impossible to do this. We would have to shed that very consciousness that makes us what we are. So we long for it, most of our waking lives.

But we can, for moments, reenter this landscape.

Said poet and rider David Ferry (quoted by Biberman): "Motorcycling

is a form of unnatural transport moving its rider toward the natural without actually arriving."

Riding, you *have* arrived. You're not "in a cage" waiting to get somewhere, where you will reengage, focus, and (with divided attention) reenter
some meaningful tableau, social, political (as the old saw goes, if more than
two people are present, politics rears its unseemly head), or historical.

What is particularly wonderful though, is this: To temporarily reenter
this world we have been sent out of by motorcycle takes little effort. Just
getting on the bike and going will suffice. Almost as if by magic, you reenter the world.

You have to. Distraction on a motorcycle can be lethal, and the dim-
mest bulb is altogether aware of this. Your animal instincts are, at first,
screaming it at you: Danger. And they're right. Most motorcycle crashes
that result in fatalities occur at around twenty miles per hour, and less than
six minutes from the rider's home. And over half of those accidents involve
riders not licensed to operate a motorcycle. Nearly three quarters occur on
a machine with which the operator has little or no familiarity.

Riding shakes you vividly awake. Or, put most simply: When you ride,
the world comes alive. You feel the air, warm pockets and cold. You stretch
a leg, touching the ground with your foot. You ride in a sea of sensation,
smells, sights, sounds (cars, trees, road texture), tactile sensations around
you (that patter on your boots warns of loose road surface), and in the bike
under you (you ride by the feel of the engine, not by your gauges). My
lovely wife, the first time I took her riding, laughed when we dismounted
at a small ice cream place in Johnson County, Iowa. "What's so funny?"
I said. Pointing, she just managed to get out, "You have squashed bugs all
over your face and glasses!" I narrowed my eyes at her: "What do you think
you look like?" I asked, which prompted her to take a look at herself in the
down-tilted glass of the ice cream stand, both of us laughing.

Riding is not some abstract experience. Sometimes it can be as blunt as
a hammer, as when, riding up a ditch on one of my dirt bikes, I encountered
a log some kids were kind enough to have set sideways there. Too late to try
to get over it, I hit it head on, the bike flying over my head, but not before

my knee put a melon-sized dent in the tank, one that I rode with as if it were some badge of honor. How'd you get that dent there? other riders would ask. Sometimes, riding could be sublime, as the evening I took my then love for a ride around White Bear Lake in Minnesota, the first week of June, just after dark, the road rising and falling, all those familiar lake smells, layer upon layer of air of all different temperatures, and the headlight opening a living line between oaks and maples, in it all the birth of summer.

A woman biker I met said of cruising on her Harley: "I hear God when I'm riding that thing."

Yes.

And maybe it is this, too, as Biberman, the Vincent owner, put it: it is as if "you had almost stepped out of your cultured self to be with the nightingale."

Yes, there is something akin to flying in riding a motorcycle, being a bird, darting here and there.

But, possibly, what riding most satisfies is a profound and simple human urge, the *urge for going*. Because it is this, more than anything, that characterizes riding. Just getting out there. Going. Anywhere. Which, of course, comes out of that need, all over again, to reenter the world, to shake ourselves alive.

And the motorcycle is the perfect vehicle for that.

## Touring, the Biggest Adventure of All

I sold my Rocket A75, and promptly was sued by the new owner, who, failing to properly care for it, blew it to smithereens drag racing. I won in court, *caveat emptor* and "fitness for purpose" saving me, given the new owner had ridden the bike for a good month. I wished him only the best, even hoped he'd repair the bike, given all I'd put into it—which I think he did. Still, I was, after a childhood of lusting after all Europe could offer in the way of two-wheeled wonders (and yes, mechanical nightmares), "lured over to the dark side." And so I bought my first Japanese bike, brand new, a touring machine.

Yamaha's XS 750 had been touted as Japan's answer to BMW's tourers in motorcycle magazines, and at half the price seemed worth checking out. It had dual front disk brakes, shaft drive, and silky power delivery from a transverse 120-degree-crankshaft in-line three-cylinder engine, much like the Rocket's, but here, dependable. For the first time in years, I thought, I'd have a working speedometer (I'd always ridden using the tachometer on my Euro bikes), shifting on the left side in a standard down-up pattern, and a muffler the size of a sewer pipe, so I wouldn't irritate all and sundry around me.

It was Yamaha's flagship model, the first of its kind. It is never a good idea to buy a first model of anything, but the dealer got me on it, and then, when I balked at his "So, shall we write it up for you?" he offered it to me for half its retail price. How could I go wrong?

This was 1977. The Big Four were all manufacturing four-strokes, world beaters in Sport Bike competitions, and the XS 750 was one of them. I bought an aftermarket luggage rack and a windshield for it.

A friend of mine had recently moved to Bozeman, Montana, and loved it. And Robert Pirsig, the author of *Zen and the Art of Motorcycle Maintenance,* had taught at the college there, Montana State. Never one to do something halfway, I decided on a tour of the Rockies, just a big loop, Highway 2 across North Dakota to Glacier National Park, down to Bozeman, through Yellowstone, through Medicine Bow in Wyoming, and home. In South Minneapolis, my sister took a picture of me on the bike before I rolled out of the driveway. (I was keeping my things in my parents' garage.) I had a tent, portable stove, ground pad, and general gear (shaving kit, hiking boots, rain suit, and so on) in my pack, bungeed to the rack, my sleeping bag set across the passenger part of the seat so I could rest against it. It was August, usually a hot and dry month in Minnesota, but I could smell rain, dark clouds a line of charcoal on the horizon to the west.

If I waited to be better prepared, I knew I would never go. Already I'd run down to Chicago to meet up with my old friend Rat from the West

Bank MC. Rat had intended to take the trip with me and had opted out, which I'd suspected he might, anyway. So I was a bit shaky on doing this thing alone. I was barely twenty, almost certain the woman I was seeing wouldn't be there when I returned. And I had a certain fatalism about the trip. I was even wearing my friend's dead uncle's engineer boots—Irv, a gun nut and collector, having *accidentally* shot himself smack dab in the forehead when he was cleaning his Colt .45.

Clad in black leather, I headed northwest on Interstate 94, and had only reached the North Dakota state border at Fargo when drops the size of thimbles began to fall. I'd spent every dime I had on the bike, so had filched my father's rubberized canvas rain gear for inclement-weather fishing, something most Lake Wobegoners have stashed away somewhere, along with Hula Poppers, Bassarenos, and red-and-white Daredevils. I got this pathetic, decades-old rain gear on, as I had outside Chicago, and remounted the bike, but this time within ten minutes I was getting stares from drivers, that rubberized canvas flapping from my back and arms in strips, giving me the appearance of, I suppose, the grim reaper. Already, in Irv's boots, I could squash my toes in water. But all that was nothing because—as any biker knows—one of the most dangerous times to ride is in new rain after a dry spell. All that dripping oil, ethylene glycol (radiator fluid), and grease ends up on the highway, and with a sheet of water on it that pavement is slick as snot.

I turned north, and headed for Highway 2, the landscape becoming by the moment more desolate in the rain. A short while later, I swung the bike off the road, toward a small mom-and-pop restaurant, my hands claws on the handlebars. Inside, the proprietress-waitress said to me,

"Getcha something? Some soup?"

The woman's husband at the grill glanced out at me, a full rack of stainless steel cutlery there, ready for action, GI Joe style.

When I went at the soup, the woman nodded to her husband, a told-you-so gesture.

We talked about the rain, the hot summer, and then came the inevitable question: "How far you goin'?"

I gave them my itinerary, and the cook said, "Always wanted to do that. Buy a bike and just . . ."

I lasted another four hours in the rain, and decided on a motel—I recall that motel as if it were yesterday, pulling my feet out of those soggy boots, the hot shower. I'd meant to use the tent, but had opted out my first night on the road—tomorrow, I thought, I'd be tougher.

Glacier was spectacular, Going to the Sun Highway on a motorcycle a revelation, high, jagged, snow-capped mountains and ice fields rising into a vivid blue sky, the very air scented with time and eternity. The Prince of Wales Hotel, an immense lodge set over aquamarine Waterton Lake, across the border in Canada, where I stopped to drink from my thermos, was some weary traveler's dream, a string quartet playing in the foyer for guests, the music carrying out onto the promontory where I sat.

It was all sublime.

Riding south out of Glacier, though, it began to hail. Hailstones the size of marbles. Riding on them was like riding on ball bearings, and I was reduced to following a Winnebago, the only safe road surface either of the two tracks the vehicle made through the hail, each at the most a foot wide.

I bought a Can Am nylon rain suit in a sporting goods store in Kalispell, and by the time I was down near Bozeman, the black dye in my leather jacket had bled through the white sleeves of the rain suit until they were a dirty blue-black.

In Bozeman, my friend, a cook, was on night shift at the Overland Express, and I saw him little if at all. But I met his roommates, Cleve and Rob, two South African motorcycle nuts and hang-glider pilots. We rode up Hyalite Canyon, yet another incomparably beautiful landscape of razor-sharp mountain peaks.

"You should think of moving out here," Rob said, and that thought struck me with the force of some revelation. "You can fly out here, ski, mountain climb, ride—it's all right here."

It was as if, along with touring—this motorcycling off track, dirt, road, and flat-track racing—my very life had jumped out of some not altogether happy limitation. Touring, you could go *anywhere*, granted you had the dollars for gas and grub. Why not the same with life? A friend of mine, a world-class snowboarder from Minneapolis, put it this way: We were the Princes of Minneapolis/St. Paul, and what a predictable and boring future that was.

In Yellowstone I was stopped by the Wyoming Highway Patrol for not wearing my helmet. I took in the usual—the Lodge, Old Faithful, and Yellowstone Falls—then hiked overnight away from it all to a lake where I caught German browns, fried them over my one-burner Coleman stove. Up not long after dawn and back to my bike, I was oddly eager just to get going again, having been swallowed up (happily) in a Yellowstone lodge-pole pine forest. Always, in the human heart, is this need for predictability and form, out of which comes a lust for formlessness and possibility, and through that possibility salvation, if even a momentary sort.

North of Jackson Hole, the majestic Tetons and Jackson Lake to my right, I turned off the highway onto a picturesque gravel road.

In the scent of snow run-off, pitch pine, and gravel talc I was humming some tune to myself when, doing around fifty, I crossed onto a band of darker gravel and the front wheel lurched to the left and the bike slammed down on its side with me under it, the gravel tearing into my back through my leather jacket and the hot engine burning my thighs.

I was so insensate by the time the bike stopped sliding, I barely knew where I was. And when I did, I was in terrible pain. In a parking lot to the left of me, two characters in a BMW with New Jersey plates eyed me, the driver grimacing then pulling out onto the highway and leaving me there pinned under my bike.

Once, riding south out of Minneapolis, a woman in a Fiat X1/9 tried to run me off the road. I'd considered, in my adrenaline-addled state of mind, jumping off the bike and through her open convertible top—after all, she was trying to kill me. And worse yet, as far as I knew, I'd done nothing to provoke her. I was reminded of that.

A rancher in a beat-up Ford 150 swung off the highway, slid to a stop, and was out of his truck like a shot.

"You all right?!" he demanded, lifting the bike off me.

The rancher insisted I leave my bike in the lot, the new layer of nearly foot-deep gravel they'd just put down having "bit me on the ass," as he put it. He drove me across town to his log house, a beautiful place, where his neighbor, a doctor, took a look at my thighs—second-degree burns on both, for which he gave me some topical ointment.

Both men had ridden Harleys, and we ate at the picnic table in the backyard, the men swapping tales of their riding days, their wives, at times, telling me not to believe a bit of it (joking, of course).

Riding through Rocky Mountain National Park, doing seventy or so, I came around a sweeper, in front of me a tanker truck, oil having spilled from it across the road, so that I grit my teeth, the bike beginning to turn broadside, ahead of me a guardrail over an abyss. I got the bike lined up the way I had flat-tracking, and just before I reached the dry pavement, hit the gas hard, so that the bike would throttle-steer to the right—that way, even if I did crash, I'd buy myself more length of road, so I could, possibly, miss the guardrail.

It worked. We flew around the bend, that XS 750 and me, like Mike Hailwood, and that evening, enjoying authentic Mexican on my cousin's ticket in Denver, we sang drunken songs with the, mostly, Hispanic patrons, which led me to consider a solution to a problem I had by this time. I was flat broke and needed gas and grub money. It was late August, and peach season. I rode out to an orchard that was advertising in a help wanted column, and there met some of the most beautiful people I have ever known, one of them Joseph Martinez, who let me pick with his family. It was backbreaking work, and Joseph warned me not to eat the peaches, which we were allowed to do.

Up the ladder, fill the basket, reaching, and reaching, and reaching, then down the ladder with the full basket, and up again, hundreds of times in one twelve-hour day, and when I sat on the ground beside my bike and opened a can of tuna, and began to eat it like that, with a fork, Joseph waved me over. He pointed to the empanadas his wife had heated on a square of sheet metal over a fire. His daughters, Rosa and Bonita, eleven and twelve, looked shyly up at me, from under dark, too-long-to-seem-real lashes.

We all ate, and I got the chocolate I'd kept in my pack for emergencies (hypothermia, really). Joseph insisted I set my tent up near his trailer, then shared with me the last plug of mescal he had in a cork-stoppered bottle. Some scary types were eyeing me, but Joseph gave them sober warning looks.

Up before dawn, I ate with them again, then rode into town and bought with my last ten dollars beef, more chocolate, and a pint of Lewis & Clark, possibly the worst whisky ever made.

Three days later, the owner of the orchard tallied up our total of baskets, divided our shares by head. Joseph tried to press some of his share into my hand, and I refused, gave him what remained of the Lewis & Clark. We had not spoken three words of English in three days.

I rode up into Wyoming, through Medicine Bow, and in Laramie made the mistake of calling my girl, who was with her betrothed—it was that kind of deal, rotten from the start.

"Who you talking to?" that other asked her. "Kate," my girl told him.

That night, the only such night on that ride, I drank myself blind, didn't even bother to put up my tent, just slung it over the bike and crawled in under, lying on my sleeping bag, so that the bugs had a field day with me.

I woke to sunlight sharp as glass shards, a head swollen the size of a watermelon. I rode into town, and turned directly in front of that Mack truck of biker lore, the driver saving me, awake and on his brakes. So, after that, no riding on hangovers, either.

I wasn't eager to get home now, given the way things stood with my girl, so I cut up through South Dakota, where I took in Mount Rushmore, then chose back roads across southern Minnesota and into Wisconsin. There I thrilled at the endless miles of winding, roller-coaster blacktop, and in the evenings drank ice cold beers out front of smoky little taverns with names like Joe's Place. I cut through Duluth, then rode on to Lake of the Woods, where I'd truly lived as a boy, a formative place, never far from me, found my Chippewa friend Delbert, and headed up to Kenora (Rat Portage), a place then still mysterious, wild, and unspoiled.

In Kenora, I attended a potlatch with Delbert and his family, where I was the only nonenrolled person, met a Crazy Dog, and danced myself insensate in the company of scores of Shinobs in their regalia.

Three days later I was dressed in tan corduroy, back at the university, in class or lab all day. If asked what I'd done that summer, I said I'd painted apartments—which I had. Here, that old biker adage coming to me: If I have to explain, you wouldn't understand anyway. I'd been away over a month, had ridden nearly nine thousand miles.

Once I got the bike parked in my parents' garage, I closed the door, still feeling as though I were welded to it—a sensation I was just then happy to forget.

A year later, having escaped to Montana, I regularly rode that bike to Glacier from Bozeman to visit a woman who worked outside Babb, for the State Highway Commission as a surveyor, a job I took on as well. I rode to Yellowstone on weekends, where friends and I dived from the cliffs at Firehole Canyon (since burned beyond recognition). I took a trip up to Vancouver, B.C., and out into the Canadian muskeg, as far north as I could go, just south of the Arctic Circle. I put 38,000 miles on that bike in three years, and in the end sold it for one hundred dollars less than I paid for it.

It had one terrible idiosyncrasy—due to the five CV joints Yamaha had used in its driveshaft, if you backed off the throttle in a tight turn, the bike stood up, due to the heavy CV shaft's gyroscopic effect, a lesson you learned on the first ride—which made the bike a kind of dog. Pretty as it was—and it was pretty, glossy silver, and blue, and black—I thought of it as a lump, and so, years later, when my crazy roommate in Iowa City, in response to my pointing out a Ducati in a magazine, said, "I've got a Ducati, wanna buy it?" I said, sure, let's see it.

Jack was on what he called a macrobiotic diet, which meant for him shoving a handful of sugar and a wad of nori into his mouth, which he would chase with a few glassfuls of Red Mountain burgundy.

A week later, Jack had the bike in the garage. He wanted $1,500 for it. A steal, he said. It didn't run, had shot cables, looked rough. Jack was leaving for Colorado in a few days, and just before he left, I told him I'd give him $200 for his bike. Roundcase Ducatis have gone for as much as $75,000 on eBay, and have become the collectible Vincents of our time.

I had the bike running in a week, sorted in a month—carb rebuild, valve job, new chain, tuning. It was all the bike the Rocket A-75 had been, and *far* more. It handled like a dream. Every time I went out on it, I ran it well over a hundred. The bike was truly magic, invited grinding, harsh use, could take a turn like threading a needle.

I thought of it as my "bite the wire" bike—it was beautiful, and it made that Ducati V-twin thrum that simply inspired you to ride fast. You couldn't help yourself. The bike sat there in the garage, saying, Yeah, let's see what you got, bring it on, let's see you break me. Try it.

Roll on the throttle out of a corner, and without a wobble, or a moment's hesitation, the bike, in some perfect logarithmic fashion, made tractable horsepower, hurling you into the next section of open road.

All this from, really, dinosaur technology. A V-twin. Desmodromic towershaft bevel-driven overhead cams (the Germans had come up with desmo in the thirties), Del Orto carbs with independent acceleration pumps, two valves per piston—putting out, in the best, hottest trim, maybe 80-plus horsepower. But it was the frame and the way the engine produced its power that made the bike special, some stroke of pure genius (and luck) of the designer, Fabio Taglioni, in it. Said Matthew Miles of *Cycle World* magazine, "You could put [Taglioni] on the same pedestal with . . . Enzo Ferrari, the car maker."

The Ducati bevel L-twin was just superior, and given there was no imaging, modeling, or design by computer at the time, it was a work of art. This machine was no more an accident than a Stradivarius violin was an accident, and like the violin, it was subtle, nuanced, *right* somehow. This bike made Ducati the company we know today. Mike Hailwood, Paul Smart, Bruno Spaggiari, and Ermanno Giuliano all rode this bike to victory over the Big Four Multis, making Ducati, for a time, the world leader in production sport-bike racing.

And it was this bike I rode, flat bars and all, to Colorado, all over Iowa and Wisconsin and Minnesota: 36,000 miles.

And then a friend from whom I'd gotten tech advice on the bike, another Ducati rider and racer, Tom, fell in a race and was hit by the rider behind him, paralyzing him from the waist down. I could have bought Tom's Mike Hailwood Replica for $3,000. I didn't. Nor did I buy my sister's BMW Sport, when she decided to sell it after her friend, crossing the Golden Gate Bridge, was unfortunate enough to have been following a flatbed truck from which all sorts of S-H-I-T fell, the poor bastard hitting that mess and going down, then rushed to a hospital and never regaining consciousness.

I was riding less, and my Ducati was the worse for wear. I'd kept the engine jewel-sharp and tuned (three carb rebuilds alone), though everything else needed work: tires, wheels, forks, brakes (the rear dragged and the front hydraulic lines were badly cracked, the master cylinder leaking). The paint was atrocious, but I liked it that way. By then that Duc was a gladiator bike, what they call in Europe a "Street Fighter."

At some point, someone had slapped a heart-shaped sticker that read *I Love Italy* on the rear fender. I was loath to remove it. My knees had worn through the paint on the tank's stylish knee insets, a layer of yellow showing through the red. The footpeg rubber was so abraided you could no longer see the *DUCATI* molded onto the face of each. Cornering, I'd ground off a good portion of the kick starter on the right side. The handlebars were slightly bent on the left from a slow fall, and the sport windshield was terminally cracked. Yes, there were other bikes I rode all those years, but as my friend Rick, the motorcycle polygamist, puts it, they had no *woo-hoo*—there was the Honda 750 I rode regularly to Alice's Restaurant in La Honda, south of San Francisco, more exotic machinery there than I'd seen anywhere outside a classic bike rally; a BMW "flying brick," in the 750 incarnation; a Yamaha 650 vertical twin; even a quite horrible, but exciting, Yamaha 305 scrambler that, ignobly, started its life with me on it by suddenly coming to life after ten years, wheelying into the backside of the

1947 Chevrolet stake-side truck we were using to jump-start it. There was even a weird nonrunner called a Centaur I bought for twenty-five dollars, a motorcycle built in the early sixties to be folded into what looked like a suitcase and put in some Cessna 170 or Beechcraft Bonanza—a plane dubbed the Lawyer Killer for its tricky ruddervator. Well over twenty bikes, good, bad, and indifferent—but loved nonetheless.

But Ducatis! I just didn't have pockets deep enough. I was a graduate student for what seemed an eternity. A new set of Continentals and a cluster of straight-cut gears had me eating rice and beans. I'd ridden countless Harleys, but had not yet been able to afford one, still haven't. And there weren't going to be any vegan, macrobiotic, brain-addled, Red Mountain burgundy-swilling owners of Ducati 916s (or Monsters) dying to unload their bikes on me for two hundred dollars. The whole game had changed. There were no backyard mechanics repairing fancy Italian bikes they'd bought for dirt anymore; these bikes now were simply too complicated, too finely tuned (from the new Passo, named after Renzo Passolini, the Tomba of road racing, to the Desmosedici). When these bikes broke now, experts repaired them, and with a half million dollars' worth of computer diagnostic equipment.

I even let my license expire, both the bike's and my motorcycle endorsement.

Still, when I felt itchy, I got on the Duc and flogged it down some nowremote Kansas back road, river roads being the best, always winding, and having good, surprising turns and sweepers, and there putting on the bike another few thousand miles of sport riding.

My charming wife, despite speaking Italian fluently and loving all things Italian—the Piazza San Marco, the Uffizi Galleries, Florence in all of its splendor, the Amalfi Coast—shortly after the bug incident declined to take further rides with me on my thoroughbred.

Life catches up with you, offers you new adventures, takes you in directions not so much as earlier imagined. Life is what's happening while you're making other plans, goes the old folk wisdom. But even given that, there is a durability in things you truly love. Absence, after too much time, may not make the heart grow fonder. But for me, things loved rise up and demand time, inclusion in my life, that or I feel I'll die.

So, a new bike was in order. And what else but a Ducati? Or a 1200 Sportster, tuned to rev and running straight pipes. But you couldn't touch one of the new EVO-engined bikes for less than a sizeable down payment on a house. And stooping to buy an AMF-built Harley was a job fit only for a masochist.

Hollywood called, then Utah (in the form of a small college), and my wife and I were back in the Rockies, this time the incomparable Wasatch. I got my skiing life back in the blink of an eye. Rescue solved all that—the Park City ski patrollers being the greatest group of people anywhere, a free pass to three world-class resorts in the bargain, and the world's greatest snow.

All of which led to my piloting Ducati's next-generation sport-touring ST4 1,000 cc up Wolf Creek Pass, and wondering if I should run it up to 150 to get around my friend on his 900 SS.

Already I'd nearly clipped the rear end of a truck riding east on Interstate 80, really just sport riding as I always had, but having been away from it for two years, having that sheet metal box go by my head just a foot or so distant gave me pause—and there were Moose's grisly tales to think about. Moose was a full time EMT guy I worked with Sundays up at Park City who rode a Harley Big Dog Chopper and loved to relate stories wherein riders of "bullet bikes" met messy ends, like the character doing about 140 who hit the rear end of a moving van, the guy's head embedded in the aluminum door so that his feet dragged along the pavement, such that by the time the driver got the van stopped, there were no "feet" on that unfortunate rider. Truly, such cautions came to me as if from God Him/Her/Itself.

Having been a ski racer, and a downhill racer at that, flying along at sixty, or even seventy on nearly nothing at all, was . . . familiar. Exciting. I was still taking the occasional run at sixty, but exercising especial caution. I knew the statistics: Superbikes, like Ducatis, while only constituting 10 percent of bikes on the road (more than 50 percent now are Harleys or

Harley-inspired "cruisers"), were involved in 25 percent of all motorcycle fatalities. And, worse yet, 47 percent of those fatalities now involved riders over forty (compared to the 27 percent back in the middle nineties); those over-forty riders were a group not unfamiliar to me.

My riding chops were coming back, but the potential of the bike was nearly overwhelming. Whereas before, with my old bevel, I'd bring it up to 100, then really punish it at speeds over that, this bike had a turn-of-the-wrist 160-plus mph capability—as simple as that. Unearned. In skiing, to navigate runs at 60, you have to stay on your skis on runs at 25, 35, 45, then 50 mph, all the while gaining skills that make running a downhill course possible—there are no Eddie the Eagles skiing downhill courses. But Eddie the Eagles are everywhere on bullet bikes, and—after two years off my older, much-less-powerful bevel—riding the ST4, I was closer to being one than I liked.

Rick got off his 900 SS and offered to let me ride it. Everything on that race-bred machine felt right. It was bulletproof, powerful, perfectly balanced. But again I let Rick lead the way with the ST4, so I wouldn't let the bike get away from me.

For the first time, I was on something that was far more bike than I could handle—if I really used what was there. And I wanted to. No doubt about it. I hung off the saddle, chin leading the way, screwed the power on, auguring out of turns just back of the apex. I rode an incautious eighty even in thirty-mile-per-hour zones.

But I didn't pass Rick, or even try to. Why bother, anyway? What would it prove? That I'd spent time on a track nearly thirty years earlier? Where, after passing a knot of far more seasoned riders on my Rocket, including my track-savvy friend Peter on his Ducati, I was asked, How'd you do that? I'd replied, simply, Skiing. It's like skiing, which had made no sense to any of those road rats—or, really, to me for that matter. Still, it was true.

Back in Salt Lake, Rick said to me in his driveway, "We've gotta get you your moto-mojo back."

I thought about that, tossing and turning that night, still bolt-awake with adrenaline from canyon racing. So, more riding—but with a new caution. I started looking for that new fix, that new adventure, some way to really get "out there"—though, hopefully, one that wouldn't kill me.

Looking for that something that would fit, I read books like *Riding with Rilke*, by Ted Bishop ("Exultant, that New Road and New Gear euphoria coursing through me, I headed west into the sun." And, "I was getting set to gobble up the next line of plodders when I saw the roof lights on the Jeep in front of me."); and *Lois on the Loose*, by Lois Pryce, a diminutive woman who took a solo ride through South America ("As the lemmings [her coworkers] began to take their positions, I wondered . . . did they too watch motorcycles whizzing by with a pang of envy and imagine what it would be like not to turn off at the same junction every morning, but to keep riding until the road or the land ran out?" And at the end of her ride? "As I had expected, the motorcycle had proved itself to be the finest way to travel. . . . On the bike, I was always in the thick of it: smelling and tasting the air, feeling the sun and wind against my skin—and yes, the freezing cold and rain too. . . . But what I hadn't bargained for was how the motorcycle encouraged friendliness, a curiosity from strangers that would inevitably turn into something more—an offer of hospitality, practical assistance or just some words of encouragement when I needed them most.") I balanced Lois's happy ride with the martial arts expert Glen Heggstad's *Two Wheels Through Terror: Diary of a South American Motorcycle Odyssey*, in which Heggstad rode from Palm Springs to Tierra del Fuego, and was kidnapped by ELN rebels who held him for ransom.

There was even a double amputee (his legs lost in a mine blast), Dave Barr, who'd set two Guinness records riding around the world, the very icon of the human spirit's capacity to overcome adversity. Making Barr's story all the more poignant was this: As an infant, he'd been left in the backseat of a car, was put in foster care, and was later adopted by a navy veteran of WWII and his wife. In Vietnam, he earned fifty-seven air medals, including a single-mission decoration for valor during combat, as a helicopter gunner.

In *Riding the Edge*, he wrote: "Wouldn't it be something to share this simple accomplishment of riding a motorcycle as a double amputee with disabled people the world over? Perhaps I could be a role model for those people who might someday suffer the loss of good health." Barr wrote a second book as well, *Riding the Ice*, an account of his adventure over Russian marshland, most of it above the Arctic Circle, and in winter, this being the only time the marshland could support motorcycle travel. Said Barr, in an interview, "If you're not willing to take risks, you're going nowhere. I took [the disabilities] and used them to give my life meaning, so that maybe someday someone will be able to say, 'I met Dave Barr and if he did all of these things as he is, then surely I can live my life.'"

All this went percolating in a stew of intentions at cross purposes. I loved to ride fast, but didn't have the heart to pay for it in the way I had when I was younger. No, I did not think myself invincible or beyond the fates meted out to a number of my riding companions. When, for example, I visited a beloved relative in a hospital, one who had fallen through a roof and been paralyzed, there was also in his room a boy my age, nineteen, whose brain had been damaged in a motorcycle accident. Time and again he lurched up in his bed, shouting altogether unintelligible somethings, which shocked as much as depressed me.

I had loved riding dirt bikes, but just the thought of being tossed from one now, fairly inevitable when you ride dirt, made me nearly cringe—all that just hurt too much, and, as I knew from skiing, I didn't heal as quickly as I had in the past.

While traveling around, say, India or New Zealand or Nepal was altogether a possibility with my wife, she being a restless spirit like myself, we wouldn't be doing so on a motorcycle.

And that was what I craved.

So, desiring more secondhand adventure, I picked up Ted Simon's *Jupiter's Travels*. He wrote, at the end of his years-long trip around the globe, that he "teeter[ed] on a knife edge between faith and despair" and asked himself, had he "really been on a long flight from reality, trying to give meaning to something that was meaningless? Was it all just an escape [he had] been trying to turn into a legend?"

I didn't really want to tear my life up in that way anymore. How many times had I returned from some monthlong trip, finding that, at least initially, I no longer belonged, not to the place I'd returned, nor the place I'd come from?

It was a profoundly painful experience, those returns, after too much time and too many miles away. I felt like Dylan's (though, really, Franklin's) proverbial rolling stone.

Yet there was no question of not going. It wasn't in me not to. Robert Louis Stevenson wrote that there are two kinds of men: those who go, and those who stay at home. I know myself for one of the former.

But then, this gem from Simon, illuminating: "People who thought of my journey as a physical ordeal or as an act of courage, like single-handed yachting, missed the point. Courage and physical endurance were no more than useful items of equipment for me, like facility with language, or immunity from hepatitis. The goal was comprehension, and the only way to comprehend the world was by making myself vulnerable to it so that it could change me. The challenge was to lay myself open to everybody and everything that came my way. The prize was to change and grow big enough to feel one with the whole world. The real danger was death by exposure."

About this time, a very good friend called from Pittsburgh. Kevin was turning forty and wanted, almost desperately, to buy a motorcycle. He was being told by his sweetheart's doctor friend that he was being "selfish and irresponsible." My only question for him was this: Would he feel as though he hadn't really lived if he didn't do this? His answer was an unequivocal yes.

So there was no help for it. Get one, I told him.

He had just the right bike in mind, a Kawasaki W 650, really a knock-off Triumph Bonneville. He would buy it if he could fly me out and I would teach him to ride it.

Five years later, he owns four motorcycles, one of them my Ducati 750, Kevin having fallen under the spell of the Italians.

Meanwhile, my friend Rick was thinking about riding Baja again—not the race, the 1,000, but simply traveling from Utah to Cabo, the southern-most point, which would include riding on "primitive" back roads, burro paths, and in places no paths at all, just desert. It wasn't a job for a street bike, nor for a dirt bike—he wouldn't, after all, be trailering his bike down there.

"Why don't you think about coming along?" he asked.

By the time I was old enough to ride it, Barstow to Vegas was history. The Baja 1,000 was too insane. Paris to Dakar was for the superwealthy and the factory-sponsored—and the insanely talented and dedicated.

"And I'm going to do this on what?" I said.

"How about a Beemer?" Rick said.

The only Beemers I knew were the touring bikes I'd grown up with, particularly my friend Richard's, a "toaster tank" 600. One evening, in the eighties, after a number of gin and tonics, Richard, another friend, Bonnie (also a rider), and I had all hopped on that BMW and ridden it around the lakes in South Minneapolis. Three up. There was a charming frisson in it, Bonnie squeezed between us while Richard piloted the bike.

That BMW was torquey, slow, and puttering—but lovely. Just the thing for helmetless loping around lakes near midnight, the moon, clouds, and sky reflected on night-still water.

Rick's suggestion made me laugh. "Yeah," I said, "mired in sand the first yard off the highway."

"That'd be one of the old airheads," Rick said. "You don't want that. You want the Swiss Army Knife of motorcycles, the GS."

Somehow this rang a bell—in exactly the way such a bell had been rung when, riding through Bozeman, it was suggested I move there.

*Yes,* I thought.

An adventure tourer. Immediately all sorts of happy images flashed through my mind: riding on fire roads, back roads, through canyons in southern Utah: Bryce, Zion, Capitol Reef, Moab. Or a ride north to my old home in Sun Valley, Idaho, a turn through the Sawtooths and up to Redfish Lodge. I'd always thought Beemers a bit odd-looking, with their jugs (cylinders and heads) jutting out on both sides. But in dirt or on gravel and unimproved roads, that very feature would be a winning one, the Beemer's boxer engine having a lower center of gravity, making it more stable. Immediately other adventure tourers came to mind, the Suzuki V-Strom and Kawasaki KLR 650. The Kawasaki was a single, which I couldn't help think sounded like a lawn mower. The Suzuki, I was told by one owner, seemed top heavy with a full tank of gas.

Still, everyone said the same thing about all three bikes: *Ugly!* Or a more reserved "They're an acquired taste." That appealed to me too. If I dropped one of these things on its side, and they all had engine protectors and handlebar guards, so what? Suddenly I was reminded of all those happy years with dirt bikes. That they had had the paint worn off the cases by my dirty boots, tanks dented, seats torn and patched? All badges of honor: all that showed you'd really ridden your machine.

Showroom bikes make me feel breathless. Sure, they're nice and shiny and in the case of Italian bikes beautiful, but what's the point? For me, now, getting out there is the whole business. If a bike isn't scratched up a bit, dinged, or worn somewhere, what is it but someone's symbol of something *thought* to be exciting?

## Off We Ride, Into the Sunset

You are piloting, now, a BMW GS 1100 Adventure Tourer, its heart burbling, just the way a boxer engine should. You sit upright, but comfortable, a windscreen cutting the pine-laden air. Around you rise Idaho's Sawtooths. On one side of the road is a pristine river, rushing, the spray carrying into the road, refreshing. You turn right, staying wide, cut the apex just so, and into a left turn, do the same, as if darting on wings. The sun hasn't come over the Sawtooths yet, and the season, spring, is in evidence everywhere, orange-red Indian paintbrush coming up through patches of snow, and columbine and penstemon, and, when you see some distance ahead a pull-off alongside the river, you check your mirrors, brake hard, and swing onto the gravel at walking speed.

You stop the bike and put the stand down, then swing off it, even now, reluctantly, as part of you simply wants to keep going.

With your helmet off, the water makes a wall of noise, though a reassuring one. An ouzel hunts for aquatic bugs, lunging into the bitter-cold water, doing what birds aren't supposed to be able to do underwater: swim. You identify with this bird.

You take your thermos from your luggage, pour a cup of coffee, bought at a little shack of a place outside Twin Falls, where old Evel Knievel tried to jump the Snake River Canyon.

Off the bike, with your attention sharpened, the landscape has a certain Technicolor vividness. The pines here are not pines. You can see this from the needles along the branches, which are not clustered; they're firs. And the flowers! Coneflowers, clematis, bluebells, mule's ear, larkspur, fleabane, and phlox. A marmot waddles down a hillside, sizing you up. Are you good for a handout or not?

The ouzel, now perched on a rock, has a grub, which it relishes. A Steller's jay swoops in, wings wafting the air.

There is something profoundly lonely in all this, but necessary. Years earlier, you avoided stopping on rides alone, because, always, your Self came crowding in then. Always insistent, wanting something: To be *somewhere else*, doing *something different*, being *someone else*.

Quietly despairing.

But now you're not canyon racing, trying to navigate winding roads at speeds that were never designed to be negotiated. Nor are you blindly pushing on, as if you'll find yourself up ahead. Some quiet joy has taken you here, and on this bike it could take you just about anywhere. Alone, like this, or with others—say you could ride the toughest noncompetition, the Iron Butt, around the Great Lakes, or . . . ? There's the Polar Bear, which would be interesting. A Silk Road ride in China. Tours of Africa, Australia, and New Zealand. Even missionaries in Idaho taking bikes for clergy down to Bolivia, a group needing riders, faithful or not.

And to satisfy your old speed jones?

You've been out to Miller Motorsports Park in Tooele, just thirty minutes southwest of Salt Lake City, and have looked into track days. One hundred and ninety dollars will buy you a full day (two twenty-minute morning sessions, three in the afternoon) of white-knuckle riding at speeds up to and over 150 mph. Add to that the prerequisite track orientation, rider/driver evaluation ($85), new sticky-compound Dunlop Sportmax Qualifier tires, two for $750 and good for all of two thousand miles (or some "Race Take Offs," tires used by an expert in one race, for $100), and some pit equipment (lawn chair, umbrella, and so on), and you're ready to go, and go fast. A bona fide Valentino Rossi experience for just around $1,000.

And if you really want to push it, put some edge on your riding skills, you could take lessons from the world-champion road-racing icon Fast Freddie Spencer himself, a two-day class only $2,395, or the full three-day for $3,195. Right there at Miller Motorsports Park. They'll even rent you a Kushitani leather riding suit for the day for $150, or the full Moto GP outfit—suit, helmet, boots, gloves—for $250.

The ST4 is waiting. Or you could dig up some basket-case Triumph or BSA, get it roadworthy and ride it in an American Historic Racing Motorcycle Association event, alongside other vintage bikes, in the Sound of Thunder twins, admission being a hundred dollars. And you could potter around on the bike later.

A fellow rescue worker, Ryan, just got an older Honda VFR, one he's only going to use on the track, and he has invited you along. And why not dream big? There could be another Ducati for you, a used 916 or 996. Why not? It's as close as your next book or screenplay. So what that your nineteen-year-old Accord now has 220,000 miles on it and looks like the snowmobile it is.

And Rick, your friend, wanted to know if you'd like to tour Europe. He's itching to go again, has the perfect set up, knows the right dealer to rent BMWs from, has an itinerary, maps, has done this ride through Germany, Switzerland, and down to the toe of Italy, where you'd take the boat across to Sicily and the wives would drop by for a week of traveling before heading back up home. *Che viaggio!*

But here, alongside this river, after a lifetime of pushing, speeding, forcing yourself along, of building faster, more powerful bikes, of riding them, repairing them, trying to tame them, comes this moment of quiet, of—just this moment—*satisfaction*. So you don't want to be anywhere else but here, right now, in this canyon with a cup of coffee in your hand, your trusty friend and lump at your side, your motorcycle.

You don't have to be anywhere, or be anybody. You are riding to live, and given that, living to ride.

And here the point of this business becomes even clearer yet, this greatest of ironies of the motorcycle. They are built for going, but the very reason for finding them irresistible is in that *while* going—up some hill, over some scramble, around some course, around the world—you've already *arrived*. Until that maniac inside says, Late, you're late, you were supposed to have reached Mudtail by noon, outer Sideflap by dinner. Or you have passed over that sometimes fine line between adventure and ordeal, when you are struggling to survive, the possibility of which always puts an edge on your ride, gives it excitement. Who knows if by noon you'll be riding on marble-size hail, or cutting through a Wyoming side wind so fierce that as you come out from around eighteen-wheelers you are nearly blown off the road.

Rarely is going also being, but it is so on a motorcycle.

William Least Heat Moon put it well in his travelogue, *Blue Highways*:

"There's nothing that we can do that's more American . . . than striking out cross country. I think as a nation we can think of few things that draw more strongly than a piece of roadway heading we know not where. This is the way we grow up, this is the way we enter our history: get out and find . . . the country.

"And ourselves."

Here are the Sawtooths around you, the Salmon River, where you'll fish for trout, a short distance north. The sky is an achingly eternal blue.

You cap your thermos and stow it on your bike. You swing your leg over the saddle, and it feels . . . just right. The bike is now some extension of your body, well worn, well tried.

You thumb the starter button and the motor turns over, then kicks into life, throbs. You glance over your shoulder, then ahead, and pull back onto the highway, navigating a broad right-hander, hanging from the tank, and the bike, like magic, making a fine, arcing turn. You roll on the gas again, until you're riding some roller coaster, down, up, left, right, and left again, the river always beside you, and just when you are really moving along, a sign pops up to your right, announcing a pass you can take after May 15, which it is. You have no idea where this unpaved road goes, not really, other than that it must connect to other roads, given the sign.

And like that, rather than pushing on, as you had thought you would, you brake hard, turn right, skirt a postcard-perfect mountain, riding, here, along another tributary of the Salmon, the bike, as if some magic carpet, carrying you—as one or another has all these years, rain, sun, snow, and furnace heat.

Out there. Into the world.

Free.

# ACKNOWLEDGMENTS

Perhaps Theresa Wallach, motorcyclist par excellence and author of *The Rugged Road*, said it best: "When I first saw a motorcycle, I got a message from it. It was a feeling—the kind of thing that makes a person burst into tears hearing a piece of music or standing in front of a fine work of art. Motorcycling is a tool with which you can accomplish something meaningful in your life. It is an art."

I am deeply grateful to all my rider friends who have made motorcycling the joy, and art, it has been for me. Thanks could never be enough, but here are a few: Thanks, Uncle Bob, for that first ride down in Florida, for getting the wheels rolling. Ray, thanks for teaching me, yes, anything can be repaired. Thanks to my good friend Richard, whose quiet and patience—and the use of his Velocette—saved my adolescent life. To my Chippewa riding pal, Makwa, Boju! Bonnie, wherever you are, blessings. Rat, I hope you're alive—and thanks for helping me navigate biker life. Thanks to Rick Pellegrino, a real rider if there ever was one, for generosity in a lean time—and for just damn great jaunts in Utah, mountain, dale, and highway. To all my motorcycle angels, the guy who dragged me out of a ditch after a hard fall, thanks! To the couple who let me sleep on the floor of their motor home when I was caught in a blizzard, thanks! Thanks, Joseph Martinez, wherever you are, all health and good fortune to you and your loved ones. Thanks Buzz and Thom for your help in Wyoming. Thanks, all!

Of course, I owe a debt of gratitude to those who helped make this book possible.

To my wonderful wife, Karen, thanks for lending your masterful ear to each draft, and—especially!—for cheering me on. *Gioia della mia vita!*

Thanks to my agent, Tracy Brown, who found a home for this book, and to my terrific editors, Peter Borland and Nick Simonds, at Atria Books. Your input has been invaluable.

Jared Stoddard, thanks for kicking my computer back into shape.

I thank the motorcycle spirits, in all their various forms—mud, mountain, track, and trail—for giving me safe passage, and wish you, reader, the same.

I thank my lucky stars.

Blessings in adventures, and in riding with the wind in your face, a trusty iron horse as your companion.